SERVANT OF SAHIBS

SERVANT OF SAHIBS

A BOOK TO BE READ ALOUD

BY
GHULAM RASSUL GALWAN
Aksakal of Leh

With an Introduction by

SIR FRANCIS YOUNGHUSBAND

GYAN

Published by

Gyan Publishing House
5, Ansari Road
Daryaganj, New Delhi-110002
Phone: 011-47034999, 9811692060
E-mail: books@gyanbooks.com

Distribution Network
gyanbooks.com
India, USA, Canada, UK, Australia, France

ISBN : 978-81-212-4544-9 (HB)
First Published, 1923

2nd Impression 2020

Printed at: Gyan Press, Delhi.

Servant of Sahibs
Author: Sir Francis Younghusband & Ghulam Rassul Galwan

SERVANT OF SAHIBS

A Book to be Read Aloud

BY

GHULAM RASSUL GALWAN
Aksakal of Leh

With an Introduction by
SIR FRANCIS YOUNGHUSBAND

CAMBRIDGE
W. HEFFER & SONS LTD.
1923

GHULAM RASSUL GALWAN

Author's Preface

TO ALL THEM WHO READ THIS BOOK,

King and Queen and ladies and gentlemen who will read this poor boy's book:

I have been always travelling with English and American gentlemen. They were all very kind with their poor servant. I will not give their names at this place. Their names and their kindness all will come in the book, and all that, how I was a poor boy, and how I got a little rich, by kindly of gentlemen. Their goodness and faithfulness I do very much remember. In the much travelling I was very tired, but, for my children, food wanted again and again, and other work I had no learning for, beside travel.

I wanted very much to write a book, but was not able. At last I found one sahib who helped me very long, till made me a man. I was sorry when first I found this sahib in Kashmir. He seemed me as very poor a gentleman, but I liked very much sahib's temper and his tent.

In travel with this sahib I was about two years. In charge of all his work. And sahib asked me my story and I told him. And after that I wrote it all, and he corrected some parts where he said he did not very well understand my English. Then I wrote it another time by his help, learning, and made a little book.

Ghulam Rasul Galwan
Akskal
Leh
Kashmir
India

Contents

Introduction

WHY Himalayan peoples should be as ready as they are to undergo hardships, and run risks of the most serious nature, in the service of any stray traveller who appears among them is not easy to understand. The payment they receive is small. They have to work for much more than an eight hours' day. And they have no insurance against accidents. Yet they readily work through long and arduous days, and willingly risk their lives. And, most wonderful of all, they are full of gratitude to their employer when they leave his service.

In this book we get an answer to the puzzle. It is written by one of themselves—by a Mohamedan of Ladak, who had worked for many years in the service of English and American travellers in the Himalaya, Central Asia and Tibet. The secret is that these men, the best of them, love adventure just as much as their employers. Written in faulty English, but with the instinct of a true artist, we see on every page the spirit which animated Rassul.

Of himself as a small boy he writes: "I was hurry for be old. And in head all times in night made rich, made meet with big man, and saw many different countries with Sahibs. All the time I played in head with the matter . . . sometimes played that went long way in world." And when he was barely old enough for hard travel he went to a caravan leader and said: "Please give me service of Sahibs. I long for the journey by Yarkand." Yarkand being a city in Central Asia accessible only by crossing passes seventeen, eighteen and nineteen thousand feet in height. And afterwards when he had obtained service with English travellers he writes: "I was much glad with this order and I said myself Now I will see new countries"—see new countries, be it noted, not make money.

The fidelity with which he served is also evident throughout the book. When he came to a pass which no one could cross except at the risk of his life he said: "Sir, if you go I must go with you. If you die, then I will die too."

And he was sensible of the beauty of great mountains. When he saw one of those stupendous peaks which cluster round the second highest mountain in the world, and it may have been K_2 itself, he wrote: "To the East was a very tall glaciers mountain, very steep, covered much ice. That looked much beautiful. Top that mountains always see over it a hat of cloud. I said myself 'Lucky man myself to see that mountain.'"

Equally noteworthy in his close observation of men and their customs, "All that I kept in my head," he says after relating the manner in which Englishmen and Chinese officials visited each other. And I have vivid recollections of the way in which men like him gaze at one with the absorbed interest of a child and take in every word one says and every move one makes—and keep it in their heads.

But most noticeable point of all in Rassul's book in his touching faith in God. It was his stand-by in all hardships, trials and disappointment. And this habit of reverence was undoubtedly what made him the gentleman he is. He came of the very poorest. He started as a simple village lad. But in every situation he behaved like a gentleman.

As interesting a part as any is Rassul's account of his "enjoyments." He was a born story-teller. Sometimes the stories were of the "lie matter" description. When he feared the anger of the Sahib when he had ridden the tiffin pony he ought to have been leading he candidly tells us he used "lie matter" to the Sahib. But most of the story-telling is of the genuine description. For these men love telling stories to each other, and do not mind how long the stories are, or how far into the night the telling of them extends. Singing, too, they love. And Rassul was clearly a popular singer, and had, also, a great delight in banjo-playing.

Altogether the book is wonderfully human and gives us an exceptional insight of the springs of action of Himalayan peoples. We see their ways of looking at things, and looking at us, and we understand them better and find they are after all not so very different from what we were as boys. It was an anxious time for me when I saw my own name appearing, but I was relieved when I found I had called the author nothing worse than a "lazy boy," and not, like one of my successors, called him "a dam fool liar."

In spite of the down rightness of this Sahib's language Rassul seems to have been devoted to him, and he seems to have been generous to Rassul. But one sees that the traveller to whom Rassul was chiefly devoted was the kind-hearted American gentleman, Mr. Robert Barrett, who instigated him to write this book, and who is at this moment again in the Himalaya.

FRANCIS YOUNGHUSBAND.

November, 1923.

Editor's Introduction

Rassul Galwan, whose story "will come follow," was born in Ladak with Pathan blood in his veins. He was my husband's servant, through two years of travel, some fourteen months of it in the saddle in Central Asia; much of it under trying and unusual conditions.

Rassul was caravan bashi. That is to say, he had entire charge of the caravan, consisting of a nucleus of some twenty Ladaki ponies, a dozen donkeys, and six men, supplemented at one time or another by a considerable number of ponies or donkeys to carry grain, or of yaks or coolies to carry the packs over passes where the snow was deep, or of camels for desert work. Rassul handled all monies (rendering very interesting accounts), bought or hired all animals and men, estimated, bought and doled out all supplies, besides acting as diplomatic representative for his sahib, dealing for him with governors and officials. All this work Rassul did very effectively, and according to a high standard of honour.

Rassul had been "always travelling with gentlemen," as his story tells. When he joined my husband he had an English vocabulary of a dozen words, and therewith an ambition to write "the story of his happened" in the English language.

The travelling of "the poor sahib" was not "sure," like that of other gentlemen. "Everywhere he like, there he go." The caravan was left to wait for days and days, while the sahib travelled alone, "from desert to desert, from top hills to hills tops," studying mountains and valleys. These periods of mere waiting, without adventure or work, without (except at long intervals), even the excitement of incipient mutiny to subdue, wore on Rassul, and my husband presently suggested that he turned his energies to the writing of his book.

To assist him in this, the sahib spoke with him "into his breaking English," using his dozen words and increasing their number; began corresponding with him by messenger whenever they were separated for any length of time; and, when they were separated permanently, gave him to read the King James Bible and a seventeenth century book of travel. The sahib corrected the first crude attempts at the story, always retaining as many of Rassul's expressions as were consistent with intelligibility, and encouraging him to keep on writing.

The thin sheets of manuscript have been following us all over the world for fully fourteen years. Unintelligible early chapters have been sent back several times for re-writing. At last Rassul has acquired a style with which we do not tamper.

His memory holds every impression made on it. We have eliminated many pages descriptive of weather and trail difficulties, of intense importance to Rassul and his sahib at the time, but not of interest to the reader of the story; and have condensed, where the day-by-day narrative style has drawn an incident out to undue length. We have also, in some sections, where a later draft showed too manifestly our corrections, used an earlier version, or "restored" the original.

The style is perfectly intelligible if read aloud. We have punctuated it with that in mind, and do earnestly implore the reader to use that method. This is not a book for the eye. It is a tale, "the story of my happened," intended for the ear.

Lieutenant-Colonel Sir Francis Younghusband and Mr. St. George Littledale, to whom we have read parts of the story, treating of events, and names, and descriptions of country with which they are familiar, agree in crediting Rassul with remarkable accuracy.

Rassul is now about forty-five years of age, and is, at present, Aksakal of Ladak, that is, chief native assistant of the British Joint Commissioner (the "B.J.C." of the story), who, under a commercial treaty between Great Britain and the Maharaja of Kashmir, is in authority over the traders meeting at Leh to exchange their goods; caravans coming in over the great main routes from India to the South, from Tibet to the East, and from Turkistan to the North.

Ladak, of which Leh is the capital, is part of the west extremity of that great mountainous plateau back of the Himalayas, called Tibet. It used to be politically part of Tibet, and is still religiously part of it, but late in the seventeenth century became a province of Kashmir.

The Indus flows through Ladak in a valley, whose floor lies at about ten thousand feet above sea level, and whose sides rise to twenty thousand. Leh lies in a short tributary valley from the north, which flares broadly toward the Indus. The city is built on a rocky spur at the point where the tributary begins to flare. The triangular-shaped valley floor, sloping rather steeply from the city down to the Indus, is terraced and irrigated, and planted with trees and many green things, and there is grass here and there in the valley, above the city; but the valley sides are barren of anything but scant low bush, and the passes across the mountains to north and south (the lowest of them, seventeen thousand feet) are deep in snow in May.

This little rock-built city, with its massive palace, old monastery, and fortification towers showing above low flat-roofed houses, and the long, straight, tree-lined bazaar, quiet enough in the winter months, when only a few thousand folk are there, but swarming in summer with traders and their caravans, was the scene of "the borning birth" of Rassul Galwan, and has been the point of departure, and the goal of all his travels, ambitions and adventures since.

Rassul himself I find thus described in letters written

by my husband on the journey, on which he employed Rassul as caravan bashi:

"Rassul's manners are perfect: the most polished gentleman could do no more than equal them."

"He is a very good person, and a father to his men."

"He is a very black, very handsome man, graceful in all his movements, his smile most charming. His voice is the sweetest man's voice I ever heard. The woman lives not who would not fall in love at first sight, but his standard of morals is very high. The women are afraid of him as of a saint."

Rassul writes me that, since his son's birth, he has determined, by his fakir's advice, to call himself Ghulam Rassul Galwan. But, in the years that his story has been coming in, in manuscript, it has made for itself a little audience, which cannot transfer its interest from Rassul to Ghulam. May the fakir forgive!

THE WIFE OF THE POOR SAHIB.

page 1

From here I am begining for next story by the help of God.

After the journey of Mr Martyen. I was a little rich than befor. my wife and I both spoked and said we dont want any journey any more now. God have gave as us enough money. now we can opened a shop. As that I was opened a shop. in that shop I selled some clothes and Tea etc.

at day I lived on the shop for food his coming home at nigth lived home. at that time my wife and my felt were both very happy. and there were the sweet took little two daughters all that seemed very happy and

One day I got a Registor letter from Captain Peterton. from the British Joint Commissioner

[Facsimile page of the author's handwriting.]

Rassul's Song

THE sun gave from east.
    It is God's kindly.
Four side round made bright.
    It is power almighty.
On poor boy look kindness.
    On poor Rassul look kindness always.
Rassul not have work or money.
    By kindly God get humble business.
If gave God, He not look
    If wise or simple,
He not care
    If big or little.

My Family

The Story of My Great-Grandfather, the Black Robber, which I Heard from my Mother.

This told my mother me. Long years before, in Kashmir hills, were herds of ponies belonging Maharaja, and were very many people to watch to them, on those mountain pastures. One those people, after, become a robber. His name Kara Galwan. Kara was his name (means: black). Galwan means robber. He was a very strong and clever a robber. He robbed in houses of rich men, and he robbed on way. He climbed high walls like a cat. Where he saw good one pony, that stole he. He kept very best ponies for own use. What matter he taught those ponies, that they understand. What he bade them do, that they did. After, about fifty men join him. What he bade the men, they do, same ponies. He kept good ponies for the riding all those men. Sometimes when Kara ride through a villages, he meet with beautiful girl on way. Then seize that girl; put her up on ponies; run very fast.

Kara gave much money poor men. Many rich men in Kashmir very hard men, never gave any money to poor men, only one or two pies sometimes. Kara like rob these hard men on way, and in house, give all their money poor men.

One time Kara climbed up into Maharaja's house. He had with him big knife that time. He woke Maharaja; told to him: "I am Kara Galwan. You must never give order catch me, if you not want me come here again with big knife. Maybe that time will kill you." Like this, did Kara with many big men. Not any men knew Kara where he lived, only they know that he lived in tent, in jungle with big trees, in mountains. Sometimes lived one part; sometimes another part. He never lived in house. Sometimes he went India for robbing-work. Maharaja always afraid Kara come again his palace. All people were frightened when they saw Kara. Rich men afraid at night in house; and afraid in day when they travelling. Short word, Maharaja and all villages men very tired with all the trouble Kara made for them.

All men wanted catch Kara, but they afraid to try, because they know if not catch, he make more bad with them than before. Kara had many different thing to kill men with. Sometimes he had with him one whip. With this whip did kill very plenty men. If could catch Kara same way men catch tiger, when he not know they would come, maybe then could keep him so that he cannot run. Kara had very good one friend. Sometimes he come that friend's house, and friend make dinner for him. One day Maharaja heard this friend matter. Then he called that friend to his palace; told to him: "If you will make one bandobast (arrangement) to catch this man, I will give you very plenty presents, and all country peoples will be glad for what you do." That friend said: "When Kara come my house to dinner, that day we catch him." This was very bad one friend, but plenty Kashmiri men do this bandobast; and sometimes good men do it, because they frightened for Maharaja. If they not do Maharaja's order, then Maharaja kill them. Anyway, that friend dig one hole, like well, deep, in own house. Over that hole put one rug. Then he made dinner for Galwan. That time Maharaja sent plenty sepoys. They all stop one place, where Galwan cannot see them.

Galwan came for the dinner. He never could think this friend will any time make bad with him. He not look very careful all place, same he look when he go one place, where he think they not his friends. Not see sepoys. Not see well. He walked into friend's house; fell into well. Down there in well, he told some matter like a song. He said: "Do not know if my friend do this, or not do. Anyway, now myself will catch own both hands, and give to Maharaja my body. Not need any man do anything with me." That time had with him very plenty things for kill men, but all gave Maharaja's sepoys. Only that whip not gave.

Then sepoys take him and put Maharaja's prison. While he live that prison, they made one gallows for hang him. Three, four days after, they took him gallows place; and he stood there on loose board under gallows, with rope on neck. And he had a wife of India. She came there that time. Then she told song, very good one song in Kashmiri language. Now, at this time, plenty Kashmiri men remember that song. Then he gave his whip that friend, for remember. Then one sepoy let drop that board, and Galwan felled, and his neck broke with rope.

That time many men run from Kashmir. They think maybe Maharaja hang them, because they like Kara Galwan, and give help him, plenty time. Some run India; some other place. My grandfather come to Baltistan. My grandfather's name was Mahmut Galwan. One brother name was Gaffor Galwan. Other names I not remember.

Mahmut took one wife Baltistan, and they all came Leh. They very poor that time when reach at Leh. My grandfather and two his sisters winnowed wheat for earn money. Baltistan, that time, my mother was in womb. She born Leh, and next one sister to her born. I not know sure my grandfather was son Kara Galwan, but I think was.

My Borning Birth in Leh and What Kind My Family We Were.

Leh is little village, surrounded by mountains. That look grey, all. There not any jungle and grass, like in wet country. There very plenty rocks and sand. For this, looks all grey. Weather not is very hot or cold, but winter more long than summer, and more cold weather than warm. And it is dry country. Up mountains, snow comes often; lies there very more deep than in villages. That place are several mountains all time covered ice and snow.

When Galwan ran away from Kashmir, and my grandfather came Leh, were three brothers and two sisters. One brother's daughter was my mother. One sister's son was Shukur Galwan. He lives now Yarkand. One brother, Gaffor Galwan, had no any children. Because their parents were poor, Gaffor keep my mother and Shukur as own children. Then they grow older. Gaffor married my mother to Shukur Galwan. That always Mussulman's custom, that brother's son and next brother's daughter can marry.

After that marriage, Gaffor Galwan went to Yarkand. My mother and Shukur Galwan left in Leh, very poor. And Gaffor Galwan very poor, that time he go Yarkand. After some years, Gaffor Galwan get very rich in Yarkand. I heard they got rich this way: one time was war in Yarkand between Chinese and Turki people. Gaffor Galwan found good money in that war.

My mother and Shukur Galwan not get rich in Leh. They heard that Gaffor Galwan was rich man. Their friends said: "You go to him. You will get a little rich, too." So Shukur Galwan went to Yarkand, too. My mother left in Leh. When Shukur Galwan met Gaffor Galwan, Gaffor not would help him. Shukur Galwan worked for own self in Yarkand; found good money. And he found there a wife; forgot my poor mother. She did write many letters. Not get any answer. She very hard-working in Leh. After long time, Shukur Galwan write her one letter. That say: "I not come back. You marry with some other man." Then my mother marry with Ibrahim, and had my sister and me and two other boys. Shukur Galwan lived in Yarkand, and Gaffor Galwan lived there too. When I go there, I not know them, because with my mother was enemies for that old matter.

When I came Yarkand with Captain Younghusband sahib, my grandfather came for look us all Ladak men. They shown him to me across the garden, and they said: "He is your grandfather." I went to him and said: "A salaam aleikum." He said: "Who are you?" I said: "I am a grandchild of your." He said: "I not have any relations and grandchildren." From that day he not speak to me any. After that, I did come several times Yarkand. He never speak with me. He afraid, if we say we are his relations, then all his money we might take when death came. He was bad one grandfather. Shukur Galwan was kind with me.

Our father's name not was Galwan. The mother, our root, was Galwan. For this we got the good name Galwan, which mean "bad-trouble-man" in Kashmiri language. Myself have written that name in letters always, when I had done the letter. But my brothers not like this name at all.

My mother was very bad angry woman with every one. My brothers could not take that angry of mother. While after, they went Yarkand. One time, my sister did marry. I live alone with mother. What mother bade me do, that did. My mother's angry was very bad, but with me she was kind.

What I did in my Young Time

Play.

My mother all times took me with her everywhere she went for winnow wheat. She always more kind with me than with other children. In summer I go every day with mother's young goats to places where was little water-springs, and little flat places all over grass. I like very much those place. We make there ponds and ditches and gardens and house. Sometimes I got other boys for come with me, build bridge.

That time I thinking in my head, in night-time, plenty about that building. Sometimes I build all alone, big one house. Maybe I work ten days that house. Must needs make first, brick, in little one matchbox. Those brick make dry in sunshine. And plenty wood things make with knife for door and window. Made all same house Ladaki rich men, plenty high. When got done my house, then myself was very pleased. Sometimes went little way off, for look house. It looked me very beautiful. Then thinking myself: "If make one garden front house, be more beautiful." There made garden, and pond and bridge. Sometimes some old man came that way; look my work. That time I go little long way from house; put ear that way; hear what they say about my house. One man said: "Look this house and garden. What boy made them, that boy very clever." I did hear this. Then I go near. They say: "Who built it? We suppose you built it. Those brick, with what make them?" Then I showed that match-box. All things showed them. They said: "You are very wise a boy." Then my felt was happy.

Sometimes I did take long grass from fields, puted it on backs of young goats. They came all the time behind me. All people laughed, when they look young goats carry grass. Mother laugh too.

There was old wall, one side of our house, more high than house-roof. That wall plenty thick, made brick. That roof, it flat roof, same all Ladaki roofs; cover over our house and next house. That house live one tailor man. I play plenty on that roof. There was one hole in that wall. There I keep my all playthings. I cut out more place that wall, make beautiful loggias. That time in Leh, wazir was European. Name was Mr. Johnson. All his family was with him. Their servants, chairs, tables, look me beautiful, that all. I want make like them. For this, plenty thinking, in night and at day. Then play plenty in day. There went for searching good paper, where English gentlemen live. There they threw one place some tin and paper. That all things I bring home, keep in hole in wall. First, made chairs and tables of tin. Then, made tops of tables and bottoms of chairs out of that paper. From tailor-place brought little pieces cloth. In plenty tailor-man's place spoke nice matter for cloth, and made friends with them, the tailor-men. Then I made some sahibs and mem sahibs. Their faces made with white dobe, their hats and boots with bocha (mean one thing make oil from). Myself was servant to sahib.

That time our house-master put new roof one side our house, that side where tailor-man lived with family. That tailor-man was of Kashmir. Plenty time I played on that new roof. Sometime, when went into fields with young goats, did take my sahib and memsahib, and played, making myself servant of sahib. Plenty I spoke with my sahib. Then always found good money. Always sahib like me. In my play, too, found for myself good wife. One day, in the nice thinking-time, in the fields, came my brother very quickly. He said: "Come quick." He made angry. I did ask to him: "Why want me?" He said: "You made plenty different things on roof; to-day found bad luck." Another word not say. I thinking: "What matter is?" When I came home, near our house were very many people, and wazir. Middle them was mother. Mother catch to me, put me quickly in.

What was that trouble, I not know then. After, I know that new roof, where I made sahib and chairs and table, fall down. There died, in that tailor's family, two women and four children. My mother first in thinking I died too. After, master of that house said me: "You make the sahib's chair and the sahib and the memsahib. For this I find bad luck. All time you do different than other boys. Other young boys make good work; find good luck. If boy make like you, find bad luck." I was very sorry for this. That man was Bhot man. Bhot men do not like this sort work. I did not make any more that sort work from that day.

In winter are many tamashas (festivals). In Ladak, lamas make tamashas. Then lamas make one thing we call storma. Those storma look, some like men, some like different animals. Some they burnt in fire, some put one place, shot with guns. When the lamas' tamasha done, then we children made one place a lama temple. Then made storma ourselves. I did make one storma like lamas'. I tried before in house two, three days, for make this thing.

Sometimes we make horses. We took in hands those horses and went round Leh. Plenty boys went. One place we put all horses. There came some old men, for look our work. Horses and stormas, these all put together. Then we asked to them which they more liked. They said for mine sometimes. Then all boys called me clever, and I thanked to them. Short word, other Ladak boys that time cannot do my work. All my work was quite different to other boys'. This all was done, when my age was from seven to twelve. After, what beautiful things I saw, I made like those things. On walls of temples came very beautiful flowers. The lamas made them with brush and paint. Those, flowers, how they looked, I kept in my head. Then, where find flat stone, I wrote them on that stone.

That time mother often took me to fort, for carry the suttoo she got, when she winnowed the wheat. I wrote all the flowers on walls of fort. Plenty I wrote bottle that they keep flowers in. Sometime I wrote a temple of lamas. What I wrote down on wall, another man not know who wrote it, only my mother and kutedar know. Mother looked my work very glad, and she called me "Galwo" (mean: "little egg"). Who men look on my work on walls, they said: "Very interesting one boy, this." Plenty men said my mother about me: "This boy, when grows up, will make very good work. Yours is good luck." And mother said very good matter to them about me, how I take her order, what I did in house. Then they more said: "Very good boy." When I heard this matter, my felt were very good. I said myself: "When make more old, then find more good luck." I was hurry for be old. And in head all time in night made rich, made meet with big men and spoke with them, and meet with beautiful girl friends, and found good wife, and wear good clothes and eat good things. And for mother made very good work, and saw many different countries with sahibs. All the time I played in head with this matter.

Going for Dung.

Soon after my age came twelve, mother must want me find fuel. I used go for the wet dung. That dung made dry in sunshine. For the dung many other boys and girls went together. Then played some games, made pakpho and pakma (bridegroom and bride). Some girls made mother. Some boys made father, and marry. Dust use for chang (beer). But I not like this play. Only I like that play which are in my head all time. In that autumn I went along the trails where see donkeys, horses and yaks. I found more dung than other boys did. Mother very pleased with me for that.

I wore long coat of wool of sheep, and one little long

hat of lamb's skin. Was part of my coat, that hat. I not had pants. For legs wore puttees of numdah (felt). Sometimes shoes wore, some Kashmiri, sometimes paboo made with sheep-wool and goat-hair. Sometimes do not wear any shoes. Wore on shoulders the skin of goats we call lockpa. The lockpa was for keep basket from breaking my coat. A big basket I took everywhere on my back to hold the dung. Three times in day I went out. Once in morning. About ten o'clock came and took breakfast. Then worked again from breakfast to tiffin. Then one more basket, in evening, bring. When found good luck, then bring four baskets, bad-luck time only two. I went outside Leh for the dung, where is no man place, not any house. I made one hundred salaam to Allah, sometimes three hundred salaam. For this I hope the dung find rich, so my mother pleased with my work. These times I played in head; sometimes play that I read Koran, sometimes other book, sometimes English book. Sometimes I not played that read in book, but played that went long way in world.

That time I made for mother that sort of servant work, did not make any other boy. All Ladaki, old, young, and beautiful girls said: "Rassul Galwan very clever."

How Beat My Mother Me.

When got mother a little angry, she beat to me, with her hand, on my head and my back. When got very angry, she caught to me, and threw me on floor. She herself rode on my back. Her face keep where my legs were and her back keep where my head was. Then took my clothes up, until my belt. (That time I not wear pantaloons, all Ladaki boys not wear them.) Then she beat to me with her fingers, and pulled my meat up between her fingers and thumbs. That pinching (scanchus) hurt very plenty more than beating, and the wounded place lived sick a few days, and in that time mother plenty abused to me.

When mother not was angry, those days she said to me: "The pinching is more useful for children than beating. If beat on head and body, that is no good. Why? When the child gets older, that time be sickly. The child body is soft. That pinching not make bad after. And in young time is hurting good. Then not doing fault any more."

Other Ladaki mothers do same my mother.

Running from Tailor-Place.

I liked very plenty read and write. But that time, in Leh, no have any school, where can read. But here were some rich men's teacher they kept for own children. If I give good money that teacher, they teach me. But I no have money. Anyway I told plenty time to my mother, about how I want learn read some thing. One day mother said me: "We have poor. I no have money to give your teacher. It is rich men's work, reading and writing, not ours. Another thing, did not read our grandfather and father anything. They were hard-working. You should do same them. That be good for you." I said to mother: "Yes. They work hard for earn. But I like reading. Maybe my luck be good. I would be learning good things. Be good for future. I must want read some thing. If you like, let me go teacher-place. I hear the reading is more good than other work. Now will be little expense. After, will find good money." Mother said: "No, you go tailor-place. That be good for future, and is no expense."

Anyway, mother gave me to a tailor-place. I went there. I were there about a month. All time I live to the tailor-shop. I not like this work any, but cannot help. And was very sorry. Why? Not was rich. If was rich, could read good things. Not rich, get this trouble.

In that tailor-shop was tailor-man bad. He beat to me, without any fault, plenty time. One day was tamasha to the Gagoon village. There is the lamas' temple. The lamas do good tamasha. Plenty Leh people going to the tamasha. That day the tailor beat to me, too.

I get very angry; run from his shop; came to home; then told mother what does the tailor to me. Mother not believe my matter; does more angry to me. I get very sorry; run from home; on the hill; up bazaar; near the raja home. From that high place, seeing the people who were going the tamasha.

That time, I thinking: "I will never go to the bad tailor-man. And mother to-day does very angry. No, I don't like go home, too. And all this people going the tamasha. Why I not go too? It be good, once, to see a good tamasha. Another, see the Gagoon villages. When I come there, I can live all night Gatoo's house, and see what do that bad tailor and mother. They did angry without my fault." In this thinking I went Gagoon.

When I pass about four miles, I get tired. That time was cold weather, and I no was shoes on my feet. Who people I meet on road, they say: "Where do you go without shoes?" I get very ashamed with this.

When I came near the Gagoon, there is a bridge. There I did tired very much. Why? I have not did any travelling before this. That time, get very sorry the poor boy for coming to tamasha, and cried very plenty myself.

The evening I arrived to Gagoon. I asked: "Where is Gatoo's house?" (One friend of our.) They said: "It is about two of miles." It is like a hundred miles to me that time. Short word, I could not get there, and then I do not know in night where I would sleep, and who give food to me.

After little while, came our friends of Leh. They see to me; then say: "Why do you came here without shoes? Now you come live with us." I went with them, very glad for getting good sleeping-place and food. In that night came my brother to Gagoon, for searching me. When he see me, he went back Leh. And I seeing the lamas' tamasha and the Gagoon villages. There were two days tamasha.

After three days we all returned Leh. When mother see to me, she say: "Why you went to the tamasha? If like, why not ask me? Anyway, you see good tamasha. I not angry."

Mother not returned me to that tailor-place. I lived with mother. When I grew older, mother gave me the order to cook, besides gathering dung. When I cooked, I get up early in morning; went for water two times. I did take with me our basket; in it put our water-bottle. That water-place was about two hundred yards far from our home. When I brought the water, I made clean the living-room.

How We Lost Our Bread and Found Jhadoo.

One time I saw a boy play with a banjo, that had made himself, with own hand. His father was banjo-man in Leh.

That banjo look me very wonderful one thing for my play. But he not could give me. That was a spoon of wood, which the Ladaki people use for cook.

When I came home, I did find one old spoon which we had, and I did make me a banjo, with own hand. But was little hard work; could not ready it in that day. I did keep it into the hole where I keep all my playthings all the time.

The following day I went to the meat-seller place, and bought a little piece of stomach of goat, and some horse-hair of tail. I did find that all thing. And I was very busy near the happy hole, in the work of my banjo.

That day was nearly done, but could not get dry the skin. In that time, mother came from the winnowing-place to home. Mother called to me. I put the banjo quickly into the hole; came to mother. She bade me mix the wheat flour for chapattis. When I done the flour, I gave to mother. She did cook the bread. That time I could not cook the bread. Mother herself did; and then bade me other work which were in house, which I can do. All that I did, but my feel was to that hole, where was my banjo. And said myself: "When mother goes out room, I will do my own good work."

When mother done her bread, then said me: "Take care, Rassul, don't let the goats eat the bread." Then mother went out room. I found time for own work, and thought that: "It is a long time now, would not come goats from hill. Until, do my own work. After, then will take the bread, and will shut the door of room." In this thinking, went to that hole where was the nice banjo, and made it. In this business I did forget the bread and door and goats.

One time I heard the noise of goats from our room. I did came down into room. There were all our goats. They had reached, while before, and had gone the bread, all. These our goats were robber, like our grandfather. I found very bad luck for me. Now what shall I do? Anyway I beat to those goat with a big stick, and myself said: "What do?"

And those day were Ramadan, the Mohammedans' one month we not eat anything daytime. We eat, evening and middle-night. Those bread were for evening, and for half-night. Mother and I were both very hungry. Why? We had not eat anything in daytime, and it was nearly evening for the dinner. Mother must surely beat me to-day. That time came in head a lie-matter. Must need tell her that the door was shut and that goats opened it theyselves.

While after, mother came in room, and she not knew what fault I had done. When mother get in room, I went nearly the door, and said to mother that lie-matter. Mother not believe for my lie. She got very angry; came toward me for beat me. I ran away out the house. Mother could not catch to me.

Then I wait an hour in bazaar, and said myself: "What do?" One thing, that time was very hungry. and where sleep? Now must need go back at home, Maybe mother forget that angry; I will find good luck. I did come home. When I reached the door, that was shut inside. Then I beat the door. Mother came on the window, and said with very angry: "You don't come my home. Where you like, there go. I don't want you any more. I am a poor woman in this country. Got little to earn living. With that brought up you children. You don't thinking I am poor. You play like a rich man's son. To-day you did this fault. Next time, when you would be older, you must rob. Then will take me the court-place. That time what do the poor woman?" And said many matter. I could not remember that all.

When mother said all that matter, my feel got very sorry. Myself said: "Why I did make the banjo? If not did, was not so much bad luck" And I said many times to mother: "Please, mother, you forget this my fault, and let me come in, and don't beat me to-day. I shall not do like this fault, never. If you see any my fault, future, then you must need beat me very hard. Let me come in, and give something for eat."

Mother said: "I don't open the door. If you find food and clothes, where you like, go there. Your brothers went. I could not catch to them. You do, same them." I said: "I never do like them. I am like your servant. What you like, that you do to me. If you want sell my body, you sell me, for your expense. You are my mother."

Mother did not give any answer. The window shut; went to bed. I left out the door. I did sleep by the our door on ground, in the hoping maybe I will get in, at half-night, when mother take food. That time was feel very sleepy and hungry, but were many play in my head: with that, feel was happy. Sleep a little, but not much sleep in the sorry.

One time I try open the door; could not open it. But I got one thing from a hole up side our door. That was a pieces cloth, one inches wide and long, like a bag. In that was a piece paper. I looked it in the moonshine. There on was wrote some thing. I do not know what it is, but it was nice one thing for play. I tied it in my belt, and sleep again.

In the sleep I heard the calling for eating-time. Then got up all Mohammedi people for eating. My mother got up, too, but not take me in. But there was near our home good one woman. She was a very good friend with my mother. She and her husband came their door and said me: "Rassul, come here, take food, and you sleep here. You is good boy and hard-working boy. Your mother does not see that all. She sees the little fault, which to-day you done. Come in." I did went to their home, and they gave me bread, meat and tea. I got happy, and they ask some question: "How the goat eat the bread?" I told all the banjo matter: what I did, that all. They laughed very plenty. After, I did show that thing, which I found, which was in my belt. When they see it, they said: "It is jhadoo. It was made one woman for bad luck to your mother. You are lucky boy, for this you found it." That time they called to my mother. Mother came there; see it; said: "Lucky boy." Mother forgot that my fault at all. And said: "I want read what is wrote on it." That thing were very bad one thing, but for me it came very lucky thing. With that mother let go me. She did not beat to me.

In the morning mother went to a mullah to learn what was on the jhadoo. The writing was Arabic. Mullah said: "If was left at your door this thing, then will the husband of your daughter not like your daughter any more. You must wash it in milk, and throw in river."

After, mother found another paper near the door. That was written by a lama. Mother went a lama's place for read it. The lama said: "It is a very bad thing. You are lucky to find it. If it get in your house, then you be mad, one time. You need put in shoe few days." (I had not been the both reading-place. I did heard from my mother these story, all.)

And who had made this bad thing? In Leh was a good merchant. Name was Kardin Khan. He married with a girl. After a few years he did not like that wife. Let go her. He married with my sister, and was very nearly with my sister. That lost wife did this bad thing. Herself could not make. She gave money to those things maker, lama and mullah. (And this thing not make all lamas and mullahs. It make a few bad lama and mullah. Good lama and mullah not like those thing maker.)

Afterwards my mother went many times and fought with that woman, who had done the bad thing. They not fight with hand, but with mouth; said many bad matter, both my mother and that woman too.

Myself got good luck; made the banjo well, and got the skin dry. The good woman friend of my mother said to mother: "Don't tell anything. You look what he has done." My mother said to me: "Let show us." I did show mother the banjo. Then mother laughed very plenty, and it showed to many people, and said: "That lose bread, but found the bad-woman thing." All people laugh who seen my banjo.

After several days I found a next play, forget that one.

Going Boyhood after Bortsa.

In every spring I went mountains and valley about the bortsa. I did go with those friends which come below: Galam, Kalam Rassul, Razak Akhun, Lasou, Samdu, Hussin, Salem, Juma, and some girls: Nome, Eshai, Jahmin, Karah, Yungsket, Palket. In these girls are Palket beautiful, Eshai was beautiful, Nome was little beautiful. Other all girls not was beautiful or ugly.

When we want go to mountain, one day before, we sew our paboo (mean: "shoes"). That paboo are made with sheep's wool, or goat's hair or yak's wool, not any leather. That break very easy. We keep strings and needles all time with us. When our paboo break, we sew. That time we wear pattoo cloth (homespun), and each child wear skin of goat on back, for not break the cloth.

For what sort food we take with us, thaltuk is wheat flour bread. Sometimes zan. This is that sort of food; wheat, barley and beans, put together. We wash it in water, then roast, same coffee. Then grind same flour. Then cook in pot. Before, put water and salt, how much wanted, then put in flour, then stir with wooden thing. When it boiling good, take from the fire. Cut for each man a slice. Sometime we take calak, that is barley, made like that other. We used to put this wooden bowls, and wet with tea, and knead well. These all we take to mountains; and beside it, take a little piece in each people's pocket.

We starting from home, early morning, about four o'clock, sometimes about five o'clock. Sometimes went to that valley west side Leh, called Chagda. There are each valleys different names. Sometimes went Laporma, sometimes Seyuchan, sometimes Feynugla, sometimes Shongsha. That side do not find any water, but two places are little springs. In big valley is Leh. Branch valleys are all those names which I wrote. Sometimes we went two miles, sometimes three miles before we reached to the valley, about seven o'clock or eight o'clock. To that place we eat breakfast; eat all together; spread blanket for table. When eat, that time speak very nice matter and laugh very plenty. Half food eat that time; half keep for tiffin, under a stone. After breakfast, some climb up mountain, some other side valley, some this side valley. We don't take the bortsa close to each other, but what speak can hear, and what sing. All we hear from other side of valley to this side. When get hungry, then take that little piece, which keep in own pocket, and that eat. Some girls singing other side of valley, some singing this side of valley. Sometimes boys up the mountains sing, and from this side to other side said with singing plenty different matter, and what came into mouth that tell.

Hussin and I climb very high place where we found the tsafat growing in cracks in rocks. We put in the cracks our pick-axe, and sometimes break a big piece of rock. When is ready to break, we call: "Take care! Don't tell you heard or saw, and we will let fall this rock for your tamasha and ourselves wood!" When the big stone falls, it go from hill to hill, the noise, like cannon and gun. It go below very far. That was very good tamasha, and there was plenty dust. Sometimes we fall some stone, without wood. When big piece falls, breaks into plenty piece.

When get enough wood, we put into baskets; tied with rope and carried on back; and came below. As we came down, we sang a song like this:

> "Don't look up the mountains at the sun.
> You will be cold: never be warm.
> If look far away husband or wife,
> Heart will be sorry, never be glad.
> Come people, quickly down."

All came below to that place, where took breakfast in the morning-time. Then, that place, eat the tiffin all together. That time speak more nice matter than the morning-time, with these girls; and sew the paboo. When we have thirst, we eat the snow. Sometimes put the snow on a stone where came good sun. Then under it dig a little place. There put the skin of goat which we wear. Then the snow melted; come into it. That we drink. Sometimes very late afternoon we eat that tiffin. After that tiffin, carry load, each people's on back. Then one would say: "Hadám malá hadámly" (what that means, I not know. I did ask other people; that not mean anything). Then other one would say: "Haslám boo nilály." And there were always rest places by old buildings with stones. When reached to that place, one boy said: "Take rest." Others said and sang other things. What came into mouth that said. Sometimes we reached to home before evening; sometimes evening; sometimes after evening.

That time drink tea, eat suttoo. One day take rest. Next day go again to mountain.

One day I go bazaar. There met many boys, which not go to mountains after wood. They joked me and said: "We eat rice and sugar and all good things. You am poor boy, which only eat suttoo. You cannot be strong as us." I said: "Poor boys' food, suttoo, is more strong than good food, which you people eat. I can climb high the mountains." They said: "You cannot go high up. You bring the wood from low valleys." I showed them our tracks on a sandy pass. (That pass is much difficult to cross. From that pass we could see many plains and mountains and Leh village, very beautiful.) I said: "You people cannot go there. Those tracks are ours." They not believe. They said: "Go there to-morrow. Make new tracks right side." Next day I did that all, what they told. And I showed those tracks from bazaar and said: "Look the sand! I did that which you people told." They said: "It is true matter. You are more strong than we are."

When Leh people saw our rich wood, many Leh people come with us. There was one those people, name Lunxum, a woman, very ugly and dirty and foolish. She did eat the dust of the earth. That made her face yellow and bad-looking. We not like her coming with us. We not eat food same place as her. She hated us. We joked to her. Once she said me: "Why you people not eat with me? You not am big man sons. You are poor, and I am poor. You thinking yourself big." We said: "You are dirty. We am clean. You eat dust." She said: "When you see me eat dust? I not eat dust. Your father and your mother eat dust, and you eat dust. You people are mad. You make come down big rocks on mountain. You sing and talk like madmen." And she afraid to us.

The Service of Kutedar[1] in Leh

THE kutedar was a Kashmiri. The kutedar paid me one basket of small wood every day for my work. My work was this kind: every morning I took two buckets water to kutedar's house in a basket on my back. After, I waited at kutedar's house, and what they bade me, I did that. I was all the servants' servant, because I was a poor winnowing-woman's son.

Often, two servants went to wood-keeper's place with me. There we chopped wood. When enough of it was ready, I did carried it to wazir's rooms and munshi's. Other servants went for their breakfast to kutedar's house; I went home for mine.

After breakfast, sometimes, big kutedar came to the wood store-room and to the wheat store-room, and my mother came to winnow wheat, and I did work for big kutedar, for servants and my mother. Sometimes, I took wood and eggs to camps of travelling sahibs. At noon all the kutedar's people went their home for tiffin, and I went my home. After tiffin came back. At night I took home a basket wood; the chips left in that chopping. Last thing, I carried there more bottles of water for the kutedar.

When I got home at night, I must need help my mother and my sister. We talked that all what happened at kutedar's place that day, and then went bed. In this business went about a year.

The kutedar's wife cooked for kutedar. She was very bad one woman, and always made herself big, and ordered to me plenty, because she not like me. Often she said bad matter about my work to kutedar, but he not take her words. Sometimes, she did throw my water, and said: "I have no water." I took ten bottles of water every day there. I must carried the

[1] Kutedar means: headman, merchant.

water about four hundred yards place up a steep hill to that angry woman. That angry of her more difficult than that work.

In the autumn, when the farmers cut their grain, and brought it, all the wheat and barley, to the kutedar, it was stored, some in Leh village, and some in the fort.

The grain-measuring business no servants understand. A Bhot man from a village did it. Kutedar needed another man for that work. I could do it, but the kutedar did not know. I had learnt it in this way: when the farmers brought their wheat, my mother had some wheat from them. She kept a bag on left side of measuring-man. I sat there to watch to that bag. That measuring-business seem to me very good play. I keep that all in my head. I know well this business, but not did try it with own hands for a long time. I went often into wheat-keeper's room to work.

One day I told to kutedar that: "I know the wheat-measuring." He laughed, and said: "Boy, you cannot. This business is hard, and your hands are too little. We will lose wheat." I said: "I will measure once, and you people watch to me." Kutedar said: "That be good. Try. We will look." That day they let me measure. The kutedar watched very close. They took one bowl full, and weighed it. That weighed seven pounds. The big kutedar was very glad and the little kutedar too, but the other servants not like it.

From that day I measured wheat and barley, and little kutedar taught me all that business: how to give wheat, and the wood to the sepoys in the fort. After a few years I became like head-man in kutedar's service. Big kutedar trusted in my hands the keys of all wheat room, and when the wheat was taken from the farmers, big kutedar did not want the other man. He wanted me alone.

The other man robbed; he took money from the farmers, and said to big kutedar: "I measure their wheat," when he not had measured it. I not did know that robbing business, but I like very much measuring the wheat. That was good play, and it gave me a good name. I got more wheat into my bowl than the other man. This was cheating the farmers for kutedar. Sometimes I afraid to God to do this, and sometimes when see poor woman or man, I did let fall from the bowl some their wheat.

Sometimes came only a few farmers with wheat and wood. At those little works kutedar sent me alone; I measuring in the day time; at night, told to kutedar, and he write that down then. In those days I not could write, but I could keep in my head: how much wheat and wood I took from farmers, and how much I paid to sepoys.

I saw many things in service of kutedar: rich wheat and barley, butter and wood, and in the fort many old guns and plenty powder for guns and bullets, and some iron guns. (Same them, I saw, long after, in Japan.) In those days all this seem me very wonderful, and my felt rich, and my stomach was full with them. I did learn there the Hindustani language from sepoys, and the Kashmir language from kutedar.

[In "The List of My Story Chapters" there appears at this point: "In My Youth Going for Coolies' Works, Building Place, and Carry Goods of Trader from Serai to Bazaar and from Bazaar to Serai." This chapter appears to have been lost, in one or another of its journeys across the world from Rassul to his sahib, for correction or back again for re-writing. The next chapter gives a glimpse of the boy definitely beginning his life work of travelling with sahibs. The work with kutedar went on, between the journeys, for a number of years.—EDITOR.]

The Journey[1] with Dr. Trall

Head-Measuring.

That day, after tiffin, my mother gave me little bag with bundles of tea of Lhasa in it. Mother said: "One bundle you drink, the other give to fakir." A fakir, very good man, lived in Kashmir. In the bag was also some bread of Ladak. Mother said: "This bread you eat when you are hungry on the road, and give some to sahib if he likes." And mother sewed up three rupees in my coat, and said: "This money, when you need, you use; and if you lose some of sahib's money that he gives you for expense, then you must use this money. Take care: before you start you must show all these things to sahib. For, if sahib is robbed, and finds money with you, then he will look you a thief."

Next morning, at five o'clock, we left Leh. My mother caught to me in her arms and cried plenty. I cried, too, with her. At last I said salaam to mother, touched mother's feet with my hands, did salaam, and said salaam to all people which were near our house, and went to my sister's home and said salaam to her. After, went to sahib and packed up sahib's things. We had four hire-ponies; three for loads, and one for sahib to ride. Sahib had a Chinese saddle, that he put on a high horse.

After a long time we came to Feyangtakpo, where I had been before. Beyond that place I not had been. I asked there of the sais: "How longer is camp?" They said: "How far we come, it is so far." I not believe to them. But they had telling truth. I never had made a long journey. Camp was only eighteen miles from Leh. That seemed to me a very far.

I reached to there at noon, and camped in a garden. We got no meat for tiffin, only eggs. I did cook the

[1] From Leh to Kashmir.

eggs, and some rice, and served them to sahib on a table. After tiffin, I did unpack sahib's tent, to pitch it. Sahib said: "Don't open it again unless it rains." I said: "Yes." Then I washed, very clean, all cooking things and table things. When I done all that, I showed my bag to sahib and those three rupees. When sahib saw those, my things, he was pleased and said me: "You are a good boy."

That sahib's business was to measure the people's face, feet, and hands: everybody's. The Ladakis thought this would be for them unluck, not would let him measure them. Sahib measured me, all my body and my face, and said: "I will give presents to those men which will let me measure." I said to the villages men: "This measuring business not is bad. If it be bad, I never let sahib measure me." And some them said: "Yes, we believe to you. We will let sahib measure us." Then I said sahib: "Measure me every camp, and let the villages people see. Then will find other men for sahib, without trouble." Sahib did this always after, and got plenty people to measure.

In one place was chorten. Surrounding it was much beautiful pictures on stones. Those stones not were heavy. Sahib said me: "You tell to a man: 'Bring me a picture and I will buy it'." I told to a man. He said: "I will bring one at night." That man stole that stone, and gave to sahib. Sahib gave one rupee to him. That man was glad to get the one rupee without trouble, and sahib was glad to get the picture. I was glad because I had found the right man.

Reading-Business.

I came back Leh, after two months, from Kashmir. My earnings about thirty rupees were, and some clothes and boots, which things gave me Dr. Trall sahib. I hid two rupees one place, where mother not find them, for my play-money. Other money all, gave her. My mother and sister were very glad for my earning. When all things counted up, it came about forty rupees. Those days forty rupees was very much in Leh. My mother said me: "You earned good wages this year in two months; so much money and clothes. Now you need not go for wet dung fuel. It is a dirty work. I do not like you do it with the good clothes. I thought when you were in Kashmir: 'God did give him good money, beginning of journey. After, he would give him more.'" I said: "Mother, I told you often before, it is very good way for earn money, but you not let go me. Now I saw the Kashmir country, I hope go Yarkand for one journey." Mother said: "It is enough, journey to Kashmir. I was very much afraid, but God kept you well. Now I won't let go you on any more journeys. Yarkand is very bad one place. If you go there, then will never come back Leh." I knew well that some our relations went Yarkand and never came back. I said: "But I will come back." Mother said: "No, no." My sister said: "Why you people talk this? When a man goes Yarkand, God knows what his luck will be. We cannot know behind-matter."

By good luck, the dung business was finished from that time. That time was autumn. I spent about three months, sometimes grazing goats in fields, sometimes helping kutedar.

That year opened one school in Leh, of missionaries. The padre sahib taught there, and there were two masters for teaching Ladaki and Urdu. And there read plenty Ladaki boys, and there went three my friends, Ramzan and Kalam Rassul, and servant of munshi Ahmad Din. I used to going the munshi's servant's house. There came Ramzan and Kalam Rassul, and they read there their lesson books. I read them too, and they taught me. I said my friends: "I will come for reading at school."

They said, "You must come. There we find books without prices, and teaching very good."

I said my mother: "I earned good wages this year. Now I will go this school for learn. It not will cost anything, and now there is no work for me until comes spring, then I will go to mountains again for bush-wood."

My mother never liked the reading-business any time. She said: "That is not our business. You learn another business, that will be useful for us. Reading-business is for rich men."

My sister told mother: "Now Rassul has no work, you must let him read. If he learns something useful, that be good. If he not learn, no matter. Let him go. If not, will make very sorry, because those his friends go, and he not go." Then mother said: "Yes, you may go."

I went one morning for the reading. The padre sahib knew me. He said: "Rassul, why you coming here?" I said: "Sir, I want the reading." He said: "Why you want the reading?" I said: "I want Ladaki." The padre sahib said: "Yes, you may read, but not now. You must wait one month, then you come."

I was sorry for not beginning then, and came home and waited long one month. I reading plenty, munshi's house, with his servant, and with those my friends, and learning something from them. I was in much hurry for the reading-month to come. The servant of munshi, Kalam Rassul, and Ramzan, could read plenty.

At last came my reading-month. I went again to the school. The padre sahib gave me Ladaki one primer, and bade the Ladaki master for teaching me. I reading that primer in ten days, because I had reading it before with my friends. When it finished, the padre sahib gave me first reader. That finished very soon. Then he gave other books. God helped me to going ahead my friends. The padre sahib liked very much my reading, and he said, "You are learning fast."

He taught us accounts. I learning this very soon, too. And the padre sahib said to me: "Boy, you did very good work with Dr. Trall at Kashmir; now, you are doing good work with the reading, very good work, and in accounts, too, better than other boys here. I think you lucky a boy." When I heard that, my felt were glad, for I believed, myself, I would be lucky, when I grow up.

I reading at school about three months; never writing anything. Without writing, making letters, but I not know that people could read my writing. I showed it some people, my writing, and they reading it, but with difficult, for my writing was different sort. I not could make good letters. When I wrote one letter, it took long time, but I reading well other men's letters.

Now came spring. My mother bade me go mountains for bush-wood. I went mountains, but what I reading, that I never forget. And in work-time I remembered those lessons.

The Journey of Captain Younghusband[1]

The Service-Getting of Captain Younghusband.

In Leh, was a man, Mohammed Isa.[2] He been long in service of travelling-sahibs, who went Chinese Turkistan. That spring he got some letters from sahibs, about going the Yarkand journey. I heard that, and I said Mohammed Isa: "Please, you give me service of sahibs. I long for the journey by Yarkand." He said: "Yes, I will give you service of sais, but you must work with me some time without pay first." I said: "Yes, I will work." And I did work for him very plenty.

At last there came Leh two sahibs, very rich. With them was a black sahib named John.[3] He made people call him John sahib. I was working always with Mohammed Isa. After that, came to Leh other two rich sahibs,[4] and arrived there Captain Younghusband and Mr. Macartney.[5] There were six sahibs for the journey of Yarkand. I was very hoping to go Yarkand; and all Mohammed Isa bade me, I did.

Now were the other sahibs ready to going Yarkand. The Mohammed Isa not gave me the service. I working

[1] This was in 1890. Captain Younghusband had been commissioned by the Government of India to explore the Pamirs, in order to learn the state of affairs there. The Chinese had recently been re-established in Eastern Turkistan. The Pamirs formed a sort of no-man's land, surrounded by British, Russian, Chinese, and Afghan dependencies.

[2] Mohammed Isa was in Col. Younghusband's service when he went to Lhasa in 1904. He died in Sven Hedin's service.

[3] Rassul wrote a delightful chapter about John Sahib and his daughters, which was unfortunately lost.

[4] Messrs. Beech and Lennard on a shooting-trip.

[5] Mr. George Macartney (now Sir George Macartney), whose father had been connected with the British Embassy at Pekin for years. Mr. Macartney is English Political Officer at Kashgar through most of this story.

there, while the other men found the service, but not me. And sahibs bade Mohammed Isa, with the caravan, start two days before them. That I heard. I said to Mohammed: "Now it is time to start for Yarkand. When will you give me the service?" Mohammed said to me: "Boy, you are hard-working in villages, but you are not strong for the Yarkand way. There are plenty big rivers. You could not cross them. You are too young. Next time I will take you. Now, I have enough men." My felt very sorry. I said: "Why did not you tell me that before? I do not you like me, what can I do? It is my luck." I said: "Salaam," and came home, and told my sister all this sorry matter. She knew that I had worked for Mohammed Isa. She was very sorry too, but my mother did not know about my working for Mohammed Isa. After two days, the Mohammed Isa and his men started for Yarkand. The sahibs stayed in Leh for two days more.

I longed to go to Yarkand. What should I do? There was no help. I said to my sister: "I will show my sahib's chit to the big sahib; maybe he will take me, if Allah gives good luck." My sister said: "Yes, you must show it; maybe, you will find good luck."

The Journey from Leh to Yarkand.

I found good luck. Captain Younghusband took me. It was very bad flood-time. Sahib let me ride very beautiful one India pony at water-cross.

Arrived Panamik one day. There the men speaking with each other said: "Here is come a Russian man[1] and he wants to go Leh, but the Capt. Sahib will not let him go Leh, and him we will take with us back Yarkand.' I longed to look him, and see what sort of man is a Russian man. I never had seen a Russian man. They showed him to me in a garden, a white man and poor.

[1] Really an Austrian, collecting butterflies.

The next day we waited at Panamik for grain, and for other business. There sold the Shukar Ali[1] and Khalik some rice which was left from our provisions, and some grain which was left, to a horsemen. They divided that money and gave me one rupee and said: "After four days we will find another rupee each man, but don't you tell any man." I said: "Yes." There I wrote a letter to my mother.

I was hungry at one place, and I opened my bag, in which were all my things, and took out some bread. Shukar Ali saw me, and sent me quickly for work. I went, and left open my bag. While I working, Shukar Ali robber my things. I watched him from a wall. I was ashamed if he see me, and hid behind wall until he finished. He taking my ink-stand, and my knife, and some bread. When I came back I shut the bag and not let him know. And said myself: "This man is very bad. He robber sahib's grain, and now he rob me, and my mother begged him for helping me."

One day camped on a plain. There was no village. That seemed to me strange, and I asked: "Why do we camp here?" They said: "There are no more villages until Kilian." On the north was a wonderful glacier-mountain. On both sides the valley were high mountains, and big stream in flood, in valley.

In sahib's camp were several officers. One doctor Mussulman, a very good man, and one Chinese munshi, and the cook was an officer on me too, and the room boy, Barha. I obeyed all them. And there was a

[1] Shukar Ali was the only Ladaki to cross the Mustogh Pass with Younghusband in 1887. Younghusband says he knew that, with Shukar Ali as a member of the party, there would always be a volunteer for especially trying hard work. When Col. Younghusband was made Resident at Kashmir, Shukar Ali walked all the way from Leh to Srinagar. to see him, and show his reverence and affection. Younghusband treated him most kindly and obtained for him, from the Maharaja, an order exempting him from service in his village. Bearing this precious paper and a large present from his sahib, he returned to Leh. There he sought out Rassul and asked him to write the Colonel a letter of thanks. This letter Col. Younghusband published in the beautiful book on Kashmir, which he made, in 1908, in collaboration with Major Molyneux, the painter.

Gurkha man, the room-boy of Mr. Macartney. He was very good friend of mine.

At other one place Shukar Ali and Khalik sold some more grain. The money they divided among themselves. I hoping I would find some, but they not give me any. I nothing said. I not like that work.

One day Shukar Ali said: "The India horse I will take." I gave him, and I walking with the caravan. We went down a steep a place and came one stream very deep flood. When that water saw the Chinese munshi, he was afraid and said me: "Help me." I took off my shoes, and holding his horse in the water. On bad one hill, he called me again for help him. I obeyed him, and he gave me one rupee. I got two rupees from him. At evening I told to Shukar Ali and Khalik about the kindness of the Chinese munshi. They not like that.

The pony of munshi came very tired one day, and he found other one horse. The tired horse came with difficult to that camp, by himself. The next day Shukar Ali told me that: "Drive that tired horse." I did not know about tired horse, and I said: "Yes." For a while he came with caravan; then he went slower and more slow. I was left far away behind caravan and sahibs. I, walking alone with the tired horse, followed the track of the caravan. It was always up hill. After a long time we came very steep a hill, that was Depsang pass. I did not know that now the tired horse can not go any more. I beat to him and pulled to him and pushed to him, but he not can go one yard place. "Now what shall I do?" I said myself: "If leave him, what trouble will there be with sahib?" I was very sorry and cried there, and plenty time lost. At last I leaving the pony there, I thinking: "Can come back and take him again." On him was halter and julay. I, leaving him with them, came up the Depsang pass. There found big a plain; saw many mountains. Myself now was alone on this big plain.[1] For a while was

[1] The Depsang Plains are more than 17000 feet high.

afraid, because I not had seen before such country. I thought myself was lost; but very soon seeing the tracks of sahib's horses, and felt was better. One place met a caravan from Yarkand going Leh. My felt were very happy. They said John Mohammed has said for you: "Let go the tired horse and come the camp." I was very glad for this matter. John Mohammed Khan was an Afghan. He travelling always with sahib and he was good a friend of sahib. Now I walking, the way seemed very long. Very tired.

One place I found Hadar, the sais of Mr. Macartney, lie down. He tired too, and he said to me: "Where find the camp? Very tired, cannot walk." I said: "Don't stay here. We must try going camp; must be near." He said: "I don't want. I not know in India I find such trouble. If I know, I never come," and he abused to sahibs and said: "They have brought me here for kill me. Why not giving me riding-horse in so hard place?" I said: "I am not so tired as you. Come with me. We both will go camp. If you stay here, then at night will come the jungle dog and kill you." Then he get up and walking with me. We went up and down several hills and came at last one little stream; that was deep. We get very wet. After that we came up on a plain. There wind blowing hard, and it was very cold, and our felt very tired. All that country looked brown, and there was much rock, and there lay many bones of animals among rocks, and there no was grass or wood. Came night. We cannot see tracks of caravan. We not know the way. We said: "What shall we do? Where shall we go?"

By good luck we found help.

In Yarkand[1] with Captain Younghusband.

After long time[2] came Yarkand.

I longed to look the amban. One day he comes. With him were some men in red clothes and high hats. Some his men carried long sticks, some men carried knives, some men carried whips. One man carried very big umbrella, red, and one man carried a gong. That gong, when they beat it, could hear far way. The amban rode in wagon. That all seemed to me very good tamasha. When the amban coming near sahib's house, all the sahibs coming out one gate to meet him. And they took him, and they sat him at table, and put tea front him. But what they said, I not know. After while, the amban went back. Many people coming, bringing melons and other fruit for sahibs. We found plenty good things to eat. The amban coming several times to seeing sahibs, and sahibs going several times to seeing the amban.

I wanted see the amban's palace and the bazaar, and begged Shukar Ali to letting me go with sahibs. Shukar Ali said: "Yes, you may go." The next day, sahib bade Shukar Ali make ready the horses for going the sahibs. I walking very fast to keeping up with the horses.

In all bazaar the people standing up for sahibs. I felt happy to coming with so big a man. It was a very far way and we coming very fast. My body got very hot. At last we coming big one gate. And there they firing off big guns for sahibs' honour. And then we went through another gate and coming before another gate, very beautiful gate, under a high roof. And there was on it a picture of lion. Here sahib get off, I holding his horse, there coming the amban for meet with him, and took him in through that gate. I could

[1] The first considerable town north of Leh on the caravan route across the Karakorum Pass, on the southern edge of the great desert of Chinese Turkistan.

[2] August 31, 1890.

not follow, and what they did in there, I not know. I was very tired with running so fast with the horse, but felt very happy to seeing the amban's house, and the bazaars. A while after, sahib coming out, and there coming amban with him. And then sahib get on his horse, and riding off, and amban going back. They shooting off more guns and I walking with sahib very fast; got very tired; got very hot. One time sahib said: "Don't come so fast; come slowly." Then I waited, and coming slowly, behind the sahibs. Now I had learned all these customs: how sahibs met with ambans, and how they sent the red papers, and how they sent presents to the amban and to his men. All that I kept in my head.

And a few times there came some gentlemen of Russia to see the sahibs. Among them was a big man, named Grombtchevsky[1], and there came with them some soldiers of Russia, which carried guns.

My Bad Luck.

After several days, the sahibs were ready to starting for Pamir. The sahibs gave to all servants new clothes. My clothes were very old and much torn, many place, and were very dirty too; but I not got new clothes from sahib. Khalik and Shukar Ali got very angry with me, every day more than before. I knew that they were saying back-biting with sahib, to making him give my place to Gaffor. I nothing said. They said: "Day after to-morrow, sahib will start." "What shall I do? I find no clothes." They laughed and nothing said.

The next morning Khalik came for breakfast and said to me: "Sahib is sitting alone on veranda. You go and tell about your clothes. Maybe sahib has forgotten you." I said: "Yes." I came to sahib and said:

[1] A well-known Russian. His mission for his Government seems to have been analogous to Younghusband's, for his. The two had met the year before in similar circumstances.

"Salaam." Sahib said: "What do you want?" I said: "Sir, all servants got clothes from you. Please give me some." Sahib said: "Boy, I have heard you not doing any work. For that, I don't want you any more. I will let go you from here." I said: "Sir, I have done very good work. In the camp I have cooked for the men and looked the ponies. You do not know." Sahib said again: "I don't want you, you lazy boy." When I heard that, my felt very sorry, and I said: "Sir, it is my bad luck. If you not want me, cannot help." Sahib said: "Go away."

I came camp and told Shukar Ali and Khalik my trouble. They said: "For this the sahib did not give you clothes. It is your bad luck. What can we do?" I said to them: "You have made lie with sahib about me. I made very good work from Leh to here. It is back-biting to sahib you have done. No matter. My God will help me and God will punish them who make lie matter about me." When I said that, the Sekandar's and Khalik's face showed me that they doing the lie-matter about me. The Khalik went to sahib. Awhile after, he said: "Sahib has called you." I thought: "Now, maybe, I will have good luck."

I went to sahib and there found more bad luck. The sahib gave me silver (ten seers, Chinese) and said: "It is your expense for the road. Maybe I will send you with the post[1] to Leh." I said: "Salaam" and came camp, very sorry.

There were about twenty Ladaki men in the service, and other men with the hired horses. They all said to me: "What happened you?" I felt very much ashamed before them, and did not like to sit with them. There were plenty fields of corn outside the garden, and I went and sat out there, I thinking about my sorrow alone, and crying very plenty, and said myself: "Among all the Ladaki men I find bad luck. Now must go back Leh.

[1] Carrying the post was a particularly responsible job, but Rassul seems not to have realised it at the moment.

All Ladaki people think me lazy man. Never find service of sahibs again. And what shall I tell mother? What shall I do. I will tell to sahib about a chit for me. If I find, then maybe get one sahib's service again. If not find, no hope for getting other service." Now I thought: "Who help me in this bad-luck-time?" The doctor sahib and the Chinese munshi always like my work, and they know my work. I would tell them all my trouble, and get a chit from sahib. I went to them and when they saw me, they said: "Boy, you no new clothes? To-morrow will start from here." I told them all trouble. They were very sorry, and said: "We will tell to sahib. The sahib does not know."

My Good Luck.

The next morning, the sahib was ready to start. Sahib called me. I came and said: "Salaam." There was the good doctor sahib. Big sahib said to me: "Boy, you are a good working boy. I did not know. The doctor sahib and Chinese munshi and the other sahibs told good things about you. I am sorry. I have made one bandobast for sending the post to Leh. And you must take the ten seers in silver home, and I will give you a horse for your riding with, and clothes, and what you want of Yarkand things for your home. You take the aksakal into bazaars and what you like, tell him, and if you want more money, that tell him. And when you come to Leh, come back to me again with the post. Then I will give you good service. If you not want to come back, tell Leh commissioner sahib. Then I will send chit for your good work. And you must give your horse to the other postman, if you not come back from Leh." I said: "Yes, sir," and thanked sahib. And no more felt ashamed to going Leh.

There were several new ponies in the camp. The sahib came and picked very good white pony for me, and brought Mohammed Yannow, the aksakal, and said to him: "Take this boy into the bazaars, and what he wants, that all you must give him, and give him a good companion for the home way." The aksakal said: "Yes, sir." That day[1] Captain Younghusband sahib and Mr. Macartney left Yarkand, and went to the Pamir.

The next day, the aksakal took me to the bazaar, and said: "What you want, tell me. I will buy it for you." He took me to the clothes-selling place. I showed him a cheap Yarkandi cloth. The aksakal laughed and said: "It is too cheap. You need a good one." I said: "This one is good enough for me." I was afraid of dear things then. He bought that coat of Yarkandi. And then he took me to the hat-seller's, and bought a sheepskin hat, and some white cloth to wear under it. And then he took me to the shoe-seller's place. I showed a Yarkandi boot which he bought, and two pairs of numdah socks, and one Yarkandi paboo. Now I said: "It is enough." The aksakal said: "The road is very cold. You need numdah and poshteen. For money you need not fear. It is sahib's order to me, what you want, all that I must give you. It is not my money." Then I said: "Yes, buy me one numdah and one poshteen." All that he bought. And he said: "Don't you want some things for your mother and your friends? Yarkand things?" When I heard that, I said to myself: "He is joking me. The sahib gave me ten seers of silver. Beside that, found so much clothes, now how can he give me more to taking home? Maybe the sahib wants to know how big is my stomach. I don't want more things now. I have found much things, and money too, from sahib. If I take more things, then sahib must be angry with me." The aksakal bought more things for the road than I told him. And when I came to the Ladaki men, they called me a good-luck boy.

And there came Khapaksha Korban, an old man, who was a good friend of my mother's. He said to me: "Among the Arghuns you are a good-luck boy. On

[1] September 15, 1890.

your first journey you found white silver yamba to take home, and a white pony to ride, and the aksakal of Yarkand to help you, and to buy you things. You must have good luck on all other journeys." And the other Ladaki men said the same. I felt very happy, and I said to God: "I thank you for your kindness. At first my luck all seemed bad, now all is good. It is your help to your poor boy."

[When the young traveller, now happily established in his chosen work, reached Leh with the post, Fate overtook him, in an experience, which he narrates in a chapter entitled, "What I got from the Woman Friend," which is too crude for print. It is impressive, as it shows the autobiographer's determination to tell truly the story of his whole life. The episode culminated in a beating inflicted, apparently in a more or less fatherly spirit, by the sepoy husband of "the woman friend." Rassul was glad to take Captain Younghusband's return post on his aching shoulders, and escape from the laughter and philosophy of the bazaar. His account of the return journey we have omitted. The chapter following begins after the post has been delivered, in Yarkand.—EDITOR.]

The Bad-Luck Journey with Hindus

IN Yarkand were many Hindu merchants. In them were Ramdos and Nandu. The both rich Hindus were ready for return to Leh. They wanted two servants. The my companion and I camped in that serai, where live the Hindu people, and we both were in the thinking: will go to Leh, but need we both friend go together.

One day, the Nandu Hindu said to us: "Do you people come with us to Leh in our servants?" We both poor boy said: "Yes, we shall come with you. One thing, we both want one place service." The Nandu Hindu took us to the Ramdos. We both said same story. That Hindu laugh. After, said: "Yes, we like you both friends. We two Hindus are good friends, too. We all friends go together to Leh. That should be happy for us." When we hear this word from him, we both poor boy got very glad.

The Hindu asked our pay. We told: "If go together, what you people pay, we like. If not go together, then we don't wanted the service." The Hindus said: "We shall pay Rs. 12 each man, beside food." We both like this pay; we got very glad for come together to Leh. Why? In us were many interesting speaking. With that speaking we never tired. And enjoy life with that speaking. Why? We both were young, and that all speaking was many foolish matter, but that was for us happy life. If not find the one service, we were in the hoping to go Leh, same that which we have before journey, with post.

Anyway we took the service, but we not know the justice of Hindu at all.

The following day was lucky day for the journey of Hindu. That day did a quarter-mile march, camped outside Yarkand town, all together. There was a fine garden full of fruit. The my friend and I gave grass and water and grain to the mules and horses. After that, ourself go in the garden, eat much of fruit, and speaking that interesting matter, and said: "We got good luck; got service together; got to earn the returned time." We both were happy life.

After two days, the Nandu Hindu said: "I go to-day"; and did give order to my friend; said: "You come with me." When we hear this order, we both friend got sorry. We told to the Hindu: "We don't want the service." The Hindu said: "We will meet at Karghalik again." That was two march away. We believe for that matter. The my friend went with Nandu, I left with Ramdos.

The my Hindu belong five mules and two horses. I was sais of them. And were two Hindu servant. One was cook, next one was for other work. I was all three man's servant. What they bade me, I did. And on those mules and on one horse no were heavy loads, only were sixty pounds on back each of animals. And the two servants riding on those pack animals. On one horse big Hindu ride. I walked along with them.

I not know journey of Hindu people at all. I know that day's camp was to Posgam. But for Posgam are two roads, one short, one long. But in the hot season there came high floods in the Yarkand river. For this in summer could not go by that short way. That know the Hindu people well. Those Hindu people advise about that road. Their advice came: that take the short road. I not like that way. I told to the Hindu: "Don't go by the short way; there be flood." The Hindu got angry, and said me: "This business not your. What we like, that we do. You are poor winnowing-woman's son. What you know?" I felt sorry. Any way, we went by that short way. After about five miles came to Yarkand river. There was highest of flood. The big Hindu said me: "You take my horse, go in river, look how deep is the water." I did that.

Water got on saddle. I looked to the side of Hindu about orders. They said: "Come back." We came, same way which we had come morning. That way came to Yarkand wall of city. That not like the Hindu. They said: "Why we go to Yarkand again? Why not go across to other road?" There no was road. Left road; came among fields of rice. There was plenty mud. Those two mules which were in my hand, they sometimes pull me, sometimes push. In this I got tired. In that trouble was about three hours, could not get way; came back on that big road again; came to Yarkand by that way. I was in the hoping: to-day will camp to Yarkand. Why? We had done thirteen miles in the wrong ways. There, late afternoon, got back to Yarkand city. When came there, did not stop; came by the long road. All the time go very fast. I run with them very fast, same a slave. That evening reached to Tegarchi Bazaar. I hope there must camp. Did not camp. From that place was to Posgam about twenty miles. That time was very tired and hungry. I did try to buy some bread. The Hindu not let me buy. The Hindu get very angry with me about the bread. I walking with them very fast again. Got too dark; not see way.

That half-night reached to Posgam. When reached, unload. The Hindu people went in a room. I did tie the animals, myself lying down one place. While after, the one Hindu came me and said: "You are sleep. Why you not take the animals to feed?" I said: "To-day I got very tired; cannot take the animals." The Hindu said: "No matter your tired. Must take the animals." I said: "Please don't tell anything to-day." But the Hindu not let me rest. Then I did gave some money to the serai man. He took the animals to feed, I lying down. That day I got very tired. That know my God and myself. The Rs. 12 pay was enough for that day trouble. I was very sorry for the justice of Hindu people: did about thirty-seven miles march, walking very fast with riding; and not let buy the bread; and, when reached here did not think this servant got tired.

That early morning I said to the big Hindu: "Please sir, I cannot walk so fast with your people. Please let go me." (I not had took any money from them.) The Hindu said: "No, you can ride on mules to-day. You must ride on mules when you be tired." I believe for this matter. I pack up the saddle to all mules or horses. After that, came outside the serai; there bought some bread and meat. Came to Hindu; put the loads on mules. Same before day, walking with them. One place I did ride on a mule. The Hindu let me ride about one mile. Then said: "Get down from mules."

Arrived at Karghalik. There was of our blood an old man. That old man gave me tea. I did ask him about my friend. He told me that: "He went yesterday. And the friend was in very sorry about you." When I hear that, I got very sorry, and thought that the Hindu did lie-matter with us. There wait two days for the debt money of theirs. I got very good food from the house of old man, and got good rest in the two day. That all trouble forget, which I done before day.

After two days' march, I tired, rode on mule. The Hindu not let ride. And said that: "You is the poor woman's son. You got food and Rs. 12. That is enough for you. Why you ride on mule?" I said: "If you people go slowly, I don't want riding. If not, I cannot go so fast." They said: "We don't give riding. Go away."

That afternoon came to a villages. That was not on the road of Leh, but their debt money was there. For that, went there.

Next day, meet with some caravans which was come from Leh. They gave me a letter and said: "Your friend was with a Hindu. He look bad luck to us. You look same. Why you people did this service?" The Hindu not let me speak with them, and not let read the letter on road.

That evening arrived at a camp. There was little cold. With the Hindu was wood. Made fire. They not let come near fire. Said that if I go near their fire, then should be dirty all their fire-place. There cannot go with Hindu any sort of other men. Why? I was Mussulman. There no was wood. I could not do fire for me; and in the work got dark; I no could read the letter. While after, the Hindu gave me some tea without sugar. For that tea I put my cup on ground, the Hindu throwing the tea from two yards high. With that got cold the tea. I did eat some bread with that tea. The Hindu sleep. I did sleep. I was very hurry about the morning, when I can read that letter.

The morning, I read that letter. Bad luck! That was full of sorry matter. That was from my mother. Said: "My son, I heard that that man had beat you very much. For that, I made complaint to wazir. When you come back to Leh, there would be a trial to the wazir-place." When I heard that, I get very sorry, and said myself: "My mother did very foolish. Now should not be happy feel, when be to Leh. Why did that? I did rob the woman. Her husband beat to me. That all my fault and the woman fault. Bad luck. The old matter are got fresh again. Anyway, need to go to Leh. What luck be, that become."

The next day I got ill; my body all feel hot. Could not walk fast. The Hindu said plenty bad matter. One time, the Hindu saw my face, and he touched my wrist. He believed for my ill. He made kind with me; said: "Come slowly." The two mule, which were in my hand, they took. But not let me ride on mules. There need many times cross the valley's water. I took my shoes off. At that place, with that cold, got more ill. One time there came some Kirghiz. They look to me, very poor boy, and my clothes were very old and broken. They said: "Come you, we can cross you on our horse." They did give me some bread. I put that bread in my belt. My feel not was eat anything that time. That evening came at camp. The Hindu camped other side Kara Kash River. I said to Hindu servant: "Please bring me a mule for cross the river. I am very ill. With the cold water should be more ill." They said: "You are our servant. We not give horse for you. Yourself come." When I hear that, I took off my shoes, went in river. When I meet with Hindu, he said: "Why you did so late? Why did you not come for own work?" Did angry and said: "We should not pay you money." I said: "I am ill." They said: "No matter your ill. You need do work. If you die, no matter. We will pay money for work." I said myself: "Who people take the service of Hindu, that are foolish." And I was sorry for the service, but could not help that time. And they not let me come near fire. Good luck. There were plenty of bushwood. I did fire, and made dry the wet clothes. And the Hindu gave me some tea, no sugar. That I drink. I had done same that illness, when the Captain Younghusband returned me from Yarkand with post. That time, the my companions did cook a little rice in plenty water, and put in it pepper, hot thing. That water I drink before sleeping. I got well with that. I told to the Hindu about rice and for pepper. They gave me those things. I did cook in my little pot; drink that, and sleep.

That morning, with kindly of God, I got well, but not very well. That morning they cook breakfast, vegetables and chapatti bread. They gave me plenty. I got well my sick.

Next day arrived at Suget Karghum. The Hindu people wait in the fort of Chinese. With me send mules and horses to grazing, and was order that there live two days. Their debt money were there, and said to me: "Food will find from Kirghiz." I did ask the cook for some tea; went to that horses' grazing-place. There was a big plain, good grass. I did tie with long rope the mules and horses.

That time was with me Kirghiz. He took me in a

tent. That tent was the head-man's tent of Kirghiz. The family of Kirghiz look me very poor one servant of Hindu. My clothes very bad. Anyway, I wait in that tent. And there made fire a middle-age woman. I did give the tea all to that woman and told to her: "Please cook me some tea soon." I was very thirsty. The woman did cook the tea. There came in some Kirghiz. They drank my tea. After, came the head man of Kirghiz and few other Kirghiz. My tea drank they. I could not get tea at all. I longed for tea, but could not get. What matter was; that in that fort there was a Chinese little amban. He was gave some punish to the head-man of Kirghiz. He was beat on his shoulders about three hundred sticks. The Kirghiz were about this very sorry, and in speaking, forget me. Why? I was a poor boy. And I understood all their sorry. For this I was patient, but I wanted my tea. Several pots themselves drank; did not give any to me. All that was my tea. I got angry. I said to the middle-age woman: "Why you not give me tea? And what kind of Mussulman are you people? You people drink tea and not give me. And this tea is my tea.' The Kirghiz people got very ashamed. They give me plenty tea with good milk; and what of things they ate, they gave me too.

After long time, arrived Leh. Met with my poor mother in the bazaar. I gave all the Hindu's things to them and went with mother, home. My mother told me many things about the woman.

Next morning I went to the Hindu for my pay. He said: "You not did good work. We not pay." I said: "Why you not pay? I will make complaint to B.J.C." Then the Hindu paid me Rs. 12, and abused to me, and said: "You mother winnows my wheat. I did give to her tea, besides her wages. Now, never again. You are a very bad man." I said: "Your justice is bad. I never saw like you any man." I did abuse to him, we both a little fighting.

That was true matter. I could not do good work with them, because they did very long marches, and went fast all the time, could not keep up. I could not walk so fast as a horse. I no had wings. And when I was ill, they not let me ride. They looked me as a dog, thinking themselves very clean people. The European justice is good. For this God has given them power.

The Trouble of Woman

WHAT DONE IN COURT.

MY mother had given a request to the wazir of Leh. It was written: "Sir. Your sepoy caught my son with his wife. He was beat him very much. That beating day my son went Yarkand with post. Maybe he will die, in way. Why they not bring my son to you? The husband made himself same wazir, and gave himself punish. I not like that."

The wazir called the husband and the wife and took their testimony. That was lie-matter.

At that time, in Leh were two wazirs, one big wazir, one little wazir. Both husband and wife were there when I came.

I said salaam to both wazirs. One man gave me a wooden thing. There was written Allah's name in Arabic language. That thing I took in my both hands. Wazir said: "Tell true what you done to the woman and what she did to you." I said: "I went often for fuel with the woman, with other boys and girls. We all were very good friends in good way. I not did bad work with her or any other woman. I was ready to go Yarkand with post. On the leaving day, in early morning of day, the woman came to my home to call me. I came out and met with her. She said: 'Come with me, my husband wants to send some messages by you Yarkand.' I believed to her matter; went with her to a dark a place. Her husband caught to me and beat to me. I not know why he beat to me." Wazir said: "Come again in four of days."

I no had money to give wazir, but my mother heard that my enemies had given to the big wazir and to his munshi. My mother had given five rupees to the little wazir, when I was in Yarkand, and now she gave some money to me, and said: "We have a cloth of Khotan silk. You take that to the wazir with this money."

There were many times coming in court, and witnesses told lie-matter. While after, big wazir said me: "You must deserve punish, but we hear from many people that you are a good boy and poor. For that we both wazirs have agreed to make your punish little. A little punish, we think, will make you more good boy than before. You must pay ten rupees fine, and go to prison for one month."

The wazir said to that woman: "You said Rassul made love to you many times. If you not like him, how could he do this? We believe you made love to him. For this you need punish too. You must pay five rupees fine, and go to prison for fifteen days." When I heard that, my felt very glad.

There came the sepoys of wazir. One then took me, one took the woman. There came my munshi friend. He writing description of both us, what face we kept, and what age we had. Then there came a blacksmith, and a head sepoy brought heavy irons for me, but not any for the feet of woman. For no punishment women find irons. Without irons, they are put in prison. The blacksmith put irons on my both feet, so I could not get away.

The guard said: "Go now." I tried to walk fast, but hardly could walk at all. I came slowly out of the big gate of the court house into the bazaar of Leh. There were many people speaking my matter. Among them was my mother and my brother. When they saw on my feet the irons, and behind me the guard, they cried very much. When I saw their sorrow I cried too. When other Ladaki people saw our sorrow, some them cried.

They said: "Pity it is, the bad woman made bad this good hard-working boy." My guard let me wait there a little.

I said to my mother and brother: "Don't you people be sorry any more. One month in prison is not hard. It will soon be over. It was Allah's will." Then I said salaam and joo to all the people, and went on. There came my mother and brothers and some friends with me to the fort. There I said salaam and joo again to all the people, and said: "Please, you people go back."

My mother said: "I will pay the wazir twenty rupees if will let go you." I said: "Don't mother, don't tell any thing more to the wazir, and don't pay more money than ten rupees." The other people said me: "Don't be sorry. This may come on any man's head." Then they all went back.

In Prison.

I went into the fort with the guard. My prison was in the fort where lived the soldiers of Maharajah. That fort was about half a mile from Leh village. The irons made sick my ankles. The guard was a Ladaki and let me walk slowly. When I came to the second gate of the fort, there was a guard with a rifle.

The wazir's sepoy said to him: "I have brought you this prisoner." He gave a paper to that guard. Then there came a officer. He took that paper, and he gave receipt to that wazir's sepoy.

Then the sepoy of wazir went back to Leh. I said joo to him, and the officer leading me to a cell, I went in. It was very dark in that cell, only a little fire-shine. The room was full smoke. I found four robbers there. They knew me and I knew them. We made friends. They were Ladaki too.

In the next cell was a woman prisoner. With her they put the woman.

That evening brought my brother my bedding and some clothes, on the back of two donkeys. They were very good clothes, which we not use at home. All the time those things we kept in the house as dear things. My brother had brought my dinner too. After, he went back, sorry, home.

At night we had a lamp, that gave very good light with Kashmiri oil. That light kept all night. The guard had given several skins of goats and sheep to the prisoners to make soft their beds. The prisoners use these skins same drums. They had made them into bags with the wool inside. When they wanted music, then they blow them full air and beat them with sticks. The noise came like a drum. Two men had wooden banjos and they knew well how to play them. All us robbers (I called myself a robber now) could sing and could dance, even with irons on our feet, and we speaking many interesting things. I liked the prison better than my own home. The guard liked our singing and dancing.

The first night I not could sleep, in thinking about my troubles. One time in night my irons got crooked; hurt my ankles. I thought my ankles were broken. There came one prisoner quickly, and fixed the irons. He said: "It is hard to sleep with irons." And he showed me how to fix them when they get crooked. Following morning, those prisoners made numdah belts about my iron rings. That gave me rest. They not hurt any more after that.

There came three guards, which took us outside the fort for a little while to wash our faces and hands, and then we came back into the fort. By good luck in those days there was no hard work for prisoners. They took us to make clean a dirty place. Then we came back to the dark cell.

My mother had brought breakfast for me. Very good things. I ate breakfast near the gate, where the sun shone.

My mother said me: "I did ask the wazir yesterday to let go you. I told him I will pay twenty-rupees fine. The wazir did not want the money." I said to mother: "I am much enjoy here." I told her all that tamasha which we had done at night. Mother was pleased about that. I asked mother: "The good clothes, which we not used in the house, why did you send those dear things to me?" My mother said: "Long before you born, in this fort was a Turki man prisoner. He wore good clothes. I heard the guards speaking among themselves about him. One day I heard, when I went winnowing wheat for the soldiers. They said: 'This prisoner is a big man. See what good clothes he wearing. We must be kind to him and not give him hard work.'" Mother said that all was in her head, and that these guards were all new, and did not know us. For this she had brought the good clothes, that the guards be kind to me. Mother had brought tobacco for all the guards, and apricots. She gave them these things, and said them treat me kindly. They were very glad for the presents of mother.

While my mother and I were speaking, all those soldiers which were at the gate, stood up and said: "Major sahib is coming." When he came to the gate he saw me. I got up and said salaam to him, and my mother said salaam too. He was a youthful man, and his face looked to me honest.

He said to me: "Do you speak Hindustani language?" I said: "Yes." He said: "For what fault were you sent to prison?" I told him all that story of woman.

Major sahib said: "One month is not very hard punish, but the irons on his feet are very heavy. This sort they put on murderers." He asked me why they gave me this sort. I told him: "The head sepoy did it, because it was his wife." Major sahib said: "I can change your irons." Then cried my mother. Major sahib said: "Who is this woman?" I said: "My mother." When he saw my mother cry, he felt more sorry and said to mother: "Make strong your felt. We will be kind by your son."

While we were talking, by good luck, there came big kutedar. The kutedar was an old man. He liked me because I had done good work for a long time in his service, and my mother had winnowing his grain for many years. I was much ashamed before him. I could not look in his face.

He said to me: "I told you once, if you wore a fine hat some woman would catch to you, but you would not listen to my advice. Now you are being punish." This he said into Ladaki language. Then he said to major sahib into Hindustani: "This boy is my own man. He was very good, hard-working and true boy. I gave into his hand the keys to all the wheat rooms, and to all the wood rooms in the fort. He gave food to sepoys. He measure all wheat the farmers bring for taxes. This work he knows well. I am very sorry about his punish. Now in the autumn there is plenty of work for him, measuring grain from the farmers. If you let him do my work in this fort, I shall be very glad." Major sahib said to kutedar: "If he is your man, then you may take him for your work in this fort, everywhere you like. He has a good face. He must be a good boy. I will give him for his drinking daily one anna's worth of milk." Then major sahib said to the prison officer: "Do not give him any prison work, and let him go everywhere he likes for tamasha outside fort. Send a guard with him. Don't take him into the bazaars. Change his irons. Let him have light ones."

After that major sahib went to Leh. Mother was much glad for all this, and went back home happy.

My First Marriage

AFTER that, all the autumn and winter I did the kutedar's work. Besides that I cooked for mother and for myself.

All that winter I heard many times Ladaki middle-aged woman speaking with my mother about my marriage. They said: "Rassul is a good hard-working boy. If he not marry soon, some bad woman get him." My mother said among them: "It is true. He must marry, but who can I bring to be his wife? What good hard-working woman is there, who will obey me?"

When I heard that, I said myself: "I must marry. If I marry, then my wife will do all the cooking for mother, and I can have time for play."

In Leh there were many good girls. I like some them and they liked me. But I could not marry any them. I had no money, no house, no fields. My name was bad: it means "robber." We could not sit at meat with good people. My mother had a very bad temper. Some girls were poor like us. They liked me, I liked them, but my mother not like them.

Sometimes said some girls to me: "We like you very much, but we am ashamed of all your trouble (which I wrote, up). Our mothers and fathers do not like that." I was sorry and said myself: "Allah, why you make me a man in the world to suffer all this trouble?"

Cooking was trouble. Mother got very angry with me, when I make careless. My felt ashamed to go for water; other boys did not do this. All this cooking and bringing-water business was woman's work. For that joked me many boys and girls.

In Leh was a good man named Rassul. He was a very good cook for sahibs. He never had come to our house. We had a relation, who lived all the time at Kargil. Once he came to Leh on some business. He was good friend of the cook Rassul. They both came our home to see my mother. When they came into our room mother bade me make tea for them. I cooked the tea, and poured into Chinese bowls.

They said to my mother: "Why don't you find a wife for Rassul?" My mother said: "Who is there? I wish I could find a good girl who would obey me. We want a poor girl like us. I don't want a Leh girl; they would not obey me. If you people know a good girl, tell me."

The cook Rassul said: "I know one girl, the daughter of Samad Shah. She will make good a daughter for you, and wife for Rassul. Her house is very poor. You will have to teach her some work, beginning. After, she will be very good. Samad Shah is good one friend of mine, and I can get you that girl at little expense, and I hope Rassul will like her."

My mother said: "I like what you say of that girl. Please tell Samad Shah that matter."

The cook said: "I will tell Samad Shah, when he comes to Leh from his villages, and I will bring his answer."

I said myself: "How does that girl look? If she is ugly, then what shall I do? Then I shall be ashamed before these Leh girls and boys. They must say: 'Rassul has got a bad wife.' But mother likes her, so I must like her." And then I remembered that my mother not had seen her, too.

Many people of that girl's villages came every day to kutedar's place. I asked them all, how did she look, that daughter of Samad Shah. They said: "She is a good girl."

My mother asked me: "How do you like that girl?" I said: "I cannot tell without seeing. But you like her. I must like her." My mother said: "If she is very ugly a girl, but I like her, will you like her, too?" I said: "Yes, I must like her if you do." Mother laughed.

My felt was sorry, and said myself: "If I could see the girl before I marry her!"

After two weeks Samad Shah came Leh. Rassul the cook brought him to our house. I knew Samad Shah.

My mother bade me make tea for them. I did that. Then my mother filled their cups with tea, and talking of many pleasant things with Samad Shah, and speaking about the marriage.

Samad Shah agreed. He said: "I will bring my daughter with me next week, and we will marry them."

The next week Samad Shah came with his daughter. I told some friends to go see the girl.

They went to meet her, and brought answer to me, and said: "We saw the girl. She is enough beautiful." I like that. That day we made ready the dinner for about forty people, rice and meat an tea. At evening they came, and a mullah came with them. The girl waited little while at house of Rassul, the cook. Her father came to our house, and the mullah made nika (matrimony). Our Mussulman custom at marriage is: the parents of the man to agree with the parents of the girl on a price. This girl's price was forty rupees. The mullah read nika and some of Allah's names, and spoke a few words and married us.

After that, we gave food to the mullah and to some other men. They went. Then came other people. All could not get into our room at one time; our room was very little one. Among them was some rich Buddhists, and the son of Hadji Nassar Shah, and there were several women.

After while, my wife brought into our room, and sat down before a Ladaki table. There was a little plate of sugar and butter, and a wooden thing in which we kept sutto. That was custom. And I wore new clothes, and in front me was a table like the other. And there came banjo men. And we all ate dinner. After dinner we sang. The mullah and the first people went to their home. We all young people left behind. We sang and danced.

At middle-night the all people went home. And the girl not did know among us which is her husband, until they all were gone. Then she knew.

The next morning many women brought money to us: some, one rupee, some, eight annas, some, four annas, some, three annas, some, two annas.

My wife was very clever. I taught her the cooking-business, and she learned quickly. What my mother bade her do, she did, same me. (But I did not like that work very much, although I was never angry with her.) I found much more time to play, after my marriage.

That winter I served the kutedar. At night, I often went to the wazir's house to dance and sing there the songs I sang in the mountains. They liked very much my singing and talking.

[The chapters which follow are selected incidents from a long journey, as sais, in 1892, with Lord Dunmore and Major Roche, over country which Rassul was destined to see again and again, in more and more responsible positions. In Lord Dunmore's book, *The Pamirs*, Rassul and the tiffin-basket are mentioned.—EDITOR.]

The Journey with Lord Sahib and Major Sahib

WATER-GETTING.

FROM Changlung that was bad one trail. For that, all our loads were on back of hire-yaks. The sahibs rode yaks. That morning I saddle yaks for Lord Sahib and Major sahib and for munshi. Tiffin-pony keep load, same before.

We started from Changlung late in morning. That was steep way and very difficult. I had trouble with that tiffin-basket. Sahibs bade me go ahead and stop on top Karwal Davan. When I got there, no was water. Why? That was hot season. I did tie tiffin-pony; went look snow. By good luck there find plenty, under two big rocks. There bring out that snow in water-proof, by tiffin pony. Put snow on rock in sun; digged place under rock for water-proof. That way got plenty good water; drank, myself, and waited for sahibs, in hoping that when sahibs came, they be pleased with my water-getting. That water-getting way I had learned in boyhood in mountains by Leh. While after, there came Rassul cook and Kashmiri table-boy, look very sorry. When they saw that snow, they felt more glad, and said: "We were sorry because the sahibs abused to us and said: 'Why not bring water for tiffin?' We did not know they would take tiffin here, top pass. If had told yesterday, would bring water, but that not tell. Now they abuse to us, and tell us: 'Walk fast till meet water.'"

I brought snow, and they cooked tiffin, and there came sahibs and munshi, very thirsty. Sahibs said: "Here have you found water?" I said: "Yes, sir." They got down from their yaks, and I showed that water-business. Sahibs laughed very plenty, and drank water and said: "Where you find snow? Where you learn the snow-melting work?" I told all that matter of mountains. Sahibs said: "This boy is wise." That make me very glad.

THE BREAKING CUP.

After tiffin, sahibs went ahead, I left behind with tiffin-pony. I delayed, so could ride on tiffin-pony. On tiffin-pony there were many water-bottles, not did use. Those things made me much trouble, some fall off, and some went wrong side, and when I want riding, that time was shut the riding-place. I wanted tell to sahibs: "Why take so many water-bottles on tiffin-pony?" but I was afraid. Anyway, one time I told this to sahibs. They said: "Yes, we don't want so many. Only need with tiffin four bottles. Let the rest go in boxes." They gave those orders to shikari, and he did that.

One time I riding, left a little behind sahibs. Beat, a little, tiffin-pony to make go fast. Beat with end of long stick. Other end that stick hit the bottledan which I carried always on my back. In it was cup of glass. One side break off. Now what do? I afraid very much of sahibs, for from that cup drank all times Major sahib water. Now what should I do? Anyway, I went on my way.

While after, I saw Major sahib. He was waiting near some water. He said, in kindly: "Rassul, here is good water. I must drink. Bring cup." I said: "Yes, sir." But I first caught that pony, and delayed to get cup. There came the shikari. He took the cup out the bottledan. It came out broken. The shikari said to sahib: "Sir, it is broken." Then sahib abused to me, and said: "How you break it?" I made a lie, and said: "Fell one place; there break it." I afraid to tell I beat pony. Why? That make sahib more angry. Sahib said plenty "Damfool," and said: "This cup has been my friend as long as fifteen years. Now you break it."

I nothing said. Sahib drank water out that broken cup. Not was broken much. Then the shikari put that cup back into the bottledan, and gave to me. Then sahib said: "I not give you present." I nothing said.

Then sahib got on horse and went ahead. Other side Suget pass, sahib drank water in that broken cup again. When he see that cup, he look me and laugh: "Look your work! You broke this cup. It was my good friend."

Next day we reach at a fort where live Chinese customs-man. Before reach that fort, sahib gave order: "All servants ride." I catch one pony, and get up on rock, for get on him. When I get on, I did sit on that bottledan, and that cup break again, in little piece. Now what do? Anyway, I went to camp, very sorry.

That place, where camp, little happy in grass and wood. We all men made fire, and sang and danced, and our felt was happy.

In morning, Major sahib call to me. When I went to him I said: "Salaam." Sahib said to me: "Look on chair." There on chair I saw many pieces of breaking glass, of that cup, which I had broken. Sahib said: "It is your work." And said: "How you break it?" Because sahib did not get angry, I tell true matter. I said: "Sir, yesterday when you bade us ride, that time when I get on pony, that bottledan came under me, and then broke it." Sahib said: "Why are you not more careful with my things?" I said: "Could not help, sir; I had to carry too many things on my back." Then sahib laughed, and called munshi, and said some things in English, and both laughed. After, munshi said to me: "Sahib is not angry about that cup, but you must be careful, not break things." I said: "Yes, sir."

Riding and Telling Stories.

Next morning Major sahib got up very late from his bed, and on half-road sahibs took tiffin. That day it grew dark before we reached at camp. The cook had got pony from sahibs. He rode that pony. I rode tiffin-pony. Now said the cook to me: "You sing." That cook was little old, one man, but he like hear my singing. It was very late that evening when we reach to camp. There was good bush-wood. We did cook our supper and feed ponies. There must watch ponies all night. We get no time for sleeping. And it rain that night.

Next day, in morning, we brought all ponies into camp and started from that place, and came into narrow valley by steep way. That evening were come plenty yaks of Kirghiz, for help us cross the Sanju Davan. Next morning all loads put on yaks to save ponies, and sahibs rode on yaks, and tiffin-basket take on yak with sahibs. I left behind with caravan. That pass is very steep and rocky, and some places there lay snow and ice. We men were behind sahibs, and there no were loads on ponies, and we all men did ride on ponies when sahibs not could see. When could see, there get down. That Kashmiri table-boy told some old stories to me, and to Rassul cook. That seemed us very wonderful. Our felt not was tired, because that was so interesting.

One time we camped in valley. There was little villages, and there was big garden with fruit of apricots. We all servants were happy, in hoping to eat that fruit, but Lord sahib said: "Don't eat any fruit in this garden." We were sorry, but could not eat, because of order of sahib. While after, Major sahib said: "You people eat fruit in this garden. Why not? I will pay for servants' fruits." We were all very glad, and climbed up trees and did eat those fruits of apricots.

Next day when sahibs took tiffin, I put tiffin-basket front sahib. When he open it, there break that cover. For that sahib abuse plenty Kashmiri table-man. Table-man said: "Sir, I not know how break it." I afraid very much. Why? That been my fault, not the fault of table-man. I ride always behind tiffin-basket, when sahibs not see, and when we went down way, my heavy came on basket, and that break. I did tell table-man: "Please, you don't show my fault." He said: "Yes, I not tell."

That basket-breaking day we had brought new pony to carry water. From that day sahibs order: "Carry water always." That Kashmiri table-man ride that water-pony when sahibs not see. After tiffin, cook Rassul ride his pony, and table-man ride water-pony and I ride tiffin-pony. And that Kashmiri man tell an old story: that, long ago, one king was. To the cook and I seemed good that story. And we three men were friends.

After four days, in crossing big plain, sahibs went ahead. That time was very hot season. Sahibs went ahead. Cook Rassul, that Kashmiri table-man and I walk behind. After us come the caravan. We thought ourselves: "Sahibs never will want tiffin in middle this hot plain." Never had got on ponies before tiffin till that day. That day got on ponies in morning. So we rode over that plain. Cook Rassul said to table-man: "Tell us stories." And he did tell very good one story about an old king. That matter seemed us very wonderful, and we did ride slowly to listen. One place waited sahibs in middle of hot plain for tiffin. We saw men there, but we did not think could be sahibs. But they seen us in their telescopes. After while, we get more close. Sometimes we said: "It is not sahibs." When we got very close, we saw it is sahibs. They were waiting for us. I got down from my pony and table-man got down, and we came near to sahibs.

Major sahib came to me, very angry, and said: "Why you ride my tiffin-pony?" Now what should I say? I said: "Sir, it is the hot season. For that I did ride." Sahib said to me: "Damfool liar, why you ride without my leave?" He caught to me, and struck me two times on my neck with his hand, and two times on my shoulder with his foot. Cook Rassul said: "Run away." I ran a little way off, and other men unpacked tiffin-basket.

When we reached Yarkand, the big ponies' backs were very sore, and so were the little ponies' backs. There we found a grass garden for them, and let go them in that garden, and we washed their sore backs, and Major sahib gave medicine for them, and we rested at Yarkand about ten days.

The Travelling-Man.

Three days after Yarkand, we came over a pass. There, on way, met a man carrying something on his back. We saw him far way. The cook of servants was in front us, all sais walking with caravan, each one sais behind own four ponies. When came that travelling man near the cook, the cook caught to him. Always the cook carried a big knife. All sais running up. I saw tamasha from far. I afraid, in the thinking maybe will kill to that man. While, after, I came up to the others. There was a leather bag full khatik, that they had taken from that poor man. The sais fighting each other for that khatik. The poor travelling man nothing said. He afraid very much, I got out of his face.

I not like that bad work. I said to Ramzan: "It is bad business. Don't you go for khatik." Ramzan does not like this business, too. While after, finish the khatik, and those men returned that empty bag to that poor man. I said to the sais: "This is bad. If heard sahibs this, then what shall we do? This matter will make bad the name of sahibs." For this matter got they angry, and the head-man said to me: "You are a good man. You not take any khatik. We am bad men. You tell that to sahibs." I said: "What for I tell sahibs? This seems bad, taking out knife to make afraid a poor man. But if you people think it be good, then it must be good. I must be bad. I must be wrong."

We walking on that plain. Ramzan and I in the talking about the khatik, other men singing. That was a long march. After while, nobody talking and singing. Why? All were tired. I had some thinking-play in my head. With that, felt were not tired. After while, some men showed us, far way, a large valley. Before evening reached to that valley. Both sides were beautiful, high, and steep and grey. There were rocks like castles. That seemed us wonderful. We said each other: "We forget our tired, in the looking this wonderful sight."

Yalgastrook (means: "alone tree") we camped that night. There is a tree and a spring of water. There was a little grass in some old fields. We pitch sahibs' tent. After, we all sais playing and running and jumping, and laughed very plenty. Sahibs laughed too, when see our play.

Beating Juma.

After few days, one day Major sahib beat Juma sais. Why? He did put saddle on horse without order of sahib. Major sahib beat him very much. Our head-man and other servants said: "This sahib's justice is bad, which he beat Juma for this fault so much. We will not go with the sahib from here. We will go back Leh." And we all servants took our things on our backs, and went to sahib's tents. We said: "We do not wanted this service any more." Munshi Ahmad Din said: "No matter this day's beating. Will not beat the major sahib any servant again." And Major sahib and munshi said many sweet matter. Then forgot their angry the Ladaki servants, and put loads on horses, and marched that day.

Rabbit-Shooting.

One day saw many rabbits, which sahibs shoot. I saw a rabbit. I did take a stone, and came behind that rabbit. Our all men joked me, and said: "If you kill, then we will make a fire in our hands and cook it." And they laughed. While we speaking, a little far, waited the rabbit. I hit him with that stone, and made hallal, and brought him back. I was much glad, and said to other servants: "Now you people must cook it, make fire in hands, which you people told before!"

Beautiful Camp[1] in Pamir.

Now in that Pamir country we pitched three tents of Kirghiz for sahibs. Two tents was for living rooms, middle one was for dining room. And at one end pitched Lord sahib's English tent, at other end Major sahib's English tent. In them kept sahibs' things. Over against them pitched the five tents of servants. On one side pitched munshi's tent. In middle pitched cook's tent, and digged there a hole for cook. Now that place looked like a serai. And in front sahibs' tent made a road, about five feet wide. Put on it sand. And, on other side a little hill, made all servants' W.C. There dug each servant his W.C. by order of sahib. In few days our camp was very beautiful.

And we put all horses in pasture. There was very good grass. We did wash sore backs of horses, and put medicine, and there was no work with ponies. All us sais brought, each man, one load bortsa, every day, and at night-time sang and talked.

Now for about a month no was any work, besides getting wood and sahibs' clothes-washing. But one morning Major sahib and Lord sahib came out their tents, and measured a place, round, about fifteen feet across it, and order to us that to build a stone walls there. We found much work on that wall from morning

[1] On the Kukturuk river. "It was owing to our camp being laid out on military lines, our making a road round it, and building a stone kitchen, that the rumour rose that the English had built a stone fort in the Pamirs. A mandarin travelled from Kashgar, fifteen marches to see it. As soon as we struck our camp in October, the Chinese demolished the stone edifice, still believing it to be a fort."—The Earl of Dunmore in *The Geographical Journal*, Nov. 1893.

until evening, building. There many times we did talk and play as we built.

One day two men caught to me and did cut off my all beard with scissors. The munshi and other men joked to me and said: "You must shave now." I did that, and munshi gave me one rupee. He and other men said: "You must give pudding to all men. If not, then will find bad luck. Beard-cutting is very bad." I did bought one rupees butter, and with some sugar from my bag, did gave pudding to all men. After, they said me: "The Hindu custom is: when father dies, cut beard, and give pudding." With this matter, they joked to me and laughed, and I laughed with them.

In about fifteen days was ready that house, but the roof was not ready. One day there came an amban of Chinese with soldiers to see that building.

One night our head-man said: "We will kill rabbits with stones." All servants did agree to hunt rabbits. I said myself: "You are a very good shooting-man with stones. At that camp you did kill one rabbit with one stone. Here are many rabbits. You can kill several." Next morning, after breakfast, I went alone. All other servants went together. I met with some rabbits, threw my stones, but the rabbit not run. I throw several stones; not could hit him. My arm got tired. At last one stone hit his tail. I saw a little blood. The rabbit ran, and waited one place. I came that place. He ran again, and waited. I followed that rabbit all day; could not catch to him. I got very ashamed. When I came at camp, other servants had killed many rabbits; and my felt was more ashamed. All servants joked to me and laughed.

Wheat-Grinding.

One day the head-man sent Ramzan and Sonam, Funtsock and me, to go Tashkurgan to buy food, with munshi Ahmad Din. We were four days at Tashkurgan.

Then John Mohammed Khan gave wheat to me and to Sonam, and said: "At Gajat you will find a mill. There grind it to flour." We both put all the wheat in bags.

After two days came at that mill-place. There was no mill-man. My companion knew the mill-business. He did turn in the water, and did grind the wheat. There was much grass there. By good luck there were much tents of Kirghiz, which were come from Russia. They were subjects of Russian; but they came running, to make them the subjects of Chinese; but they were new for the Chinese country.

We camped in that mill the next day. My companion said: "I will grind the wheat. You go to those Kirghiz' tents to sell my things." He gave me some needles and some buttons and other things to sell. I took them to those Kirghiz' tents. The Khirghiz took me into a large tent, and they said: "Your coming is lucky for us. To-day is a big day for us. For that we made good food. You are a traveller-guest. That be good luck for us."

I said: "I am such a man. My home is far away. I will pray, for this honour. God will help you, and more make luck for you." They were much pleased with my matter, and gave me very good food: much meat and other food. I was a little hungry, found very good food. I was much enjoy; was sorry my companion was not there. I did showed the selling things. They nothing bought. I came back to the mill. That evening was done the wheat grinding, and there come some Kirghiz to visit us; brought us good food.

The next day we met with our head-man and with all men. Munshi Ahmad Din said: "The wheat-grinding is much difficult. For this, I left you. You made very quickly this business." We said: "Yes." And Ramzan was glad to see me again, and Kalam Rassul was glad, too. Ramzan, Kalam Rassul and I speaking at night of that all, what we did at Tashkurgan; were much pleased to be together again. And they said: "After several days, we will start from here."

About Meeting with Russians.

And every evening we made big fire, and sat, surrounded by that fire. There came the munshi, and we talked much, and laughed. One time, the munshi said among us: "After several days we will start from here, and go to Russia, and their soldiers are bad. Maybe will kill to us. If you people see them, then you people will run. That is very cowardly for men. That is as a woman." All men said: "We will not run." And nothing said. I said among them: "I will never run, and I will catch to some of them." The munshi laughed at my matter, and said: "You will run, too." I said: "When we come to that place, you will know I am not afraid, and I want very much to meet such soldiers." All the Ladaki laughed at my matter.

All that night we men sang very much. We four or five men slept in one tent, and I slept with the head-man. Once, at half-night, we did hear a gun's voice. That we all heard in our tent. And the head-man said: "Did you people heard it?" We said: "Yes." And the head-man bade me to go out that tent, and ask others. I got up, in much frightened, and came near the door of our tent, but I not could go out, for fear, and I called to the cook. He said: "Yes, I heard that." And that the munshi heard. He called me; and the cook and I went his tent. The other men stayed in their tents. Then they called to Lord sahib. Then they did found it was a Kirghiz, who did shooting a wild dog. We came to own tents again, and sleeped.

Next day, munshi said to me: "You got up before them, every one; but you could not come out of your tent; and you called to the cook, as a woman calls." I said: "Yes, I afraid a little." He said: "You will be more afraid of the Russian soldier." I said: "No sir."

We were in the Pamirs about two of months. One day the munshi said: "We will start back in few days." Our head-man bade to us to shoe all ponies. We did that. The all ponies had grown very fat, and it was difficult to catch to them. And the Juma sais was very good man to catching to horses with a rope, and we caught to them all. And the cook Rassul did gave me two skin of sheep, and I made a little poshteen to wear, but it no had any sleeve. Then we started from the Pamirs.

One day on a large plain, were many horses' tracks. Those tracks not were our horses'; the shoes were large, and different from ours, and all were fresh made in the night. Ramzan said to me: "What is it?" I said: "These must be of Russians tracks." Ramzan was afraid and said: "The Russians will kill us." I said: "No, no they cannot kill us. Our Emperor King is very strong. How can they kill us?"

Ramzan did not believe to my matter. I saw in his face he was afraid. We came to camp and that news gave to our companions. They were afraid too. But the head man never was afraid.

The next day, other men brought in the horses. That morning I sleeped. Before arrived the horses, I got up. All horses came in. The men said: "All horses are all right, only on one horse's back is no saddle. It is Galwan's fault." The head man abused me a little: "Why did you not tie it good?" I said: "I have tied it very good; I don't know how it loose." The men who went for horses, they said: "We searching very much in the valley; could not find it." The head-man said to me: "You go into this valley, and you find it yourself." I said: "Yes, sir."

And I rode off on that horse without a saddle, an went into that valley, where grazing the horses that night. I crossed a little spur, and found another spur. Now the camp was little far way. Now I came into a flat valley, surrounded by mountains. When I reached the middle of the valley, what did I see? A man on a white horse, running very quick towards me. When I saw him, I ran towards him, very quick. There I saw: from the left side came one, and from the right side came one. All three mounted, came towards me. Now I said to myself: "These must be Russians. The horse's saddle they taken off." I was glad to meet them.

We meet presently and behind me was another man. I was in the middle of all them. Each man carried a gun, and each man a big knife-sword. The man in front me was a Russian. The other three were Kirghiz, but their clothes were like Russian.

The Russian, with his right hand, his beard put into his mouth, showing me very angry a man, and he put on a bad face, and he said in Parsee language to me: "Who are you and where do you go, and where do you come from? You must tell true. If not we will kill you now. We am Russians." I returned in Turki. I said: "I do not know any Parsi words." They said, in Turki, the same as before. I replied to them: "Your government's custom are quite dark, if you kill a poor man without fault. You must kill me, I suppose. I have nothing to tell you, no news." He said: "No, if you tell true, then we will not kill you."

I said: "Why you tell me, you will kill me? Why not you make question, in friendly? I will tell you that way, but no other. I am not afraid to you. You people could not kill me. Our government is very strong. I am the subject of the English. But our government's customs have been light; never to kill a man without fault. I am a very little man, but if you kill me, then our government must search the blood-tracks of even a little man, when they hear it."

They speaking each other in Russian. I saw they were ashamed, and they replied to me: "Our custom have not been: to kill a man without fault. And our government is light too, but here we have been at war at Surmatash, which way you came, with Afghans. If you are an Afghan, then we will never let go you. If you are not an Afghan, then you are our friend, and you may tell us true matter, in friendly. Who are you and where came you from? And where do you go?" And the Russian gave me a cigarette, and they smoked.

I said: "We are India men, the subjects of England, and two big English sahibs, named Lord Dunmore and Major Roche, came from India to Yarkand and Pamirs, from Pamirs to here, and from here will go to Murghabi." And they said: "Why you people come to this country, and why got to Murghabi? You must tell true." They said with fiercely. I said: "I do not know why the sahibs came here, and why go to Murghabi. If you want more matter, then come you people with me to our camp. There are big men."

They speaking with each other in Russian. Then said to me: "We don't want to come to your camp. We believe to your matter, but at Murghabi are officers of our. We think they will not let come you people. If they let come you, then we will see you there again. Now we are friends." I said: "Yes, I think you people are my friends."

My clothes and coat were Ladaki pattoo, white, a very good one which had made my mother, and on my head was a Ladaki hat and on my feet a long sock of numdah, and a paboo of Yarkand, and one pugaree, same Afghan. They thought very interesting my pattoos coat, and said me: "Where was made this pattoo?" I said: "In my home." And they said about that pugaree: "Maybe you took it from the dead Afghans at Sumatash."[1] I said: "I am not a robber like the Afghans. Is the Russian a robber too? The English men not are robber. I have brought the pugaree from home. In India they use many kind of clothes."

They laughed and said: "You are a wise boy. You are not a little man. You must be a big man." I

[1] Lord Dunmore mentions seeing blood-stained and bayonet-pierced greatcoats lying on the ground at Sumatash, near the place where the dead Afghans had been buried, after the battle.

said: "I am sais." They said: "No, no you cannot be that. Your work must be with the sahibs. If not, how can you speak so much with us? Maybe sahibs taught you this all matter to tell us." I said: "No."

And then I said: "I came into this valley to search for my horse's saddle." They said: "Yes, we have it. We will bring it."

Then one man went for the saddle. We four men came towards our camp. While after, that man brought the saddle. I said: "Give it to me, I will carry it." They said: "You are our guest. We will carry it."

And the Russians gave me other cigarettes. I, smoking them, came near our camp. About three hundred yards far our men saw us. Saw well Rassul Galwan with four mounted men; and what happened, not know.

Now I said to the Russians: "This is our camp. You come with me." They said: "No, we will not." And to the one man which carrying my horse's saddle I said to him: "Give it. I will put it on my horse." They said: "No, we will put it." Then I wanted get down from my horse. They not let me get down. The two men caught to me, my two arms and my one leg, and held me in the air. They said: "If you get down, then we be ashamed." And the other two men put the saddle on my horse, and they put me on my horse's back again. There we were a few minutes, so that the all our companions from our camp saw. And the Russians shook my hand, and said: "Good bye." I said to them: "Good bye."

They went way, and I came to camp. When I reached to camp I was a very dear man. They took me to sahib's tent, and the sahibs said: "What was it you told the Russian men?" I told that all, what had done those men, and what I told them. Sahibs and munshi said: "Wise boy."

In Kashgar[1] divided all horses. Half horses took Lord Sahib, and half found Major sahib. And some men choosed Lord sahib, some Major sahib. They said: "Lord sahib will go by Russia to England, and the Major sahib will go to Maral-bashi."

Finding More Pay, and the Going of Lord Sahib.

That evening, in the munshi room, Ramzan Ali and Mohammed Isa were together. I said to the munshi: "Sir, all men get for a month ten rupees pay. Why have I found only nine rupees? What fault do you see in my work?" The munshi said: "You are a very hard-working boy. You must have good pay. You tell about your pay to the Major sahib. Now you go. He is in his room."

I went to sahib's room. There was the door shut, but I knew the sahib liked my work. I did open sahib's door. By bad luck, the door gave a hard noise.

Major sahib said: "Damfool, who are you?" When see me, said: "What you want?" I said: "Sir, my pay is little, I want more pay." Sahib said: "Yes, I like to give you more. How much you want?" I said: "Ten rupees, same the other men." He said: "How much is it now?" I said: "Nine rupees." Major sahib laughed and said: "You want only one rupee more? Yes, I will give you ten. You are a good boy."

I was very glad and came to the munshi and said: "Sir, I found one rupee more pay." The munshi said to me: "Foolish man, you asked for one rupee. Why you not ask the sahib for twenty or fifteen rupees? The sahib would pay. The sahib is very glad with your work. That I know." I was a little sorry not to tell more, but I said: "Sir, it is enough for me." The munshi laughed at my matter.

Now they said: "The Lord sahib will go to Russia

[1] I have omitted the account of the visit to Murghabi. Major Roche had no Russian passport, and parted from his companion at Yarkand, hoping to have a shot at a long-haired tiger in the Maralbashi country.

to-morrow." We all servants were in good hope of getting good presents from the Lord sahib, but he gave only old clothes. I found one old coat. We all men were sorry for this. When he went, we all servants said salaam to the Lord sahib, but he nothing said. When he said salaam, he looked away to the gate.[1]

Now there were left several Ladakis without any service, and they had not found orders to go back to Ladak. They said: "What shall we do?" They told to munshi. Munshi told to Major sahib. Major sahib said: "Why do we let go these poor men without fault? All men must come with me. I will pay." They were all glad and said: "Major sahib is a more good sahib than Lord sahib."

Now the munshi was left in Kashgar with Mr. Macartney. From that year he waited about eight years, maybe more, in Kashgar. I was very sorry to leave the good munshi.

[1] Dunmore, in his paper read before the Royal Geographical Society, on his return, says: "A better set of men, hardier or more willing, I have never met with."

The Service of Major Sahib

THE FIGHT OF CHINESE.

THE day before evening, we came to camp. When got there, we heard that the Chinese men there beaten our sahibs and our head-man. There were camped some Chinese soldiers, in that serai, before us. We got much angry with the Chinese soldiers, to beating our sahibs. We unloaded, and went to the sahibs. The Major sahib was angry, and said to us: "If you people beat the Chinese, I would be glad." We all young men liked that order of the sahibs. Some us took tent-poles, some long Kashmiri sticks and made ready to beat the Chinese soldiers. There came a Chinese officer to sahibs, and begged them to stop us. Then sahib ordered us: "Don't fight." We all young men were sorry for that order. At night we talked much, and said that: "If we had fought with Chinese, we beaten to them."

That night came many Chinese soldiers and a Chinese officer of theirs. They planning to beat to us, but we did not know.

The river always every night covered itself with ice, and, if we not make holes in that ice, the ponies not could drink water. We dug holes with chopper (axe) every day. That day, Kalam Rassul and Sonam went to that river to make holes. In the hand of Kalam Rassul was a chopper.

When came into little bazaar outside our serai, Kalam Rassul called to us and said: "The Chinese beating to us." And I went out with two men. There were four Chinese men on horses. We followed them. They ran away very fast.

When we came back from far way, that little bazaar was full Chinese soldiers, and there were some our men. They beat to the Chinese and the Chinese beat to them.

There Kalam gave me a stick. I forgot the other men, and myself was surrounded by Chinese soldiers. I beat to them, and they broke my stick. And one their sticks hit my arm very hard. There were many Chinese. Our all men ran. I ran, myself, and got into an old house. I hid in that house.

Now all the Chinese went to their camp. Kalam saw me where I was hide. He said: "Come out now. Here are no Chinese men."

I went to him, out of that house, and there came four Chinese, those four which we following before the fight. Now Kalam Rassul and I ran, and came up on a plain outside that village. My hope was: that I get to sahibs' serai, by plains way. Two Chinese came in front me, two came behind me on that little plain, and they beat to me with their sticks; four men. I had no hope to escaping again from those enemies. After they hurt me very much, I begged to them and said many times: "ko ko"; but they not would let go me. There were no helping-men. Which side I moved, there they hit me with sticks. I lay down on the ground, but there they beat to me too. I thought: "These people will kill to me." Then I did same a dead body. Myself did not move. Then, by good luck, they went on; but I not could get up. The time was sunrise.

While after, there came the sahibs and our head-man and others. I was lying down. Sahib looked over me, and said: "You hurt much?" I said: "Yes sir." Then sahib said: "I will kill one Chinese." In sahib's hand was a pistol. Then took me some of our men, same a dead man to our camp. What I see there? Some men's heads were wounded; some men's hands. Ramzan, my good friend, was wounded on his face. Now was ready our breakfast, but no one like to take breakfast.

While after, sahibs came to me and said: "Rassul, don't you be sorry. Here is only you, one, lying down. There among the Chinese, are seven men, lying down, same you, and their amban lying down too." I felt happy with that matter, and the sahib gave me some medicine and ordered our head-man to put me in a wagon.

Now I had found two times such bad luck; one, that woman's husband's beating-day; the next, this day. Here I was hurt much and nearly to die, but this did not seem me such bad luck as that woman's husband's beating-day. He not did beat me much, but that seemed me very bad. Even now I am afraid, when I remember that first bad-luck day.

After Major Sahib's Service

Spending Pay-Money in Kashmir.

When reach to Kashmir, Major sahib gave pay to Kalam Rassul, and to me. I got four months pay, rupees forty, and rupees ten present. Same that get Kalam Rassul. We said many thanks to sahib. Then sahib went in boat. Sahib said many times salaam to us, from that boat. We said many times salaam. And we were sorry to be separated from sahib.

Now we seat one place, look our money. It was one hundred rupees for both men. And I had some more money beside that. We both were felt rich.

Kalam Rassul said to me: "We will make some smart coats as munshi Ahmad Din, and each man boots and pugaree." And he said: "When we go Leh, will wear them." (Foolish.) I like to do that all what he told, and he took me to a shop. There buy soda-water. And we both bought some pattoo, and gave to a tailor.

In Kashmir we wait several day after sahib. There in my head was a foolish thinking of youth. I liked to wear good clothes as a babu, and good pugaree. That all I did bought. And Kalam Rassul said: "We go in a boat for play, and drink soda-water sweet." At that time one bottle soda-water price was one anna, the sweet sorts one anna and half. Now what Kalam Rassul told, that all I did. There ran some money. But by helping God, I not did like women. Kalam Rassul did. He finished much his money in Kashmir. I was much rich than him. I did bought a Kashmiri tea-pot, which called: "samovar." That price was seven rupees. It was for home, to keep for remember that travelling of Lord sahib and Major sahib. And I bought some Kashmiri shoes for mother, and for my wife, and some for wife's mother and father. Beside those things, I left about rupees thirty. Kalam Rassul said: "Give me some money." He said: "Will give back in Leh." I gave him some money, a debt, and he said: "We will buy for each us, each stick which is, inside, a knife." I said: "Yes." Bought that. I did bought a present of Chiense for Hadji Nassar Shah's sons.

Now I said to Kalam Rassul that: "We will go back Leh. If we wait here a longer, then we will be a poor in buying things. Then what shall we take for home?" He said: "Yes."

There came a man; said us: "One sahib has called to you people." We went with that man. He took us in a boat. In that was an old sahib. The sahib asked us questions, read my chit, and said: "Two sahibs will go Yarkand by Leh. I will send you people telegram." We said: "Yes, sir." And was much glad with that news. They were Mr. P. W. Church and Mr. E. L. Phelps.

We made ready our all things for Leh. We found two coolies. We fixed their wages from Srinagar to Dras, each man rupees two. And they carried our things upon their backs.

We came to a bazaar. There bought one rupee's sugar for fakir sahib. Arrived Ganderbal that evening. There we wanted some fuel and some cooking pots. Our clothes seemed as a big babu. The villages men run when they see us. We not got any things there. In one veranda were a few woman and an old man. We went there, and said to that old man some lie-matter into Hindustani language. "That we are not babu and munshi. We are Hadji, and our father dead. We are of rich families in Yarkand. Now will go Yarkand. Please you give us cooking-pot and wood. We will give money." They gave us fuel and cooking-pots, but not take money. We were much glad with lie-matter to get that good luck.

The Visit to Fakir.

Next morning, came to that villages where was the fakir sahib. I said to Kalam Rassul: "Now came fakir sahib's home. We will go there." He said: "I will not go there." Then Kalam Rassul and the coolies wait under a large tree.

I went to fakir sahib. There was sit the fakir sahib among much people. I know him before. I said: "Salaam aleikum." The fakir said to me: "Aleikum salaam." I put that sugar in front him. Fakir sahib looked my face, and laughed, and said to a woman that: "Bring for this man suttoo, in my cup, full." That woman brought a large cup suttoo. The fakir sahib gave that cup suttoo to me, and said: "You eat it." I eat a little; could not eat much. The fakir sahib said: "Why do you not eat up this all?" I said: "Sir, I could not eat this all." Fakir sahib said: "Then you take it with you to your family, and God will help you." And nothing said. A little after, said: "You go way. There is hurry." There not let me sit. I said: "Salaam aleikum." And came out that home.

Came to that tree, where was waiting Kalam Rassul for me. I said that all to him, what happened at fakir sabih's home, and I gave little suttoo to him, and some to those coolies. Other, kept in my bag for my family.

Wearing Rich Clothes in Leh.

After several days came Leh. Here found well my mother and wife. I gave my earn-money to mother. There were about rupees forty things, and rupees twelve cash. My mother was very glad to see the Kashmiri tea pots, and the Russian clothes, which I had brought from Kashgar for mother and my wife. But mother was angry with my earning. Mother said: "Before, you brought good money in few months. Now you was about one years. Only you brought a little money, only rupees twelve." I said: "Mother, these things are from my pay." Mother said: "You were with bad companions, with Kalam Rassul. He never obeys his mother, and you had learning from him bad work. Sorry, you not thinking, that now you have a wife, beside yourself." I said: "Mother, I no had did any bad work. Only is this my fault: I had bought these good clothes. In it ran some money." But mother was angry. I was much sorry and said myself: "Why I bought these clothes?" And: "I will never do like this."

Now after few days, my mother had heard that Kalam Rassul no had brought one rupees for his wife and for his mother. Only he had wearing beautiful clothes. With that was a little good luck for me. The angry of my mother was little, and she seemed that: "My son is more wise than Kalam Rassul."

Now what sort of a man was in Leh the poor woman son?

There I was full youthful. The my beard has came beautiful. And the talking and song were more good than before. And my clothes were of Kashmiri pattoo, all grey colour. On whole body was like English. But on head was pugaree, sometimes white, sometimes Kashmiri thin pattoo. With those clothes seemed myself as a big babu. But no had in pocket one rupee. Sometimes felt much ashamed with those clothes. Sometimes felt was enjoy with those clothes.

Kalam Rassul did sold all his beautiful clothes for the expense of home. I had not such bad luck as him. By the help of my mother, there was enough expense of house, with her earning, beside mine. But the telling of mother always said: "Look at that bad Kalam Rassul! He sold all his clothes. It is much ashamed but you not needed sell your clothes. You wear them, yourself. But you must be careful in other time. The money-coming is very difficult, and running of money is much easy."

In Leh were several parties, some rich Mussulman parties, some Buddhist good men parties, some Buddhist rich boys' parties. We were a parties, some poor boys. We all had no other work at that time, beside the hope, if come travelling-sahib, we go with them. I had other friends, too, beside my poor boys' parties friends. The sons of Hadji Nassar Shah and Hadar Shah, very rich Mussulmans. And was in Leh, munshi Pallgos, a rich Buddhist man. He was in a honour service of Maharaja Jummoo.[1] His son was my friend. I used to go play with those rich men's sons. When I sit with them at night, they came to ask my mother. Beside order of my mother, I cannot sit with them at night.

In that winter, in Leh, had opened a school of Maharaja Jummoo. I always like to read. I said to mother: "I have learning the Buddhist letter, some writing and reading. Now I have no work. I will go to the school to read Urdu." Mother said: "It is foolish work. You may go."

Now came spring and summer. One day I had sit in school to read. There came a sepoy from wazir, and said: "Called to you and to Kalam Rassul the wazir." I went to wazir, and he had get a telegram from Mr. E. L. Phelps, and Mr. P. W. Church, that was English. The wazir does not know English. There was a pundit munshi. He know broken English as me. He was told to wazir that: "Rassul Galwan and Kalam Rassul keep in punish until sahibs come Leh." Wazir said to us: "What fault you people are done with sahibs?" I said: "We have nothing fault." The wazir said: "Why said that the sahib?" I show him that that old sahib had sent that telegram for us, as that he had told in Kashmir. He said: "Yes, that be true matter. The pundit could not read it." Then sent that telegram to a padre sahib. There found my matter true. Then

[1] "This ruler has for his full title *Maharaja of Jummoo and Kashmir*. The title is not complete as denoting all the territories ruled by him. These include Ladak, Baltistan and Gilgit."—Frederic Drewin, *The Jummo and Kashmir Territories*.

the wazir said: "You people are servants of these sahibs from to-day." We said: "Yes, sir." And we was much glad with this news.

[Rassul's memory seems never to let slip a detail in all these earlier journeys. We have omitted much, trying to select those passages which have lingered most vividly in our own memories, in the years since we began to read this manuscript, and, also, those which mark successive steps in the steady progress of the "poor winnowing-woman's son" toward "rank and honour." Mr. Phelps and Mr. Church, whose journey followed after the winter at school in Leh, early appreciated the possibilities of their man, and gave him opportunities to develop them. In 1900, they made a second shooting trip to Central Asia. In 1901, Mr. Church published *Chinese Turkistan with Camera and Rifle*.—EDITOR.]

The Journey of Mr. Phelps and Mr. Church

LEARNING HUNTER-WORK.

ONE day I went with sahib in the woods of Kara kuchan. Sahib said to me: "Rassul, you are a good man. The sais work is no good for you. I will teach you the hunter work, then you will find rupees thirty pay with other sahibs." I said to sahib many thanks. Sahib said: "From to-day, you look our guns and telescopes. I will tell that to shikari." I was much glad. From that day the Kashmiri shikari teach me the gun-clean-making and the skin-making. His name was Rassul Dar.

THE CHINESE MURDER-WOMAN.

At Kara kuchan we heard that, at Maral bashi, are kill one woman to her husband. And said: "Now she reach here to take to Kashgar." We like very much to look that woman.

By good luck, arrived there that murder-woman with some Chinese soldiers, and camped in that serai, where we had camped. That murder-woman dress was all red. They said: "It is custom of Chinese; when do murder, wear red." That woman was young, and she spoke very good to those her watcher-soldiers, and she laughed with them, in talking.

When she saw us, she said to us: "What you people looked me? It was my luck, because I did kill my bad husband, and myself will die soon. That does not matter. Came in the world one day. Die every one." And she no was any sorry. We looked very strange woman. We heard that she had other one man friendship; therefore she kill to her husband. She has beat with a kitman, which is Turkistan digging-thing of iron. When hit that, her husband head was breaking off. After, we heard that woman kill in Yarkand one Chinese with a big knife.

Losing the Ponies.

Now we start from Kara kuchan, arrive Maral bashi. Sahibs and other some men and I went shooting into the woods. One day we get a fat sheep from sahib, and rice, and we came into a beautiful wood, and camped under tall trees. Our felt were very happy, and it was tiffin-time. Rustum and Kurban said: "To-day must cook lama poktak which put in soup." When we done the lama poktak, we put into our cups. There frighten the ponies, run into the woods. In half-minute lose all ponies. We left lama poktak, and run follow ponies.

Ramzan and I came to a large, deep woods; there not see ponies. We do not know which side run the ponies; and in that woods was much long reed, which, riding on ponies in them, could not see over them. We both men travelling in the reeds, and going top little hills of sand, and looked round; nothing see. While after, we saw, two sides, two tracks among reeds. Ramzan went one side, I went next side. I travelled with that track. A long time after, lost me that track. Now which way shall I go? Anyway, I travelling and going on those sand hills, looked round; nothing see, beside reeds and deep woods; and I do not know, that the sun was sit down. Now I came back toward camp. I do not know which side is camp; but, by a little remember, which way had come, by that side went back, in the hoping I come camp. There get much darkness. Now I seemed, that it is at last day to die. Why? I heard there come much tiger. Myself said that: "Now must eat me up a tiger." Sometime said myself: "God is always with man. He help me." Felt a little happy in travelling. Came to a sand-hill. I went top it, to look fire of camp. There nothing see. Thought myself that, if travel more, then more lost way in darkness. It would be good if sit here for the night. To-morrow will find way, in light day. In the hoping, there lying down. While, body was hot, not felt cold. While after, much felt cold. If make fire, there was rich wood, but I no have matches.

In that sorry time, came in my ear a voice, which called some men. I get up, and went on top that sand-hill. Good luck! There see a fire, and that voice came that side. I answer to that calling, and went to that fire. There was Mr. Phelps and some other men. Mr. Phelps said to me: "Where you was?" In the speaking, there reached Ramzan too. Then I told to sahib all happening. Sahib said: "Here no was hopes to getting the ponies, but the two beard men found them, Rustum and Kurban; but I was much sorry for you and Ramzan. Were more dear you people than all ponies." We both men said: "Thanks your coming to look us."

Now came camp, and laughed each other about the lama poktak. That night not sing any in the talking, and each other said: "These sahibs' justice are very good."

Now I not remember here. Why? In these woods not was any trouble, and was much happy. Therefore not much remember to this place. Anyway, there we was about a week in hunting. There get some antelopes of that country. The Kashmiri hunter teach me those antelope skins-and-head-taking-off. I did that all.

In Serai with Chinese.

Now we came back to Maral bashi. There meet with John and other men. There reach some Chinese big men, and many carriage were with them. They camped in that serai where we camped.

Now a Chinese man has come in our room to drink water. And what water left in his cup, that he had put back in our water-keeping pots. And the Gaffor has told to that Chinese: "You made our all water bad." That Chinese had get angry, and had beat the Gaffor with his hand. That had hit to Gaffor eye. Gaffor had hit to Chinese eye. Now there has come many Chinese to beat them. Gaffor and Cook Rassul run, and come in sahib's room where other men were, and told us that fight-matter. When we heard it, we some hold stick, some tent-pole, and we went all to beat the Chinese men. There came the Chinese big man, and shut that gate, and begged us, and said: "Don't fight each other." And there came sahib, and, by good luck, stopped that day's fight. Then Chinese big man ordered to his servants. They went to next serai. That serai get all to us to live. Sahibs were much glad to going the Chinese in next serai.

At that night we all servants were in singing and in talking. There came a big voice, and heard a voice of bugles and soldiers. Now they came in our serai. We came out our room. There were Chinese soldiers and many carriage. While, we afraid, and thought that those Chinese, with which we were fight, now they come with soldiers to kill us. Some our men run there, out serai. There sahibs were afraid, too. Sahibs came out their room in fear. I meet a carriage-man of Kashgar. I did ask that man. He said to me: "Was a big colonel of soldiers dead, at Kashgar. Now take that dead body to China, and his family." I said: "What is the soldier?" He said: "It is custom of Chinese. For this dead body honour, come soldiers."

My felt better. I gave that news to sahib. Sahibs were glad. Sahibs went back in their room. The Chinese camped in that serai. That night the soldiers making banjo of their. We could not sleep.

The next morning were many tamasha for us. There were many died body in their carriage, but the big

Chinese died body were in carriage alone. To that carriage was covered black silk cloths, and head-side was a white chicken in a wooden cage. Now there came the amban of Maral bashi, and other big Chinese, and they bring feast to that died body and to his family. And food-taken time put in front the died body all kinds of food on a board. With honour put them, and tobacco, too. And the ambans and other Chinese big men came. There they make salaam to that died body. Their forehead put on floor. That time shoot, as guns' voice, many things, and burning there many papers. That died body there was few days. For us was good tamasha.

Now one day we had making clean the ponies' place; there came a Chinese, where were the both sahibs. That Chinese went front sahibs, then he speaking English with them. The sahibs were much glad to see that Chinese. They took him into their room. We looked very strange, the speaking Chinaman English. That time bringing the telegram from China to Kashgar. That Chinese was officer of Chinese telegraphs. Now many times that Chinese came to sahib's place for dinner.

Hunting with Sahibs.

Now we came to Shamal. There Mr. Church used to take Kurban with him for speaking Turki with the village hunters. Mr. Phelps always take me with him. The Shamal people kept some large birds, kite, which those birds hunting many little animals. To some those bird kept always their eyes shut. Mr. Phelps saw some them, which carried some men in their hands. He said me that: "To-morrow we will look these birds' play." The people said to me: "At that night, not fed to the birds. Keeping hungry is good." The next morning we went with some birds in woods. We every one were mounted ponies. When see a rabbit, the people let go that bird. He come from high up sky, come down on the back of that rabbit. Then the man catch that rabbit, and let the bird eat some meat of that rabbit. This way they killed pigeons, and other little animals. That day I found much play, we mounted, going follow the birds.

Now I going with Mr. Church to hunt. We used to go very early morning, and when we came to woods, then Mr. Church and his hunter-man going to hunt, and kept me with ponies. I wait one place until sahib came back. There was much cold, but Mr. Church not did let me make fire; the smell of fire go to the animal. A few days not let me make fire. After, the hunter said: "Does not matter if make fire." Then I make fire, and get felt warm. But the sahib nothing get. One day sahib get a stag. Sahib order was to me that: "When heard a gun's voice, then come toward that side." That day I heard few guns' voice, and went to that side. There Mr. Church had killed a stag, not very big, that were ten branches. But that animal seemed me very beautiful. Never had I seen that kind of animal. Then we took off that skin, when the Mohammedan hunter had killed. We put some meat into fire, and eat up, and then came to camp.

After that, we went in jungle with part caravan, same before. There found much play. Some place there were ice on the river. We play on it. We every night make large fire, and we sit, surrounded by the fire, and sing and talk. And there came the both sahibs, and teach us many play of English. We like that all to do, and we laugh much with sahibs.

The Fire-Burning Tamasha.

One day Mr. Phelps went one side to hunt in jungle, Mr. Church one side. Both sahibs not taken me that day. There was a Buddhist man. He and I went for wood in jungle. There we saw a much deep jungle.

We both said: "We make fire for tamasha." Sometime said: "Maybe sahib be angry." Anyway, one time I like to burn that. I did put a match. That jungle burning very far way. A while I afraid, but seeing very wonderful tamasha. We both came quick camp. We told that wonderful fire matter to all companions. They said: "It make bad. If see sahibs, they be angry." I was sorry but I said to all men: "This fault I have done. What matter become about it, I take. But you people come with me to look the good tamasha." They came with me the fire-burning place. There were many place beautiful smoke, and some fire high, some lower. It were burning a large place. They said: "It is much beautiful to look." While after came Mr. Phelps. He came to our camp, with angry, and said: "Foolish! Who burned the fire? It made bad my hunting." And said: "Tell truth." I get up from my place and said: "Sir, it have been my fault." Sahib said: "Why for you made it?" I said: "For tamasha." Sahib said: "You told true. Therefore I pardon you this time. If you do like this again, then I will beat you." I said: "Yes, sir." Then sahib said: "Truly it was much beautiful to look. When we start from this woods, we must make a large fire as this." We said: "Yes, sir." Then sahib went into his tent. I was much pleased to done that my fault.

Our Men.

Now, few days after, we came to a next jungle. There sahibs ordered that: to gather woods one place, and said that: "Before start from this place, we will burn it." We gathered a large wood in few days. Now came that starting-day. At that night we burned it. There tamasha was very good, but there was nearly to burn our tents. The fire was far way, but the hot came to camp. That night were much enjoy in dance and sing.

Now I write here what kind of men were our party of Ladaki servants. There was Kalam Rassul, were always a good stage-player. He always making his pugaree big, and, if he find, always he wear good clothes, and on his neck red clothes. And he put on his face some Yarkandi woman red and white thing, to look beautiful himself, which we joked him about it. And he was in dance wonderful. He known many kinds of dance. He dance with two big knife. That dance every one people liked; and he was much joking, which we always liked his talking. He was for work very lazy, and he will not let do work to other men. Where find money, there he spend. No was any grief about his family. But for sing his voice was not good.

And Lascow was one, in wearing clothes same Kalam Rassul. He do not know the dance, and was good working boy. But he spend money wrong way.

Mhamdo was one, which he like to wear good clothes. He was good for work. He spend money wrong way. He was in sing very best, and in few dance.

Kurban was weared good clothes, and he was in dance good. And he know many sing, and he can speak Afghani, Parsi, Hindustani, Turki, but he was lieful man, and spent money very soon. But three of men's work he could do alone, very hard-working man.

Rustum not wear so good clothes as other, but he sing good Turki and dance. He was truth man, and he does not spend money much wrong way, and he was very hard-working man. Iashit Siring was a Buddhist boy, which he sing good Ladaki and dance. He was a little lazy.

And was Mudihi a cook of sahibs', which he spent money wrong way.

And Rassul cook was rich than any servants. And he was wise, too.

And was Sharkhan, an India man, which he spent money wrong way.

And Gaffor, he was old, not was bad work to him.

And was Tongam Raman, a poor man, which he was our cook.

And Ramzan, which he not wear so good clothes, and he was hard-working boy.

John, which was our caravan bashi, was an old man. All his beard were white. He was most black man.

My clothes were old and I was much careful to my money. Why? In last journey, I had lost some money with Kalam Rassul in Kashmir. Therefore my mother has told me many advice, and she has told that: "Now you have wife." I always remembered the matter of mother. But I was very good in sing, and I known few kind of dance, too.

In Yarkand.

Now we after few days, reached to Yarkand again. There were our great deal Ladaki friends, and my brother and Shukar Galwan.

Now both sahibs were young. They always like to play. One day, they said: "We will play the polo game, and you servants must take each man a pony." There, in Yarkand, outside the eastern gate, there is a large green plain. Every day we went there for the polo game, and there came also some Kashmiri men and Ladaki men, who lived in Yarkand. Beside that, many Yarkandi people came to look the tamasha, but there no one, beside the two sahibs, know how to play well. Some sais knew a little. I had played many times, but I could not play well, but we all liked it. The sahibs heard, that there were near Yarkand many Balti men who lived in a villages. The sahib called in some Baltis for polo, but they could not play well. The sahibs asked some of them which way they came. Some said by Ladak. Some said by Mustagh. Then the sahibs asked many question of them about the Mustagh pass. There was among them a little old man, named Wali, who had been with Colonel Younghusband when he was Captain. And he had been guide to Captain Younghusband to the Mustagh pass.

Sahib said to Wali: "We will go over Mustagh pass, and that way to Baltistan, and we want you to come with us." Wali said: "I can not go over the Mustagh again. Why? When I went with Captain Younghusband all the villages people of Baltistan were angry with me, to showing the Mustagh pass to a sahib, and they made me swear, not to bring any other sahibs by Mustagh.[1] Now if I go with you, they would be more angry with me. Perhaps they would kill me." Sahibs said: "It is an old matter, your oath and your promise. They cannot hurt you in our company. You must come with us. We will give you a good present." Then Wali said: "I will counsel with the other Balti and will bring the answer after few days."

And after few days Wali came to the sahibs and said: "We will go with you." Both sahibs were much glad with this news.

Now Wali counselled with sahibs about Mustagh. Wali said: "Let sahibs take other three Baltis with me. The other Baltis will carry loads on backs." Sahib said: "Yes." Then sahib fixed pay for four men. Sahib said: "We will go first to Pamir, then to Raskam, then Mustagh." The Balti said: "Yes, that will be good." Then they said to sahibs: "We want money in advance, and one pony." Sahibs agreed.

One time we saw the Chinese celebrate their new year. At that time I had not seen like that before; it seemed me very wonderful. There were many men carried wooden boards, wrapped up in red cloth, and words written on. And there was a large dragon of paper. That carried several men. And there was a boat of paper, very beautiful, and in that boat was a beautiful girl (but that was not a girl, but a boy dressed like girl).

[1] Col. Younghusband speaks in terms of high praise of Wali's courage, endurance and faithfulness. He confirms the statement that the natives on the other side of the pass were very angry with Wali for bringing a sahib over. In fact, he says that their wrath was so great that Wali (himself a native of the village) and his companions, afterwards went all the way around by Leh and the Karakorum to Yarkand, instead of directly back.

And there was a lion dance; that lion going in a dance to the voice of banjos. Kalam Rassul said among us: "I have learned a good stage play for Leh. That Chinese paper boat I can make in Leh like this one."

My Knees-Illness and Enchantment.

Now the trouble with my knees, which had come to me in Maral bashi way, got more bad, and more.

One day came my brother and Shukar Galwan. They said: "This evening we will give the dinner which we promised. All Ladaki must come." And we all went for our dinner there. That night joined us all the Ladaki which were in Yarkand. After dinner, everyone sang and danced. That old man Shukar Galwan said: "It seemed us we have been in Leh." And he made a prayer for us all of young men. But my knees were very ill that night. I could not dance, but only sing.

By day by, that illness got more bad, and more. I could not walk a yard place, and at night I could not sleep; that seemed my arms with a rope tied. But I could speak. Sahibs came to look me, and gave me a bottle of medicine. They said: "Put that on your knee, and rub." I did that, but the knee got more bad. I got very weak. All men and sahibs thought Rassul would die in few days. Many times I wanted to sing with our men, but they not let me sing. I could not walk alone. The Ladaki helped to make my bed. And Ramzan, my good friend, was very sorry about me, and slept always at my feet at night, ready to help me.

One day both sahibs came and sit in front me, and all servants were very kind to me; said many good matter to me. From that day Mr. Phelps brought his chair with him, and sit in front me, and asked many questions about Pamir. Sahib said one day: "You not am ill. It looks us they have made a jadoo for you." I was very glad sahibs come to look me, but

I not knew they got bad news from Leh, that my wife was dead there. Sahibs had ordered to all men that: "Keep this bad news from Rassul."

Now there came all the Ladaki, which lived in Yarkand town. With them came an old man. He said: "This must be enchantment. The Yarkand country very bad place for enchantment. You must get a fortune-teller." Some Ladaki went to a fortune-teller. At evening they came back and said to me: "We have got him, and he has found in his book, that, on a Wednesday, you met with a demon in a wood, and that demon got angry on you. But could not harm you. On next Wednesday, you had come to a water brook. That the water was dirty, you drank. That time the demon harmed you a little, and this illness you now have. But it will leave you in one night. Here will come two fortune-tellers on Wednesday night." I said: "Yes." They said: "Will need all kinds of fruits which are in Yarkand, and from seven houses seven pieces of wool, and one hundred small sticks, and a blue goat, and a measure of corn-flour and one cock." I gave them ten rupees which I had, and said: "What you need, buy it from bazaar."

I was much hurry for coming of the Wednesday. At last it came. On that evening came two mullah fortune-teller. They looked at me and said: "You are strong spirit man. You will be well this night." And said: "To-morrow you will be taken out this house to a road. After, you will be brought in other one room. You must not look back when you return from that road." I said: "Yes." Then they put those fruits and the cock, that all of things, in front me. Then the two mullahs seven sheets of bread, one side of each, they burned black. Then, into each sheet of bread they put a small stick. Then they hung on each stick one of seven pieces of wool from the seven houses. Then they lighted seven lamps. Then they stood me up by wall. There two of our men held, on right side, and on left side.

Then those seven breads and seven lamps they put under me. Then the two fortune-teller men read many things aloud. I got very tired. After, they laid me down. Then the big mullah took one kind of fruit and read some thing over it; then struck me with that fruit on my head and on my feet; then he gave that fruit the other mullah. That mullah read some thing over it, and struck once on head of cock. Then he throw that fruit down before the cock. With each of seven fruits, same did. That cock never move, but sit in same place. After, that mullah took in his hand a stick, and read over it, and struck me with it, and gave it to other one mullah, that read over it, and struck cock with it. There were one hundred sticks. That reading lasted all night. I got a good sleep that night, though many times waking. At last the big mullah took in hand large one knife, and read over that, and struck me with hilt, a little hard, as if he got angry. I was afraid. With that knife, he hit me many times. Each time when hit, my felt better. I liked that beating.

Next morning, before sun rise, the mullahs took out of that room the seven sheets of bread and all the fruits, those sticks, and that cock, and a wooden bowl of clean water, and a bundle of dry grass, for lighting fire. Then they carried me out, on a man's back, out garden gate, to a place where met three roads. I sat there on that man's back, which carried me. Then the mullah swung the cock three times around my head. Then he passed three times round my head the water in the wooden bowl; then the fire. Then those people, who held the cock and other things, went away. I was brought back. I did not look behind. They brought me in other one room. In that room was ready soup made from blue goat, and that corn-flour. There were two large pots of soup. And there they brought some poor people to drink that soup, and all my companions. We all drank soup together. Then the mullah said: "You go to sleep." I did sleep a little, and when I waked, I got up alone. There was no illness left. It was as if a man make loose ropes that tied me. That day my felt well, but I was weak. The mullah said to me: "The weakness does not matter. But when you go to stool, then at that time will come blood, but don't be afraid. And for seven days you must every morning eat cream." I thanked very much to both those mullahs, and gave to both mullahs tangas twenty, and said: "I am a poor man. If not, must make a good present." Both mullahs were good men. Said: "Does not matter. We not did it for money. We did it for God, and this boy is in the full youth time, and is good boy. We are very glad that he goes out well from our hands." Then they went to their home.

Sahibs came to look me. Sahibs said: "The mullahs did enchantments for you." I said: "They caught my devil." Sahibs not believe. Anyway, by the help of God, I got well.

Now the sahibs were ready to start for Pamir. Mr. Phelps said to me: "You are weak, but if you eat eggs, then you will be strong." And he told the cook to let me have three eggs each day.

Going to Mustagh Pass.

Now, after many days marching, there arrived the four Baltis from Yarkand, the guide of Mustagh pass. Now sahibs said to Rassul cook and to me: "You both men come with us to Baltistan, by Mustagh." I was much glad with this order and I said myself: "Now I will see new countries."

Now we going up way in a valley, which that valley was full of glaciers. There was right side glacier, left side, steep a hill, covered ice. We asked some people: "Which way shall we go?" They showed us that steep hill. We thought those people joked us, but their matter was true. But that road was much difficult, to go over it with caravan. There fell two of ponies with load, and broken there the boxes. There looked from the pass to below, there spread the sahib's things, some red, some white. We came down and took that all thing. Some thing could not get. Now fell other ponies. There dead some ponies in felling. Now we took off all ponies' loads, and broken the frozen ice, and making road. Then we took one ponies, three or four men. This way took all ponies top the pass. After, all baggage carrying up on our back. When we carrying them, we sing and joke each other, and laughed. That trouble were as a play for us. Many time we came top the pass with baggage, and go back for other things, down. There was much cold, but we, carrying the baggages up on our back, felt warm. Among us was the Kurban, very strong man, and he carrying up on his back much heavy things than any us, and he singing more than us.

Now, top that pass, came a hard wind, which bring snow with, and hit to our face and body that snow. Then travelled down from that pass by a snow plain. When done that snow plain, reached in a warm valley in much darkness. Next day, see that was a large valley. One side run beautiful stream, and were many trees green leaves. It was summer. We each other said: "Look to the power of God! We had winter yesterday; to-day get the pleased summer."

Next day travelled down by that valley; came to a old villages, which were many tall trees, and houses, and fields, and burial grounds, and mills, and garden,—everythings were there. But there no were any of human people. The guide said: "Here many people lived, and many time the Kanjuti people were came to robber them.[1] Beside robber, killed many men. Therefore not lived here any people." And said: "Here will live people again. Why? The Kanjuti are came under English government."

[1] It was because of Kanjuti raids that Younghusband was sent out to investigate these regions in 1889, with a view to their prevention. Kanjut is another name for Hunza.

After next day we came to next large, beautiful, old villages, which there no was any human in that villages too.

Now the Raskam[1] valley are a large valley, north and south high mountains, which looked grey and black. In valley, both sides, were much jungle, bush-woods, and some place good grass; and in Raskam valley many place we get some brown stones and white. There must be some dear stone, gold, silver, copper, bronze, and other things. The Raskam valley is very enjoy valley, but that road is very bad as Hell, which middle summer cannot go any people in that valley in flood-time.

Now the Baltis, the guide of Mustagh pass, said: now came near Mustagh way. Now sahibs made arranged for Mustagh pass. The Baltis said: "Eight days food wanted." And said: "From here to other side Aghil Davan, a pass, take ponies. There is good road, which could go caravan; only one place find a little bad road in a narrow valley. After Aghil Davan cannot go ponies, all baggages carrying up on our backs." There made ready three ponies to go with us until Aghil Davan, and two men with ponies, Kurban and Ramzan. Sahibs ordered caravan to go through Yarkand river over Karakorum, and to Leh, and said: "Kept here some stores and flour. If we not find way to Mustagh, then we will reach back to this place." I had in a bag some things, clothes for my wife and other thing. That all I sent with Ramzan to my mother to Leh.

The next day we said many salaam to John, and to all men. They said good-bye to us. We left that place and started toward Mustagh Pass; came to a place where joined two valleys. There the Baltis guide said to us: "The south side valley is our way." That valley was a big valley. East and west were high white mountains, and into that valley much white gravel, not big water. In that valley were very much big and

[1] A corruption of Rast-Kan (a true mine).

little rocks, very difficult road to taking any ponies. In it, many times, the ponies felled down.

Sahibs and two Baltis were ahead, we four Ladaki were behind with that three ponies. A little head than us were next two Baltis. The Rassul cook was older than we were, and he was wise man, too. He always said to us that: "The Baltis are deceitful men. They brought us in wrong valley." I do not think right the Rassul matter. Travelled with ponies with much trouble up that valley. And we said each other, that it were more good if have not brought ponies, if this all baggage were carried up on our back. Now came to a place, which cannot go ponies over these large rocks. At that place, the cook Rassul said to me: "Yesterday, the Baltis not said us, there are this kind of road. You must tell." I did called to a Balti and said: "You people brought us a wrong way. Don't make lie with sahibs." That Balti answer very quick and said: "Yes it looked me wrong way. You people go back down. I will bring sahibs and Wali Balti." The Rassul cook said: "The Baltis are clever. They made this mistake to look sahibs' temper. If sahibs make angry for this mistake, then we will find best road to Mustagh. If not, then this people never show good road. I know well the Balti people."

Rassul cook told that to sahibs, but sahibs not thinking right that matter, and nothing said to Baltis.

Now going back. By and by came up top the Aghil Davan. Came down from that pass, and early camped. At that place lay a biscuit tin. Sahib said: "It throwing here Captain Younghusband." Baltis said: "Soon can see Mustagh valley."

The next day Kurban and Ramzan went back with that three ponies. Now we travelling on a small plain, there could get no way to go down to the valley. Now we turning back to near pass. There was a little valley. We get way by that valley. We get way by that valley with difficult. There came a wild donkey toward us.

Sahib shoot him, and kills; then all that meat we hidden under a rock. Sahibs said: "If we not find way over Mustagh, then will help us this meat." Cook Rassul said to me: "Telling this matter in front Baltis was not good. This Baltis never show us the Mustagh. They told us in Yarkand: 'We had did oath and promise not to take sahibs.' They will take the two hundred rupees with deceitful."

The Rassul was a father for me. What he bade me, I obeyed him. That was advice of my mother. I had travelled with him, with Lord sahib and Major sahib. The Rassul joked me. I joked him. His custom was, that when he tell good things, he abused in every words. That all his abuse seemed to me very sweet. Named was Rassul, and my name Rassul, same name.

Now, from one place, see a foot of mountains, to left side. The Baltis said: "From that foot of mountain, will turn up to Mustagh valley." The next day we came, much early, to a beautiful place as garden, and several little old house, and many fire place, which many people were camped there a long before. Which that place name we were hear a long before at Yarkand, and called to that place Suget. At that place did not camp. Went up a little, what view see. Toward south and west was pass of Mustagh. To the east was a very tall glaciers-mountain, very steep, covered much ice. That looked much beautiful. Top that mountains, always see over it a hat of cloud. Mr. Church said: "In India side are four tall mountains. Among them one is this." Which he give a name. For that I not remember. (The Baltis called to that mountain, Masher-Brum.[1]) I said myself: "Lucky man myse l to see that mountain." To the west side: mountains, and grey hill of soil. Between east and west, wide valley; full of glaciers. Under that glaciers came all the water of Mustagh out, then going down. We camped a little down that glaciers, at that night. The Baltis

[1] Over 25,000 feet high.

said: "Our way is left side. After two days, will cross the pass."

Next day we travelled up left side, over glaciers ice. There were many dangers place. Many place were hole of ice. If look down a hole, no see bottom; and many cracks of ice, which, if fell into such a crack, then no hope to get the dead body. There always much rocks, and very bad going up and down. I said: "My God, you help us in this dangers place." The Rassul was much afraid. He said: "I have no hope to escape from this dangers place." I said to Rassul: "God will help. You must make up strong your felt."

The next two day we walking on ice. There many place were beautiful iceberg. That all looked as chorten of Buddhist. And right side of valley on a big rock was a real chorten of stones. We did ask the Baltis: "Who had build that stone?" The Baltis said: "It had made Mohammed Isa,[1] at that time, when Captain Younghusband was travelled here."

There no were place to make a camp. We pitched sahib's tent to front a rock. With us were several long sticks. We made them tent-poles, and then spread waterproof into tent. At night the sahibs said to both us Rassul: "Come to sleep, into tent." To the Baltis gave some waterproof.

Next day we throw some things, some heavy blanket. Now we started from that place. There was a branch mountain of Mustagh Pass. The Baltis said: "That is Mustagh Pass. When we came half the pass, there said one Balti: "My head got sick. I cannot go over the pass. Please, you let me go back down." Sahibs and I said to him: "Where do you go back? If sick, come with us. That is good for you. Must come to-morrow to villages." That Balti not agreed, and lying down himself on snow. Sahibs said: "We will lost time, if we look at him." And went on. That Balti lying down. When we came a far from him, that sick man

[1] Mohammed Isa turned back at this point.

get up and going very fast to down. We see that from the pass.

When I come top the pass, sahibs were a little down. Cook Rassul said to me: "I did told sahibs I will not go down such a dangers place." I said to him: "What did sahibs said?" He reply me: "Sahibs said: "I will go." I said: "If sahibs go there, we must needed go." The Rassul abused to me, and said: "I do not like to kill myself. If you like to kill yourself, then go with sahibs by this way."

Now what see from that pass?[1] The right side and left side highest mountains, covered with ice and snow. In front that pass was a valley, that was dark with clouds and mist. I said myself: "If is this road bad, how say the sahibs will go by this way?" I went a little down. There were both sahibs. They said to me: "Come, look the way." I went with sahibs. What see? Under that pass was a lake. Three side of the lake were very steep rocks, covered with very hard ice. There was no going-place. If go a two yards place, there was no hope to escaping. If fell, go down into that lake. Sahibs said to me: "Could go or not?" I said: "Sirs, here is no place to going." Sahibs said: "We have came here by order of Government, to look this way. We both sahib die, does not matter. But we must go this way. If you like, come with us. If not like, then don't come with us. But ourself must go." When I heard it from sahibs, in my felt came strong spirit. I said: "Sir, if you go, I must come with you. If you die, then I will die. If you not die, then I will not die."

[1] Col. Younghusband agrees with all points of this description of the Pass and the approach, except the lake. His own crossing of the Mustagh Pass, in 1887, near the close of an overland journey from Peking to India, is most satisfactorily described in his book: *The Heart of a Continent*. He says, himself, that a proper mountaineer would never have attempted it, but he, in his ignorance, though much upset by the aspect of the pass, thought it was what an Alpinist would expect; and, finding that his men expected him to take it, he did so in silence. He learned later that only their reverence for an Englishman's powers gave them courage. They had no ice-axes, only improvised ropes, and most unsuitable soft native footgear.

Sahibs said: "Which way we will go?" I did showed a place, and said: "By that way will go." Then the both sahib said: "Bravo!" And said: "We looked your spirit is little or big. Now we know you are a good man. We do not like to kill ourself in this dangers place. We must go back to Shahidula, then to Leh." I said: "Yes, sir."

Turning Back from Mustagh.

From that pass we turned back. There see from the pass the Masher-Brum mountain very close and much beautiful. From that place we came by our old road; arrived to our last camp.

That night we had no any wood. The sahibs made tea in tent, with oil, which they had a tea-making thing (as that, which I had one in ship). For that night we drinking some tea and some biscuits. Now we had only about three pounds flour, and some meat, some cocoa tins, some coffee, and were some soup tins. There we were seven men.

The Rassul was half dead in the afraid. At that night sahibs said to me: "Singing-day is to-day. You sing." I did sing in tent. The Rassul abused to me and said: "It not singing-place. It is cry-day. You must make remember it is die-day." I said to him: "We never die. You must make up your felt strong." Rassul said: "What shall we eat food, and where shall we go?" I said: "We shall go to Shahidula." Sahibs said him much matter to make his felt strong. Rassul not believed, and said: "It is nearly to die."

At that night was much cold, and our foots get much cold. The sahibs' foots were more cold than us, in English boots. There the Rassul put one sahib's foot under his stomach, the next sahib's foot I carries in my stomach to make warm. That night passed with much difficult.

The next morning, which get up, there was much cold and wind. With wind rise the snow. That was a bad enemy for us. There we drinking some tea and eat some biscuits and breads. Now sahibs said: "Throw many things, tent and clothes, and other things." Sahibs said: "Your heavy blanket must throw here. You both men can use our clothes."

The Rassul carried sahibs' table things, knifes, forks, spoons, and were many silvers things. That all he carried on his back, and other flour and meat into a leather bag. I carried upon my back two rugs, two poshteens and other some things.

Brandy-Drinking.

Now at that place cannot stand with the cold. The sahibs drink there brandy, and asked to Rassul and to me to drink brandy. "We said: "No, sir." Sahibs said: "If you people drink it, then you will not get cold. Must drink some of it for the dangers place. To make save own life, it is order of God and Mohammed sahibs." The cook Rassul drinking up half a cup, and then sahibs gave a half cup to me. My felt said: "Drink it." I did drink. There burning my mouth. With much difficult, it went down into my stomach.

Now the sahibs went ahead than us. Now the Rassul and I were felt warm and happy, much enjoy with the brandy.

When we passed the snow-plain, came to the glaciers. There, until a far way, no were danger. When we done the snow plain, reached to a small lake. That lake was much clean water over ice. The Rassul said to me: "To-day we did drinked some brandy. With that, felt get enjoy, and warm, too, and I did forget the dangers. Now here is much clean water. We will drink some brandy with water, same sahibs." I like that matter. The bottle of brandy was on my back in the sahibs' bed. I took the bottle, and drinking some again, with water. We left there a long time at that lake place, with kindly of brandy. I did put the bottle into sahibs' bed again, and carried it upon my back, and travelled again. There the Baltis, everybody, walking slowly. We both Rassul head were bad with the brandy. There the Rassul lost all the table things, knife, fork, spoon, everything. Where that thing lost, we do not know, by kindly of the brandy. That all thing were of silvers things. We searching them, could not come hands. In doing that, there lost much of time. Sahibs went ahead, a long before; which we not see sahibs. That day was to reach to a dry place from the glaciers; but we left behind, by kindly of brandy.

Now we were much hungry. We had some flour, but there no was any wood on the glaciers. We had been much trouble to walking over ice, among rocks, with the hungry. Now there get night, darkness. And when we wait for a rest, there get sleep very easy. Now we nothing wanted, wanted sleep only. I said to Rassul: "It would be good, if we wait here for this night." Rassul said to me: "We cannot wait. If we wait here, then sahibs will die in this night, without food and clothes." I said to him: "Sahibs never die for a night." Now we walking again. Came under a pass of ice, which were over it many holes and cracks. I said: "It is that place, which you was afraid, when we went up at that time." And I said again: "Sahibs will not die for a night. If we travel in the darkness to the dangers place, then we will die, and sahibs will die too, after." Now Rassul agreed to wait there.

Now there no were any eating and drinking-work; was sleeping work only. I did went under a rock to go sleep. There I did opened the bed of sahibs which were upon my back. There I got empty the brandy bottle. The cork was lose, and all brandy was gone, and all were came on the clothes. I was much sorrow about it, and afraid to sahibs for that fault. Now I did put some clothes under me; some I weared upon me, and I did sleep. But all the clothes were full of smell of brandy. With smell my felt much enjoy at that night. At that night I get much sweet sleep, much wonderful, which never was I sleep so sweet, before that night, and after that night, in my life.

Our thought were to get up early. When I opened my eyes after the sweet sleep, there came high up the sun. I get up. Other were sleeping. I did waked them up. Every one get up, and we walking without any foods. There was a little bread for sahibs. Now it were two days, no get foods, only get some tea and biscuits. We were much weakness, but my felt was stronger than Baltis and Rassul.

I get top the pass. After the ice, on a dry small plain, see a smoke under a large rock. I said myself: "It are sahibs." I was much glad to done the danger, and to see sahibs; but I was afraid with my fault, to lost the brandy bottle, and to the fault of Rassul, to lost the silvers things. There came the both sahibs very quick to me. I said: "Salaam." Sahibs said: "How are you? We thought you people dead." I said: "Sir, by help of God, no one die, but we get dark. Then we wait to a place." Sahibs said: "It made much wise work. If had come, then must be die, at that dangers place, in darkness." I said: "Sir, we were sorry for you, which you were no clothes and foods for this night." Sahibs said: "Does not matter. We get wood. You people came all right." I said: "Sir, we have done two faults; one, lost the silvers things, next, the brandy bottle." Sahibs laughed and said: "Does not matter. We thought you all men and all things lost." And sahibs said: "There is some bread?" I said: "Yes, sir. Have some bread with Rassul." Sahibs said: "We am hungry."

BAD-LUCK-TIME.

Rassul said: "I will give to all some food." The Rassul made a cooking-pot the basin of sahibs (hands washing thing). In putting full water, and put some flour and meat, made as soup, that we five men drinking. For sahibs was soups in small tins. That made. Now the sahibs said to us: "We go very quick to that place, where we killed the wild donkey; there find meat. And will go quick to that place, where we separate with caravan. There will find some foods, which we was told to John, to keep some foods there." And sahibs said: "To-day, we will go for camp to the Suget, where we see the beautiful place, and old house."

Wali Balti said that: "My eyes got ill. My son and I will come behind you. Leave there our loads. We will bring them. We will reach to Suget this evening."

We did leave their loads with Baltis, only we took three cartridges, in hope, if meet some animal in way, to kill. We do not know it were next deceitful of Baltis. We arrived to Suget; camped there. There was a little sugar and flour, that always the Rassul carried upon his back, and some tins of soups and vegetables for sahibs. Now the two Baltis not come to that evening.

The next morning we drink that soup of flour again, and wait for the two Baltis. They does not come. Sahibs said: "If we wait, we will die without foods. Keep here some flour for Baltis." We did put some flour in a handkerchief, and that hung on a tree's branch on way, and started ourself, and walking.

Now the cook Rassul said: "Now, if God help us and we reach to Leh, we must needed make to repent to God, which we drinking wine." And said: "Now we have much hungry. We will drink the tins soup. That is a strong things. When we come to Leh, we will make repent about it." I said myself: "I beg God's pardon for the wine-drinking. That time was very cold. That one drinking help us very much. The next drinking brought us bad luck. Now you said for tins soup. I never drink it. It did not get us such a hungry which you think. We have a soup of flour. If I die, does not matter." The Rassul get a little angry on me for this, and he not drink, too.

Now we came to that place where we hided the wild donkey's meat. There were no meat, only were bones. All the meat was taken the Baltis, who running from Mustagh. We were much angry and sorry for that meat. Why? Our long hope were on that meat. Mr. Church said: "Take the thick bones. In them will find butter." We did carried them on our backs, and walking. Camped, where were much good water and bush-wood. We made a good fire, and lived, surrounded by that fire; sahibs, we two Rassul and that Balti. Now our camp were very poor camp, as that which came a very poor coolie's going to a travel. We were same that.

Now the Rassul broken those bones, there got a little butter, that put into a cup. The Balti, which one was with us, he robs that bones-butter, which was into cup. Mr. Church see that, and said: "The bad Balti robs this little butter." I said the Balti: "Why do you robs it?" He said: "I do not robs it." The lie Balti! On his finger was that butter, and on mouth. We believed that the Baltis are lie, and sahibs abused the Balti. After that the Balti said: "Yes, I did robbed it. I cannot stop with the hungry."

At that night we get a little good soup with the bones. Now we had a very little flour, and had some sugar and pepper and some cocoa tins, which in that cocoa put hot water. It go good. In it were milk, sugar, and cocoa. At that night the sahibs made a wall to go sleep for night. Each sahibs had each rug of fox-skin, and there was a red cloth, which was cotton in it. That one cut off, and half put under one sahib, the next half put under next sahibs, and under their head put their boots and going bed. The Rassul and I put under our head stones, on that put our sash, then we both wear upon us a waterproofs.

The next morning that Balti said: "I will wait for

other Baltis, and we will catch you people to Oprang." That Balti waited there. We carried the loads on our backs. By bad luck, that day, the sahibs carried some loads upon their backs. Now we four men only. Always the sahibs going ahead, they talking themselves; we two Rassul travelled together behind sahibs, and talked each other.

The Rassul said to me that: "How get my matter? I told you that the Baltis are deceitful. That you foolish man does not believed me, and the sahibs not believed, too." I said to him: "Your were quite right." And he said: "How will we reach to a villages? We no have foods." I said to him: "God will provide food."

[Pages lost. Rassul has been on a vain hunt for meat.—EDITOR.]

A little before evening I came on my way. Now the sun gone down. I left way until sahibs about twelve miles. I said myself: "Foolish man, why did you thinking all that wrong? No get meat, and lose time. Now, how get to sahibs to-day?" I travelled in these, all sorry. Now get much dark. There no was moon. I came to the big plain. There blow the wind. Now the cold and darkness and the hungry were on our luck on those days. I afraid to wild dogs. Sometime I afraid to demons. Sometimes felt better, and said: "The God is with me." And was a big hope on the rifle. I took out the rifle from glove, and walking alone in that night in darkness.

A very longer after, I saw a light of fire, far away. I said myself: "This fire made sahibs." Sometimes said: "It made a demon." (Which I had heard in Leh from some lamas; demon make fire.) But my way was towards that fire. If I say it was camp-fire, camp was in a deep place, which cannot see. A longer after, I came near that fire. There saw some men walking in the fire-shine, and heard some voices which called to me. I did returned the calling answer. While after, I came to the fire-place. There were both sahibs and

Rassul. The both sahibs came to me, and embrace to me, and said: "Don't care for Baltis, but we were much sorrow for you." I was much glad with all that kindness of sahibs, and then I told that all story of my happened. Sahibs said: "Those animals be got wind of you."

The Rassul was angry. I said to him: "Why do you are angry?" He said: "Sahibs gave me trouble to carry wood up the hill. I told that; not needed fire. You will reach. Sahibs not believed me." I said: "Don't be angry. Your matter were right. I must reach, myself."

Next morning we found that yakdan, which we left. There were a little enough stores for sahibs, and, beside flour, there were some suttoo too. Sahibs said: "We do not want flour. The stores are enough for us. The flour and suttoo kept for you people." Then sahibs carried part of the stores and some clothes upon their back. Rassul carried that flour and suttoo. Rassul never give the suttoo and flour to me. And I carried much heavy stores.

Now Mr. Phelps said to me that: "Give me your paboo, and take my boots." I said: "Sir, in my paboo have very much lice. You will find trouble with them." Sahib said: "That not be more trouble than this short boots."

Now we travelled from that place, we travelling by the tracks of our caravan. Then came in a river. Now we saw the caravan crossed that river of Yarkand. That water was much deep, cannot carry sahibs. But we carried sahibs' loads upon our backs, sahibs going in their foots in river. Both side that river were the gravel. Those hit very bad to our foots. Sahibs said to Rassul and to me: "You people are our faithful servants and friends." The Rassul said to sahibs that: "Sir, you people was rich, and were taking good foods. At that time, you people not thanks to God to his kindness. You forget God. Then God gave all this punish to you." Sahibs laughed, and said: "It is true of your." That night dinner, our flour soup was a little good than before. In that were some wild vegetable. It had been a long time, no any meat and butter.

Next day we wait one place for tiffin. That place I see the cook Rassul. He ate himself, by hidden to me. When I see that, my felt much sorry. And I said to him that: "You were always as my father, and my mother was begged to you about me. Now why you eat, by hidden me? Rassul said to me: "We get that a bad luck time, which, if had father and son, the father not look to his own son, and son not look to his own father. Must save own life. I how help you?" And he was brought some vegetable. He does not like to give me that, and said:" You must get yourself vegetable. I said: "We have no such unluck time as you said. God will give foods."

We started from that place, came to a beautiful place, many trees as a big garden. I saw much wild vegetable, which we eat, I wait there to take them. There sahibs and cook Rassul went ahead than me. While after, by good luck, see a house under a mountain rock. I went toward that house. There see a big gate. Mr. Phelps came out from that gate, and said to me: "Good luck! In this house are few room. To a room was locked up. I did break that door. There get a large bag, full of rice, about five maunds." I was very glad to this news. Then we went into that house. There cooking-pots and other things, and was in one thing some oil. The Rassul cooken rice and that oil. By kindness of God, we eat enough rice and camped there. The next day we wait there for rest. The Rassul there cooked much rice to take with us, in the little table-cloth of sahibs, which not used. We sleep under trees on green gras , very enjoy. Now I said to Rassul: "Look the power of God, which he gave us all this rice in no-hope place." Rassul thanked to God.

Now sahibs said: "How much rice we ate, and will take

with us, we will pay money when we meet with men." And sahibs said: "This house belong a fort of Chinese."

Now we counsel, that where shall we go. The our caravan were went by Yarkand river, that go east, and from that fort to north gone a small valley. By that valley was a small road. We said that must be Kugiar road, and we agreed to go that road; must meet some human. Then, where we like, will find road. At that time, only we wanted human. We took rice for eight days and started by that small valley toward north. Camp in that valley. Now our camp were as poor coolies' camp. When the coolies camp, they take off their dirty clothes, and take off their lice from their clothes. We were poor as coolies, and at those days we had much lice as coolies. And Mr. Phelps say: "Your lice cut me very much, but it is more easy than the short boot."

The Rassul laughed and said to me: "Look at the sahibs! Now the lice taken from sahibs' clothes, looked me as coolies. It is the power of God. If not, how the sahibs find such kind of trouble?"

Now we always take coffee and cocoa, that were very good.

Now we travelling up that valley, came under a hill. Now up a little valley we found a little road, which there were many dungs of ponies and yaks. A little after, came over a little pass. Top the pass, was some thick snow. That looked bad road to go down. Now we searched way to going down. I get remember of young-time, which I were going over mountains in Leh. In that remember I showed to sahibs a place. I said to sahibs: "I will go by this road. If I can, then you people come after me." Sahibs said: "Cannot go by that place." Sahibs were in this talking. I did went by that way. I fell down, hit a little, but, by helping God, I get down safely. Then behind me came sahibs and Rassul down. We crossed that pass. Sahibs said to me: "Bravo! You get good road below, and there are good fuel of yaks' dungs." We did made there tea and wait a little for rest. We were so tired, we seemed one those day as a month.

FINDING HELP.

After rest, we walking down by a valley. One place we saw some wet dung of yaks. We looked that very lucky. A while after, see several yaks, and thank to God.

A little after, we done that valley and came in a large valley. By good luck, we saw several men in that large valley, which they had made a little fire. When they see to us, they get up from their place and came toward us. We said salaam to them; they said salaam to us. And I said in Turki: "Where do you people came from, and where do you people going?" They said: "We came from Pakpo and will go to Baza Dara Fort." And then they looked from our foot to head, and we known in their face, that they afraid to us. And they said: "Where do you people came from, and where do you people going?" Then said sahibs to me: "Tell all our happened story to them." Then we went to their camp, and I said all the our story. They said: "We thought you people are Kanjut robbers." I showed them two sahibs. I said: "Are very big sahibs." By bad luck they not know what is sahibs. They were as animals. Called to this kinds of people Wakhi; their language is a Tadjik. And they said: "How many men are behind you?" I said: "Are no more men, beside we four men." They not believe; must thinking, this people are robber. Rassul and I told many good matter; then they believe to us, to not be robber; but they never thinking the sahibs to be big men. We showed to them the sahibs' gun and the fox-skin rugs. We asked them: "Please, you people come with us to next villages, and give us some yaks to carry our loads." They said: "Cannot go with you people. Must go very quick to the fort." We gave some rupees to them. They not know what things is rupee. We said a rupee is so many tangas of Yarkand. They not believed. They not agreed to go with us. We do not know what shall we do. Then they said: "From Pakpo, where do you people be going?" We said: "To Karghalik. There we will pay amban the price of the rice which we took from the fort." Then they said: "Don't tell anything for that fort. If you people say there at that fort no were any people, then amban will punish to us." Now I said: "The amban must be angry to not watching the fort. The next angry will be to not helping these big men." With this matter they afraid more. They said: "Please, don't tell to amban." And said: "We can let go a man with you, and two yaks until Pakpo. From Pakpo can find other man and yaks." Sahibs was glad with this matter. And we bought some butter from them, for that dinner of night. And they gave us some breads. We were much glad.

Now next day we started from that place with that young man, and with yaks. There came few other companions with us to go to their tents. Now seemed me the yaks were very fat and young; cannot ride on their back. Cook Rassul said to me: "We will mount on yaks." I said to him: "I must walk. That be more good than mounted. These yaks are young, foolish, and fat. They must fell us." Rassul said: "You are as a woman, which afraid to mount a yak." I said: "It is true. I am afraid to mount a bad yaks."

Now, by good luck, we no have loads up on our back. Without loads, walking seemed me as a mounted. We walking down by a lovely green valley. At last we came to a water-brook. There were high water, and many rocks in stream. They said: "Here will cross this water." I said: "Yes," and took off my paboo from my foots, to cross that stream. Rassul said to me: "Why do you take from your foots your paboo? You must ride on yaks." I said: "No, I not wanted yak. I will cross it by my foot."

Rassul abused to me and said, "Woman!" Then he said to a man: "Bring a yak!" There brought a yak. Rassul said to me: "You are foolish as woman, and these people are women, as you are." I said: "Yes, we are all woman. You are a man." Then Rassul rode on a yak. When he get up on the yak's back, that yak jumped, and took him outside that water-stream, and felled him among rocks. That seemed me wonderful tamasha. The other men and I laughed very much, and we did crossed that water-stream. Then came to front Rassul. What seen there? Rassul lying down, front him was much blood, and in front him sat Mr. Phelps on a rock, and he laughed very much. I laugh very much laughed, which Mr. Phelps' and my laughing never stop. Rassul abused to me, and he said: "If I get this unluck, you laughed. You do not help to me." But both sahib and my laughing never stop. Now Rassul said to me: "Bring tak takmo." (That is a grass name, which grow Ladak. If put that grass, then will stopped blood.) Now where I bring that grass? There not was it. And I said to Rassul: "From where came all the blood?" His face put down, never show me his face. At last, he showed his face. We known, that into his nose was came one horn of that yak's, which he has mounted, and nose was cut, and came much blood from his nose. His nose was big before; now get more big, with the wounded sore. Now Mr. Phelps said to Rassul: "You ride on my ponies, I will walk." Rassul said to sahibs: "No, sir, God pardon my fault. Now I will never ride, to a ponies, and on a yaks." He did not ride.

Now we travelling by that lovely valley; arrived that afternoon on a next pass.

Next day, sahibs said to me: "You go ahead, and make ready good foods until our arrival." I said: "Yes, sir." Now Mr. Phelps said: "Now give my boots to me, and you take your paboo." I said: "Yes, sir."

Now I went ahead. There were very bad road. A long time after, came to a dry place, where was much green grass, and was a large road. Now see the Pakpo country, a large, wide valley, surrounded by that tall mountains, top covered snow. And that all valley and hill much green land of grass, a large pasture; in them grazing flocks of sheeps and yaks. That all seemed very beautiful. Now my felt much enjoy to seeing them.

A long time after, see several tents. When I came nearly tents, came many dogs, in much barking. I much afraid to them. There came several men out tents. When I meet with them, I said: "Salaam." And I shook their hands. They looked from my head to foot. My face were very black, and my hair was come long, and dirty clothes, and in hand long stick, on one end of it long iron, and on my back English gun. And I knew in their face they sorry to my coming. Why? In those place were coming many time robbers. And they said to me: "From where do you come, and where shall you go from here?" I told them all our happened, that all. They took me in a tent and gave me bread and butter, cream and milk. I said to them much sweet matter. I get a friend among them. I said to them: "Big sahibs will reach now, and you people pitch a tent for them, and put in that tent good rugs and put many foods: butter, bread, cheese, cream and other things." They made ready, that all. And they said to me: "We no have wheat. We have corn bread only." I said: "If you not kept wheat bread, then bring corn bread." Then I said: "Bring a good sheep." There made ready all that good things which they haved. Now I said: "We will got to Kugiar, and to-morrow we wanted four ponies." They said: "No kept ponies. To-morrow our man will go to Ak Masjid, and he will take several yaks. You people can ride on them." I said: "It will be good." Now they said to me: "Friend, your hair look much dirty. We will make clean until sahibs come." I said many thank. Then made a man my head clean. I got very good rest there, and felt much enjoyed.

A longer after, sahibs and Rassul arrived. Sahibs were much glad with my arranged, and sat on dastarkhan. Now the people came inside our tent and sat front sahibs. Mr. Church said to me: "You tell, by sweet matter, to those people: 'Don't come in our tent.'" I did said to those people, as animals: "You people go now into own tents. This no good, to sit into a bigguest tent." They said: "Yes."

Next morning they brought several yaks and a young man to go with us.

After several days, we marching, came a mounted man toward us. When he come near, Rassul and I know him, which we were seen him many times at Leh, among traders. He is a old man, which his beard was very long and white. I went before him and said: "Salaam aleikum." He said: "Aleikum salaam," and he know me. Then he came sahib, and said: "Salaam." That man name was Muhmad Feazulla. He know very good Englishman. He has brought some good breads, and some fruits, and that all kept before sahib. And sahib said to me: "Tell him all our story." That all I told him.

He said: "Yesterday few men had seen you people. They told me that there were come at Ak masjid four poor men and they said: 'We am English sahibs,' and among them one said: 'My father is Shukar Galwan.' When I heard this matter, I thought they must be a sahib. Why? I know to Shukar Galwan, and I known his son are travel with sahibs." Now he said: "That my tent is a little down. We will camp at night, there; then go to-morrow to Kugiar."

At Muhmad Feazulla's tent we got all good things to eat, and sahibs bought some very good numdah, very soft wool, and some pattoo cloth of camel wool, and gave one numdah and one long coat to Rassul, and some gave me. Muhmad Feazulla made all that arrangement for hire-ponies for us. And we washed clothes, and took bath, ourselves.

Then we came Kugiar, each man riding ponies. Then I went ahead to Karghalik. There I went to the house of Shukar Galwan, and told them all our story. They were very sorry, to heard all this our hungry trouble. And Shukar Galwan said to me: "If you live with me, you will never find such trouble again." I said to him: "I like very much the trouble."

Then Shukar Galwan said: "These sahibs are a very big guest for me. I longed that will give a good dinner, but who will cook the English food?" And he was sorry to no be my elder brother there, which he knows some English foods cooking. Then he puts there a large table of Chinese. On that table puts many kinds foods of Yarkandi, and all kinds of fruits. At that time was riped new apricots and mulberry. That all made ready, and he kept on that table a small bottle Chinese brandy. Then he kept on next two table sheep-meat, few chickens' meat, many kinds vegetables, eggs, butter, honey, many thing without cooking. He said: "This all is my feast for sahibs. Why? This sahibs are a large guest for us." I was very glad to be that all ready for my sahibs, from my relation, and look for myself a little honour.

Arrived that afternoon sahibs and other men. Shukar Galwan went a little way before sahibs, and some men of amban. When sahibs seen that table, all interesting things, and good rugs, sahibs were very glad. Sahibs said to Shukar: "What are these all?" And Shukar said: "This all are, sirs, my feast for you." Sahibs laughed. And said: "You made much trouble for us." Shukar said: "Sir, I have no trouble. You are a very big guest for me. My son is your servant."

[On arriving Leh, Rassul received the long-withheld news of the death of his wife. His hunter sahibs were very gentle and friendly with him, giving him much honour at Leh, attending a great tamasha to celebrate the safe termination of the journey, publicly testifying to Rassul's spirit and ability, and putting on his head, in the presence of his Leh friends, a fine pugaree.—Editor.]

My Second Marriage

AFTER Mr. Phelps and Mr. Church journey, I came back home. And what I earned, that all I gave to mother. But some I kept, for my play. Now my mother said to me: "You have earned very good money in this journey, and we have now rupees two hundred in hand. You need not cook. I will cook." Several days after, mother brought a middle-age woman to cook for us. Her name was Sharup.

Now I, many time, go to play with No-No Sonam Wangdus, and with Razak Akhun, and with Kalam Rassul and other friends. When I went to other friends' house to talk, at that time, I had to get leave from my mother, for, without mother's leave could not sit at night. Sometimes friends came and sit at my house. Sometimes I was invited to dinner by No-No Sonam Wangdus, sometimes by other friends. Sometimes I made a dinner for all friends. And that money which I had hidden from mother, that I spent for this.

And many times my friends used to tell me about my next marriage; and they mentioned many girls' names which were in Leh. I not like them. And for a long time I said: "I will not." And my mother asked me many times about the marriage of mine, and she gave many girls' names which I not like. I said to mother: "I will wait."

Now my first wife I not had liked very much. That my mother knew. Yet she was not so bad, and after her death I remembered her much. But cannot come to hand again. And my mother said to me: "You must look very careful for next marriage, so that there would not be that kind of trouble." I said: "Yes, mother, and I like that kind of a wife who will obey you, the same as myself." Mother said: "That will be all right, if you teach her."

Now in doing and thinking all this, we were two months and a half. One day at breakfast my mother said to that woman, who cooked for us: "Do you know any girl, outside Leh town, which Rassul would like, and who would obey me?" That woman answered to my mother, and said: "At Shushat village there is a beautiful girl, and about the same age as Rassul, and a very good honest girl, and she will obey you."

When I heard that from that woman, I liked that girl, without seeing. I said to my mother: "I like this one." My mother said: "Without looking, how can you like? No good. Before, you must look. Then we will send to her mother."

I felt: must make quick this work. I said to my mother again: "This one, whatever kind of a girl, I like her. You must send words to her mother and brothers." In few days my mother sent words, and some tea and butter. This was Ladaki custom. There came reply that they like to give me their daughter. And I heard that my wife had liked me, without seeing. I was much glad with this news.

At that time at Sheh villages came a tamasha. That village was very near to my wife's villages. My mother said: "You go to that tamasha, and there will come that girl, also, for the tamasha. Then you can look to her very careful." Beside that, I wanted go to that tamasha also. There Kalam Rassul wanted go for that tamasha.

We brought food and hire-ponies, and went to Sheh. It was about ten miles. When we came, there were many people gathered, but my wife had not come. There we made two days' tamasha, because I had hope that next day I would see her. And at the tamasha many women and men danced and sang.

And when the big tamasha was over, every one at night made a little tamasha, at own camp. Kalam Rassul and I gathered some friends, and sang ourselves. Kalam Rassul said one time: "There is no enjoyment here. We must have some beautiful girls to sing." I said to him: "That is good. Where will we get them?"

He said: "I saw that several girls lived in next house. If they came, then we be happy enough." We knew those girls were very beautiful in Leh. I said: "I do not like to bring them. I think we had better sing by ourself." They said: "That way is not a happy one. We can give one rupees or two rupees worth of chang to them." I said: "Then you people go and bring them."

Kalam Rassul and other men went to those girls' camp. After a while they came back, in much sorrow. I said: "Where are those girls?" Kalam Rassul said: "They abused to us, and said: 'We are not singer woman, who would come to sing at your camp.' Those girl got very angry." Kalam Rassul begged me, and said: "If you go those girls' camp, they must come." (At that time, by help of God, I had good luck in Leh. Everyone, old men and young men, like Rassul, and everyone, old woman and girls, think that Rassul look honest and good man. Beside that, many good girls liked my talk and song. Everyone was kind to me; but later I was unluck, and no one like Rassul. That came after.)

Now I went to those girls' camp. They had shut their door very tight. I said from their door: "I have come." Quickly they opened their door. I said: "It will be a great kindly, if you come to our camp, and will sing together. We shall all enjoy much, then, this night." They said: "You came to our camp. We can sing here. We cannot come to your camp. For there are Kalam Rassul, who is a bad man, and others." I said: "What can they do bad with you?" Then they came with me. We bought chang for one rupee and half. Kalam Rassul drank, but I did not drink. We brought banjo man also, and sing and dance, and much enjoy ourselves all night.

The next day my wife came for the tamasha, but I not know which girl she was. I ask a boy of Shushat. He showed me a girl, which I like very much, and wanted to marry her, but she not know me. All that day I looked the tamasha, and at evening I came back Leh. And my mother said: "Did you see your wife?" I said: "Yes." Then mother said: "We will try to bring her quickly."

Now by good luck, in several days, all the business of my marriage we had ready. Now my mother and I counselled together, that we will not spend much money on this marriage, because already we held one marriage before it. Then all my friends came, and No-No Sonam Wangdus was as a head-man among them, and he said: "This marriage you must make a big one. If you have only little money, we will help." They said: "We will make big dance."

Now this was not custom of Mohammedan; but, at that time, my best friends nearly all were Buddhists, and all my friends like very much to dance.

Now we made a day for bringing my wife. It was custom: from my side, send several good men, bring her my home, and their expense I must pay. Now I send No-No Sonam Wangdus, Habibula and a mullah to read nika, and other friends and my brother went with them. They took every one a pony, and one pony for my wife.

When she came near Leh, there went Ramzan Ali, Razak Akhun, Kalam Rassul and other friends, with banjo and with many lights, about a mile to meet her I waited in my home. And I had on very good clothes from feet to head. They brought my wife with much banjo noise. And they danced with swords before her. There was a big tamasha at Leh that night. And with my wife had come her elder sister, and waited a week at my home. This was custom.

Now my house was very small. While after, all guests went to their houses, and some working-people waited there. Now my wife and I came in a room together. We both had never spoken to each other before. She was much ashamed. I thank God that, in all the kindly of God, he taken from me one wife, for which I felt full of sorrow, but gave a very good wife again. And my wife was glad to get me. She thank to God.

The next day we took one other man's large house for few days. For that, we had spoken before. And near that house there was a small garden. My friends pitched a very large tent, for tamasha, at night, in the garden. And Kalam Rassul said: "I can make arrange to Chinese tamasha, and make that boat of paper, that we saw in Kashgar." There was at that time a friend of mine, a rich Hindu son. He gave all the paper for that boat.

And next day many Ladaki women came: bring some, a tea-pot tea; some, a pound butter; some, annas four; some, annas eight; some, a little milk; some, a plate of suttoo or flour. We had kept a clerk to write that all down, what each brought. That was, that all could be returned to them on their happy day. It had been a custom in Ladak. So there we gathered about rupees thirty. And at that evening we made dinner for about one hundred people, rice and meat and tea. After that dinner the banjo men made a high noise of dance in that small garden. There gathered very many people, and there danced my friends many kinds of dance: Yarkandi, Balti, Gilgiti. Then Kalam Rassul and Razak Akhun brought that Chinese paper boat. In that Kalam Rassul sat. The Ladak people never had seen anything like that.

All Buddhist people and my friends like that tamasha very much, but the good Mohammedi did not like that tamasha, because it was not custom for Mohammedi. But at that time I was not ashamed, and follow my friends' custom.

Next day all my marriage was finish. And we went to our own house.

Now the No-No Sonam Wangdus gave five maunds of fire-wood and the rich Hindu's son gave the paper for that boat, but besides that we spent about rupees one hundred, and in that bringing of friends came about rupees thirty. This made a name for my friends, for they said: "Rassul Galwan made a good marriage and tamasha out of that money that all friends gather." My mother and I were much sorry for this matter, that they did not help, but to add to their name.

I passed several days in enjoyment that I had got a good wife.

Now there came a letter from Mr. Littledale to B.J.C. That was: Ramzan and Razak Akhun and some other Ladaki to go Kashgar. Ramzan Ali[1] and Razak Akhun had been with Mr. Littledale in his last journey in China. Now Ramzan Ali was in service of B.J.C. He sent in his place Kalam Rassul. Now Razak Akhun, Kalam Rassul and Hussin, three of men went to Kashgar for Mr. Littledale. I was left in Leh. And my thought was, that I would live a year with my good wife. I wanted to travel a long way to look at other countries; but now I liked more to live in Leh, and was very happy.

Now, about twenty days after, the wazir got a letter from the B.J.C.: that a very good servant who had travelled in Chinese Turkistan, and knew some the language, and was a truthful man, should be sent Kashgar for Mr. Littledale. The wazir knew me well and he found my chits better than other men. He liked very much send me Kashgar. I not like to go so soon after the happy marriage. Wazir was a very wise man. He said: "You must think out this matter." I told my mother. My mother not like me to go so soon for a long journey, and my wife did not like also. I said to wazir: "I cannot go." Wazir said: "You must not ask your mother and wife. They are women. You think for yourself, what is best." I said: "I will answer to-

[1] Ramzan Ali was caravan bashi for Lord Dunmore. When Lord Dunmore met Mr. and Mrs. Littledale on their way to Pekin, Ramzan Ali joined them, Lord Dunmore saying that they had in Ramzan Ali one of the best men in Central Asia.

morrow." Now I thought myself: "Which is best?" I wanted very much to live with good wife. But I felt that I would not find such a sahib and big sahib again. And would see many interesting countries, railway and steamer, and will find rich money also. Now I came to Wazir, and said: "I will go by your order." And Wazir gave me a very good parwana (passport) to help me, and one yak without hire.

I said to my wife: "My mother's temper is bad. You must not mind that, and you must not do bad work with other men. Then I will be as your servant for long time." My wife said: "I will take mother's bad temper, and don't you think that any bad work will be done. You be very careful in your journey." And we few night in the spoken. We both cried, and I said: "We are not rich. If we had enough money, then I would not go away from you." We cried again and made our pillow wet, and I gave her five rupees to hide from my mother for her needs. And I said: "I must make you a very good present." She said: "Does not matter present. If you come back well, that is enough." That night was a very hard night for us. Now I begged my mother to be good to my wife. And I said to mother: "This wife I like very better than the last one." My mother said: "I must look after her very careful. You must not be sorry for us. You be careful in your journey, and I will pray to God about you."

[The journey with Littledale shows Rassul, at last, in actual, though not in nominal charge of a caravan. We have given the account of the journey practically entire, because it was in itself a thrilling journey, and because it shows, at a high point of development, Rassul's resourcefulness and devotion. St. George R. Littledale, in 1895, penetrated into Tibet from the north, getting within forty-three miles of Lhasa, before the hostile Tibetans succeeded in stopping him. The return journey, to Ladak westward, was through country never before traversed by Europeans.—EDITOR.]

The Journey of Mr. Littledale

GOING TO MEET MR. LITTLEDALE AT KASHGAR.

Now I started on my next long journey in the name of God again. At that night camped at Ganglose. Next day I started early in morning. When sun came up I got up on Kardong pass, and looked back at Leh village, and felt sorry and happy also.

Other side pass many caravans coming up. There there is a little part of ice. My yak man said me: "If cross that ice before come the caravan, then will be good for me. Why? We have one yak only. If wait until cross all caravan, then it be very late for us." But the caravan was coming and was nearly under that ice. The yak-man said: "If you say, 'I am B.J.C. man,' then they will wait below, until we cross the ice." I took the yak-man's advice in the matter, and called from the pass: "You people stop until I cross the ice." They not stop. The yak-man said: "You must abuse to them; then they will stop." So I abused to them in Turki. But they not stop coming up. So we met with the caravan in middle of ice. They all were big Afghan traders. When we came near them, they caught to me to beat me, for that I had abused to them. I knew them, and some them knew me. Now I said myself: "I will find bad luck." I quickly begged them, and said, "I did not know who are you people; you must pardon to my fault." By good luck they let go me. I thanked to God, for get safe from the danger of beating, and I was sorry and ashamed. I kept in my head: that to abuse people is no good; it must bring bad luck; sweet matter will bring good luck than bad matter.

Now everywhere the parwana help me and where I camped, there the farmers brought me flour and some butter, and milk and fire-wood. One man stayed at my camp to make fire and bring water, same servant. What I bade him, that he did. The next day I travelled about three miles, and early came to Taghar. There the numbardar brought me flour. And he brought an old woman for my work. And the numbardar said: "Here were not any men. While after, a man will come. Until his coming, then you kept this old woman." I said, "Yes," and the numbardar made my camp in a large house. Now at my work I was always singing and joking and laughing. That old woman looked me very interesting boy. Now I made tea, and I filled that old woman's cup first. She said many joo. I liked that, and I sang many kinds of song, because, at that time, was my work singing and dancing. After, numbardar brought a man. But that old woman said: "Please let me sit with this good young boy." Now there came one named Azum, a young sepoy. He lived with me at same camp, and he got flour and other things, same me. And for both of us got from the farmer no price. But Azum could not sing like me.

Now we were there two days, because I waited for my brother, which came behind me. After few days my brother came there with several other of caravans, who were going Yarkand.

Now after few days we came under Karakorum Pass. There we met a Ladak caravan, which came from Yarkand, and was going to Leh. They brought good news from Yarkand to my brother. They said my brother's wife had got a son. With this news my brother was pleased, and I was much glad.

We every day made a long march, which started early in the morning and walking until evening.

Now we met with two Hindus which had came from Leh and were going to Yarkand. At that time Yarkand was very cold. Those Hindus not had enough clothes. But they had hire-ponies and they took the Kugiar road with us. (Now for the Kugiar road I was better guide than all caravan. One caravan which went before us from Panamik, we caught up with that caravan on way. They had used up their grain, and many their ponies were dead. They said to me: "Your words were right, which you told us at Panamik, which you advise us: 'Take more grain.' ")

Now my brother and I said to the Hindus: "In this cold weather, you people must not riding on ponies from morning until evening. You people must walk If not, your feets and hand will be lost in the cold. You must walk until body is warm. Then you ride again." The Hindus said: "We had not paid the hire of ponies to walk. We never walk." My brother and others and I knew well that in this way they must lost their hands and feets. We spoke many times to the Hindus, but they not take our advice.

After some days we came to a pass. There we camped under two large rocks. That night both the Hindus cried and said: "My feets and hands!" Now we thought their hands and feets would be gone. If at that time they would put on hot stone it would be good. We said that, but they did not like to do that. Now every night both the Hindus made such noise we could not sleep at camp. We must go separate place for sleeping. One Hindu was a little young. I was much sorry for him.

After few days we came to Kugiar. There we heard that Mr. Macartney had came Karghalik to make free all the slaves. At that time were in Yarkand and Khotan and all places many big men who had many slaves. All those Mr. Macartney make free. Now I was much glad at the news, that Mr. Macartney and munshi Ahmad Din had came to Karghalik, and was hurry for come Karghalik.

After two days from Kugiar we reached Karghalik, and we two brother camped at Shukar Galwan's house. Shukar Galwan was much glad to see me again. (And when I had come to Karghalik from Mustagh with Mr. Phelps and Mr. Church, at that time Shukar Galwan had a preliminary for his some land with a Karghalik man. Of that I had told Mr. Phelps and Mr. Church, and they had wrote a letter to Mr. Macartney about that matter. Mr. Macartney wrote to the amban of Karghalik, and Shukar Galwan had got much help from that letter. Therefore he was very thankful to me.)

Now I went to visit Mr. Macartney, and munshi Ahmad Din. Mr. Macartney was walking outside his camp. I said: "Salaam." Mr. Macartney knew me well. He said: "Did you came safely?" I said: "Yes, sir." And then he asked me all the news of Mustagh; what happened there with Mr. Phelps and Mr. Church. I told him all that story, and all that the Baltis did with us. And he said: "Both sahibs wrote me about the bad Baltis. I punished a Balti name Masuliem, who run from Mustagh. Other do not get me." And then he said: "I will give you service if you stay with me." I said: "Sir, I have came for Mr. Littledale." And I told all that story, how the wazir sent me. Mr. Macartney said: "I do not know of the coming of Littledale." Then he said: "You go to Kashgar and wait there, and I will see you after twenty days."

Then I went to the munshi Ahmad Din camp, and met with him. The munshi was much glad to see me, and he asked me for much news of Ladak. I told him all the news of Ladak. The munshi always was very kind to us. He said: "You go to Kashgar and live in my room. That I have ordered for Razak Akhun and Kalam Rassul also. After twenty days we will come back from Khotan; then I will give you people another house to live in. Until I come back, you people can live in my room." I thanked him for all this kindly of his.

In two days we came to Yarkand, and camped at my brother's house. There we saw the little new man. Both of us brothers were much glad to see him. And there I waited in Yarkand two days; then hired a araba man to take me to Kashgar in his araba.

In five days we reached Kashgar. About 10 o'clock at night, we came to a gate of Kashgar City. At that gate the araba man said to me: "You go now to your place." I said to a man: "You show me the Chenar Bagh (that was the name of Mr. Macartney's garden). I will give you one tanga." That man said: "Yes, I will show you." It was very dark, no moon. About 11 o'clock I reached Chenar Bagh. I was much glad to arrive there. Now I said myself: "The Ladak men do not know my coming. I must play a joke on them." And then I sang, in Ladaki, through the window. All the Ladaki were in the room of the munshi. When they heard my song, they thought it wonderful, and came all out and met with me.

Then after welcome I went in the room, and there were the munshi's room all clean: were rugs were on floor, and good fire-place made room very warm. Now they brought tea and my dinner; asked for Ladaki news. I told them all that I knew, and they said: "Why do you came here?" I said: "For Mr. Littledale." This matter Razak Akhun and Kalam Rassul did not like. That I saw in their face, but Hussin liked very much my coming for Mr. Littledale.

Waiting in Kashgar.

Now I live with them in same room. And Hussin cooked for us. We had not any work at Kashgar to do. But all the nights and days, talking and singing were our work, for we were all full of youth.

Now Kalam Rassul had very good one banjo. I wanted very much have one, same his. Then Kalam Rassul took me to banjo-maker's place, who made 8 tangas the price for a banjo. And the banjo-maker said it would be ready in few days. After few days my banjo was ready. I was much glad to get that banjo like the Ladaki. Now Kalam Rassul and I made many times the banjo. But we did not knew the banjo well. So we learned it.

After about fifteen days, Mr. Macartney and the munshi Ahmad Din came back Kashgar. And then we got another room in the Chenar Bagh. After some days there came some guest from Hunza. Our room we gave to them and we got next a room very small. We were four men, and it was very difficult to get in it, for we had some fire-wood, and if we kept it, then we had no sitting-place. So I thinking a help for this. I dug the ground and put in it our water vessel, and, for all the wood, I tied some ropes high up under the roof, and there hung all the wood. This way we got enough sitting-place. But the fire-place was in the wall to cook, and that small room was very warm. Kashgar is very cold in winter. That room was very close to Mr. Macartney's room, and we not like that, for all night we sing and talked. Next trouble was this: that when we opened the door, it made a very bad squeak. These all we did not like, so near a big man, but could not help, for beside that room there was no other room. I did put oil under the door, and, with that, the noise did not come so bad. Now Kalam Rassul and Razak Akhun and Hussin said to me: "You are a wise man to fix the room." Beside them, all who came in our small room looked very interesting,—the way of wood keeping, and the water vessel,—and all laughed.

Now we were at Kashgar all the winter, about four of months, with no work. When we wanted money for our expense, that we got from Mr. Macartney. And the munshi Ahmad Din was always kind with us, we many times going to him and talking, and always he helped us. Beside that, he gave always very good advice, which was very useful for those who took those matters as from a father. I had made of his advice in my head, and that I used many times. And the reading Urdu and English I tried on his advice. I was very glad to have him in Kashgar.

Now Hussin was cook for us, like our servant. Razak

Akhun, Kalam Rassul and I went every afternoon to Kashgar City to play, and came back at evening. Now we had no work. Therefore we said each other: "We must do some thing. But what shall we do?" I said them: "It would be much better if we read somethings." They said: "What we read?" I said: "Hussin knows the Koran, Kalam Rassul and I know Ladaki." I said: "Let Hussin teach the Arabic Koran to us, and we will teach Razak Akhun and Hussin Ladaki." We all four men agreed to do that. We bought a Arabic primer-book from bazaar, and we had a Ladaki primer-book with us. Now we read it from morning until afternoon, and our small room was like a school. Mr. Macartney and the munshi looked at all that, and laughed. And the munshi said: "You people have made a good school." And said: "It is very good. We did this many days, Razak Akhun and Hussin learning some Ladaki, and I learning good Arabic. For me this helped much, for I had read some Urdu books at Leh. But Kalam Rassul got tired, and then he let gone this idea from his mind, as did Razak Akhun. But Hussin and I were not tired. We both kept learning some.

Razak Akhun and Kalam Rassul had been very good friends with me from my young time. Hussin and I were very good friends from young time also. But Hussin was not clever as we were; and Kalam Rassul and Razak Akhun, if I tell any wise matter among us, broken off.

Now Razak Akhun and Kalam Rassul had the custom: among people, make themselves as big men. Razak Akhun was a little wiser than Kalam Rassul. Kalam Rassul liked very much to wear good clothes. He many times used to wear my clothes and my pugaree, which I had got from Mr. Phelps and Mr. Church. I let him wear, in hoping he would be good friend to me. Now Kalam Rassul, Razak Akhun and I went always to the bazaar. Their custom was, that, if we met any Chinese men or Russians, to act like big men, and as if of bad temper. My custom was: I to show a very soft temper. Beside that, I had written some Chinese good words in Ladaki, to speak with Chinese; and when I met with Chinese, I made salaam to them, and honor, and I used these Chinese words, which I knew a little.

Kalam Rassul and Razak Akhun all that did not like. They said to me: "Why do you make ourselves like low men before Chinese people? This is not good, telling salaam to them, and speaking such sweet matter, as you are doing. We are English government men. We must show them bad temper, so they be afraid of us." I said to them that: "It is not good to show bad temper. That is bad men's work. Then they would never think us big men. If we show good temper, they must think us big men's servants. Beside all that, wise matter is this: Sweet matter will help more to men than a very big order or power." They said: "It will not." I said to them: "We shall be a long time on this journey. You people use your bad temper. I will use my temper. Then see which one helps us. Then we will use that one." They said: "Yes, we will do that."

One day we three friends were walking in bazaar. There we saw many people going to one side. We asked some them: "Where are you people going?" They said: "Here is tamasha of the Chinese. We are going there." Then we three friends went there for that tamasha. When we came there, there many boards had made a high place On that was a large tent, which had two doors. One side was a opened place. The Chinese wore many silk things and wore very interesting hats. There came many interesting things, coming out from the one door of the tent, and going in by the other. And there they made very good music, and they sang and danced. This I saw in many place in Chinese countries, but at that time it was new to me. It seemed me very interesting.

Now, at one side, were sitting there many Chinese men on chairs, and in front them was a table. I had good luck. There were some Chinese men. To them I had spoken good matter, and had made salaam. I not remember them, but they had seen me from their chair. By good luck, there came a few of these Chinese men and shook my hand, and took me with them and gave me a chair to sit on, and put in front me a Chinese cup of tea (no sugar or milk) and some seeds of melons. I was very glad for that.

But my two friend, Razak Akhun and Kalam Rassul were left at that place where we were before. Now I could not speak Chinese, but I made the men understand, that: to bring my two friends. Then they brought Kalam Rassul and Razak Akhun, and gave them chairs and tea. We were a long time there. My two friends thought it very strange, the Chinese do so much honor to me. Now I said to my friends: "Which temper helps, sweet or bad temper?" They said: "To-day your temper helps. Your matter was more right here than ours." And they said: "We must keep now like your temper from to-day."

Now at Kashgar there came Christmas day. Mr. Macartney made a big feast for all the big Mohammedan men of Kashgar, and we got a very good feast. That day next, he made a good feast, from breakfast until dinner, for all the Chinese, the ambans little and big which were in Kashgar.

Next he made for the Russian consul. That day with the Russian consul there came several sepoys. The consul went in house; they left outside. I wanted to make friendly with them.

The munshi Ahmad Din always kept in his room tea and bread and many kinds of fruits. If it was big day he more kept. I went to munshi's room. There were many things, but not was anybody there. I did bring many of those tea things and fruits into our small room. Then I did invite those Russian. They came into our room and there were very good things. They were much pleased with me.

Now to the munshi's room had come guests, and there were none of the things. The munshi's servant had seen all the things in my room before the Russians; so he got angry with me, and went quickly to tell the munshi.

Now the Russians went away. Then the munshi called to me and said: "Why did you take my guest-things to your room?" I said to the munshi: "Sir, with the Russian consul had came several sepoys. Mr. Macartney took the consul into dining-room, but his men no one asked. This I thought was a matter for shame. Then I took those things and puts them before them." The munshi was much glad over this matter, and said to me: "You did very wisely. They must need here have tea, but your room was small. Why did you not bring them here? Anyway, you did good work." And said to his servant: "Foolish man! For my guest, why did you not bring new things? We have much." And he abused to his servant.

Afterwards the munshi's servant and I laughed very much, for he was joking man, and he said to me: "You made the fault, and the munshi abused me." I said: "Yes, another time you must let me take all the things which I want." He said: "Now I will never give you anything!"

The French Sahibs'[1] Story.

One day arrived there Mohammed Isa and Abdurahman from China. They had been long before with the two French sahibs, one of which sahibs had been killed by the Tangut people in the Tangut country. We were

[1] M. Dutreuil de Rhins and M. Grenard. M. de Rhins was a man of forty-five, who had been an officer in the French Navy and mercantile marine, and was, of course, a stickler for discipline. He had devoted some years to the study of Tibet, and was projecting a three years' journey. M. Grenard published the results of the journey, at Paris.

much glad to meet with Mohammed Isa. Now he asked us the Ladaki news. We told him all the news of Ladak.

Now they told to us all the story, how the Tangut people killed the French sahib. Mohammed Isa and Abdurahman told the story of French sahib this way:

The French sahibs went from Cherchen through Akka Tagh, from Akka Tagh to Tibet, Tengri Nor (Lake). From Tengri Nor Lake, the Tibeti people turned them back. Then they, a little longer after, reached Tangut country. And there it was the duty, every night, of the servants, to watch the ponies by turns, two of men. Now on way, had died many ponies, and there was left few ponies only. Sahib brought some yaks for carry their luggage.

Now they came to a little villages of the Tangut. (The name of that villages I not remember.) There were some houses and a temple and lamas. And there was a serai. Sahibs camped in that serai. And there it was raining all day and all night. Sahibs were there, in the waiting, three or four days.

One night the rain was very hard, and it was very dark a night. But all the servants did that pony-watching duty. That night were a Russian and a Yarkandi servant on the watching duty. But on their watching they had felled asleep, and the Tangut had stealing two of ponies, the riding ponies of sahibs.

Next day morning every one knew that there were lost two of ponies in that night. Sahibs told to head men of that villages, that: "We did lost two of ponies here in this night." The head-men told to sahibs that: "This place is a many people coming and going place." And said: "We do not know who rob your ponies. If we knew, we could catch him. We do not know. Whom shall I tell? I cannot help." Sahib said: "If we do not find here our two of ponies, then we will take two ponies from this villages. Why? We lost our ponies in this villages." The head-man had told to them: "This is not custom to taken our ponies. We have not robbed your ponies." Sahibs had told them: "We have a very big parwana from the Chinese Government. Everywhere we got good help. But in this place we have lost our two of ponies. Must take two ponies."

There were two of sahibs, one elder, one younger. But the elder sahib temper very bad. He said in many places, when angry with village people, to shoot, kill them. In French words he said: "Bom, bom." What that means I do not know.

Next morning the sahibs ordered all servants: "To-day we will start from here, and we will catch two of the ponies of this village." The Tangut had let go their ponies to drinking water, and there came some boys with their ponies. The two sahibs and their Russian servant went to that river where drinking the Tangut ponies, and there caught two of ponies. One of them was a horse; with it came a young pony with its mother. So that there came three ponies. Sahibs brought them in the serai, and saddled them to ride.

Now the boy which was with those ponies, he cried, and, in calling to his father, went to his house. There came the head-man of the village, and that man to whom belonged the ponies, and some other men, to the sahibs and said: "Please let go our ponies." And spoken much about the ponies. The sahibs did not return the ponies. Then they said to sahib: "When you start from here, you look. Now your life will be finished here very soon."

Mohammed Isa said to sahibs: "You must return the ponies. This must bring bad luck for us. This is a bad matter." The elder sahib said: "Po, po." And the Russian man said: "They cannot do anything to us. But we need to be ready." Then the elder sahib ordered to all servants to keep ready their rifles and cartridges. Now all servants made ready to shoot, if the Tangut shoot at sahibs. And then they puted loads on yaks' backs, and started from that place. The time was about noon. It was much raining. All the caravan went ahead. At last started the elder sahib. With him was Mohammed Isa. Now from the monastery and temple all the lamas made their banjo, and all villages people made loud cries and calling. Mohammed Isa said to the sahib again: "Sir, this making cries, this all looks bad luck. We must need return the ponies." Sahib said: "You are as a woman. If they shoot, we can shoot them. We have more good rifles than they have." He started from the serai and came outside the gate of the serai.

Then the Tangut people began shooting from their house walls, in which were holes for shooting. Now one their shots hit the serai gate wall; next one shot hit the elder sahib in the stomach. Sahib said to Mohammed Isa in Turki: "Very bad, very bad. Now bring my rifle." When Mohammed Isa gave his rifle to sahib, sahib did shoot two times toward that house, from where had shot him. Then the Tanguts shoot very much from all houses. But did not hit any man. Now sahib lay down. There was wall, about two yards high. Mohammed Isa took the wounded sahib, and keeped him behind that wall. And the sahib said to Mohammed Isa: "You go back the last march and take this report, and tell the Chinese munshi, and go very quick."

Now there the Tangut shooting very much. The young sahib and Russian man run. Then all servants run behind them. The elder sahib lay under that wall. Not was any one with him. Then the Tangut took all things of sahibs. And all these divided among themselves, and did burn the papers and maps.

And Mohammed Isa return. Said the sahib not had died. After two days the Tanguts tied his hands with rope and threw him into river. There swam the sahib. Then the Tanguts put a stone on his head. Then he died in that.

Now the poor young sahib and all servants ran away. The Tanguts coming after, a little far way. After, did not come. Sahib and servants came all one place. Now they were very destitute, and had not any food or any money. But Abdurahman had a very little suttoo in his belt.

Now Mohammed Isa had came to the Chinese munshi, and told him all this bad luck. The Chinese munshi had answer to Mohammed Isa: "These people are very bad. I cannot tell them anything. If I order them to do anything, then they kill me also. But I will report it to Chinese government.

Then Mohammed Isa following his companions, and at a place met with all men. Now some had a little money in their pocket, and with that they bought a little suttoo. And among them was one cup only. And they had much trouble.

After several days, they came to big monastery. There was a big lama, and he was a very good and wise a lama. He knew well European people. And he had heard the bad luck news, before they coming. When the young sahib and all servants came there, the lama gave to them good foods. Besides that, he gave several ponies, and for all servants cooking-pots, and foods to last until they could reach at a Chinese town. And he had told to the young sahib: "If you can send me some money for all these things, you may send me. If you cannot, does not matter."

After leaving that monastery, they came to a Chinese town. There had come money for the young sahib, and the young sahib sent to the good lama for his ponies, and all that his helping work. Then they reached at Sinning. There the young sahib paid all servants' wages and had gone to France at his home.

Now Mohammed Isa and Abdurahman had come from Sinning to Kashgar, and a few months after, they arrived at Kashgar, and met with us. We were much pleased to see them, a long time after, and we like very much to heard the story of French sahibs.

Arriving of Mr. Littledale.

After some days Mr. Macartney got a letter from Mr. Littledale, saying that they will arrive at Kashgar after few days, and he said to send two Ladaki servants to meet him. The Razak Akhun and Hussin went to meet sahibs, Kalam Rassul and I waited at Kashgar.

A few days after, Mrs. Littledale, Mr. Littledale, Mr. Fletcher[1] arrived at Kashgar. The sahibs rested few days and counselled with Mr. Macartney. Kalam Rassul was sent to Yarkand, to bring paboo for servants.

Now, in the room of Mrs. Littledale, all boxes were opened; all other things, all silver rupees and all things they had, spread on ground. And there they bought much Chinese silver. Now about these Mr. Littledale asked me how to keep them. I said: "Some we will keep in each bag of flour. Any robber will not think the silver is in flour bags." That Mr. Littledale liked, and Mr. Littledale asked me many things, and that he liked me, that I knew into his face.

And sahib wanted to find more Ladaki servants. I said: "Sir, we will find some at Yarkand, and some here." Now there was Abdurahman with Mohammed Isa, and some of his money and turquoise was in the hands of Mohammed Isa. Abdurahman wanted to separate from Mohammed Isa, so came all his money and turquoise in his hand. Now the munshi Ahmad Din asked Abdurahman to take the service of sahib. He agreed, and the munshi told to him: "For your pay, you will find rupees fifteen per month, and clothes and food." Abdurahman agreed to this pay. We did not know. We heard that Abdurahman was to come in our service, and we were much glad to get him. Why? He was a hard-working man. And we asked him about his pay. He said: "Rupees fifteen." We said: "Very bad. You have made us all servants very cheap."

[1] Mr. W. A. L. Fletcher, a nephew of Mr. Littledale, was an Oxford crew man. Later, he distinguished himself, both in the South African and the World Wars. He died as a result of being gassed.

We in much sorry for this matter. Munshi Ahmad Din and Mr. Macartney said, with much sweet matter: "These sahibs are very big men. You will find very good help in all your work from Government afterwards." And they said: "It is the last journey of sahib." And said much sweet matter, and the munshi also. They said: "We told the sahibs you people would go for rupees fifteen. If you not agree, then it will bring us great shame before the big sahibs." They we did agree, in the hoping, if we did good work, we would find good luck from Government.

Now we got some pay there. I sent rupees one hundred to my mother, and letters, with the all news of our journey. Now Mohammed Isa and Abdurahman had brought much turquoise from China. My rupees thirteen was in the hand of Mohammed Isa at the time of Major sahib journey. I bought, for that, turquoise from him. And some money was with me, from home, and some from the pay. I bought turquoise. I got sixty pieces good turquoise, and I sent them to my wife.

Now Kalam Rassul got back from Yarkand, and there came Galam Muhmad, a Ladaki boy. He begged us, to let go him with us. Razak Akhun and Kalam Rassul not did like to take him with us. I knew him before. He was a strong and hard-working boy. I spoke to sahib about him. Sahib said: "If you like, we will take him. If he cannot work, then you will find trouble. Why? His part of work will come on your head." I said: "Yes, sir. I will do it, if he cannot work." Then sahib gave him service.

Doctor-Work for Sepoys.

Now there arrived four Pathan sepoys. Mr. Littledale said to me: "Three sepoys are not able to go. Their foots are frozen. They will wait here a week, and you wait with them. Why? Your head is good." Sahib gave me rupees two hundred for expense, and said: "More money you will find from Mr. Macartney." Then sahibs went. I was left Kashgar with the sepoys. Mr. Macartney gave a room to us, in a serai, in Kashgar town.

The next morning there came the Russian doctor and brought a small box with him. Several things were in that box, and one bottle medicine. The doctor put in a basin water, and put in the water two or three drops of medicine, from the bottle. Then all the water in the basin came white as milk. Then the doctor washed the sepoys' feets with that water, and all the white skin off; then put other medicine. Some medicine was on some cloths; that he put on the sore; then put on it cotton. Then tied cloth. And all that he showed to me. And the munshi Ahmad Din said to me "You watch very careful the doctor work. After, you will be their doctor." Now I did put in my head all that work of the doctor. After, the doctor let me do it, and he sit in front me.

After three days, at night, the sepoys said to me: "That rupees two hundred which you got from sahib, why do you keep that money? You must divide it among us. Fifty rupees will come each man." I said to them: "This money is not to be divide. Beside this I will find more money from Mr. Macartney. I will buy poshteens for you people and other things, and must give good food to you people. Then I will give a bill sahib." They said: "Why do you spend it? We can spend it ourselfs. Money you must give us, fifty rupees each man. The other money, which you will find from Mr. Macartney, we will divide, after."

Now the sepoys, in speaking, nearly were to fight with me. There I was alone, and they were three men. I said to them: "It will be better to divide the money among us. So save me the trouble-work of giving bill to sahib. But I cannot divide it here. I will give to each man rupees fifty in front Mr. Macartney, to-morrow." They agreed to this matter.

The next morning, we went to Mr. Macartney. I knew well he will be angry with the sepoys. Therefore I walking behind the sepoys. When we came to the Chenar Bagh, Mr. Macartney and the munshi were at the gate. The sepoys said salaam to Mr. Macartney. After them, I said salaam. After, the sepoys said: "Sir, Rassul got rupees two hundred from sahib for our expense. That we want to divide among us." When Mr. Macartney heard this matter, he got much angry. Then said to the sepoys: "This money is not money to be divide. Rassul will spend it, and he will give a bill to sahib. And you people must obey to Rassul. He is as an officer among you. And you people must cook for him, and in every matter must obey him." Then sepoys said: "Yes, sir."

Then we came back to our camp. Now the sepoys nothing said about the money. Then I bought poshteens for the sepoys. There was one sepoy named Badullah, very tall a man. For him I could not get a poshteen in Kashgar town. Then Mr. Macartney gave order to a poshteen maker.

Now, in some time, I learned enough doctor work for the sepoys' feet. The havildar both feet, and foot's fingers were very bad, and one foot's thumb was gone. Other two sepoys, all the fingers of their feet were bad, but there was hope to get well.

Now Mr. Macartney gave some money to me, and I got more warm clothes for the sepoys and always gave them good food to make them strong. After a week there came a araba, which Mr. Macartney arranged. Then Mr. Macartney said: "Don't let the sepoys walk beside cart, and don't let them mount on ponies." I said: "Yes, sir." And he said: "Now you are doctor for the sepoys." I said: "Yes, sir." Then I said many salaam. Mr. Macartney said: "You must do good work with this sahibs." I said: "I will do my best work as your advice. By the help of God, sahib must like my work." Then I put the sepoys in the araba, and I sat with them.

Now what food the sepoys wanted, I gave them, and every day I made doctor work for their feet, but the sepoys not did let me do much work with their feet. The sepoys always were a little angry with me. Why? They thought: "In the hand of this man came rich money. In our hand did not come any money." The havildar and Badullah were very bad men, and both were very greedy. The sepoy named Purdil was young. He was a good man and was not greedy. Beside that he was a little friendly with me. The havildar was with me an enemy, and he wanted to make me bad before sahibs. Now he said: "The carriage is no good. I will ride on ponies." I said to him: "I can not give you ponies. That is no order of sahibs."

Meeting with My Mother's First Husband.

Now after five days, we came to Yarkand, and there we waited one night. After Yarkand, I came to Karghalik. Here Shukar Galwan made a very good dinner for me, and the sepoys also. And Shukar said to me: "You do not need to travel after this journey. I have much land. You shall be possessed of them, and in winter you shall live here. In summer you can take eight or ten ponies' loads of goods to Ladak. Why do you take so much trouble with Englishmen?" He was very kind with me, although he was a very great enemy of my mother. (That I have wrote, up.) And my mother had told me: "Shukar Galwan will surely show you greed. You must return him hard words." I said to Shukar Galwan: "You are a rich man, and have much lands. This is what you have earned from young time. Now you have come to old age. If God help, I will find land and be rich when I come to your age. I do not like your lands. Beside that, my mother had brought me up. Now shall I let go her, and look at your land? No, thank you. I do not want your lands."

Meeting with Sahibs and Making Arrangements.

At Karghalik I got hope Mr. Littledale I could catch before Khotan. After five days I met with Mr. Littledale, one march this side of Khotan, at night. I heard that the all servants made tamasha at every camp, and on that night was tamasha also. At that time Mrs. Littledale and both sahibs were sleeping, so I could not meet with them. That night I did meet with all servants. After welcome, they took me to a house where was the tamasha. There in a big room were many men and several women, and some banjo men, and the village begh, and a begh had come from the amban of Karghalik.

The next morning, I met with sahibs and with Mrs. Littledale. They were much glad at my coming, and Mrs. Littledale said to me: "Rassul you are good boy. Now you wait at our table and look after our room." I said: "Yes, ma'am."

Now Razak Akhun was caravan bashi. He had been on last journey with Mrs. Littledale in China. Therefore he got caravan bashi. Kalam Rassul was cook for sahibs; Hussin was waiting at table; and the others looked to ponies. Now Mrs. Littledale ordered me to wait on table and Hussin to look to ponies. But that the other servants not did like. Razak Akhun and Kalam Rassul said: "You must look to ponies. Here Hussin will work. We will tell it to Mrs. Littledale." I said to them: "It is the same to me, where I work. You tell Mrs. Littledale." Now Razak Akhun and Kalam Rassul went to the room of Mrs. Littledale. There were the sahibs also. I listened from the door. They said to sahibs that: "Rassul is very good for looking after ponies and donkey, no good for table. For table is Hussin good." Mrs. Littledale said: "No, no. I must have Rassul for my table-boy." Then Razak Akhun and Kalam Rassul cannot help themselves.

Now at Khotan we bought ponies and mules. There

were about thirty mules and ponies, and we bought also about fifty donkeys.

Mr. Littledale always said to us: "You people must make tamasha here, and at Cherchen, everywhere are village. Why? For a long time you people will not see any human being, and no villages. Beside that, you will find much trouble in the desert."

At Kashgar, Razak Akhun and Kalam Rassul had talk with me. They said: "We must take commission from the spending of the money. We must need make some money this way." I said to them: "This not good, taking any commission from sahibs. We must work honestly with sahibs. For that, God would be glad." They said: "If you want to do honestly, then you make yourself fakir. Here you must need do that, what we shall do." In this matter we talked very much. Then I said: "Yes, I will do that, if you friends like." And they said: "Whatever money you spend, you keep some commission, and what money we spend we will keep commission. Then we will divide between us. This is the oath between us." I said: "Yes."

This matter we had spoke of at Kashgar. Now at Khotan, from Mr. Littledale came about three hundred and fifty rupees in my hand, for which I gave bill to sahib, but from it I made rupees twenty commission, because of that oath of my friends. Now I put the rupees twenty before Razak Akhun and Kalam Rassul, and I said: "What I made in the matter of our oath is this. Now what you people have made, let know me." Razak Akhun answer to me. He said: "We not have taken any commission and have no money. The rupees twenty keep for yourself, and from to-day don't keep any more, because of the promise and oath, which we made at Kashgar." And he said: "I do not like to take any commission from sahib." I knew well, from our companions, that in his work from Kashgar and Khotan he had made good money. But that money he spend in a bad way. I kept that rupees twenty for myself.

Short-Time Marriages.

And every body was singing in our camp. In Chinese Turkistan it has been the custom that any man can marriage for ten days, a month, or for one day, for as many days as he wanted. But unless a mullah does read nika, one will not find any wives. Now all our men made marriage there. Some my friends married three or four times. Now I wanted to marry one. And to our camp came an old woman who washed sahibs' clothes and ours. That woman knew Abdurahman. When Abdurhaman had come to Khotan with French sahibs, at that time that woman had washed their clothes, and she had helped for the marriage for all servants of sahibs. Beside the servants, the elder French sahib had marriage also for a long time. That all arrangement had made this old woman also. Now she arranged for us our marriage. I told that woman: "I want to marry with a girl who has not any sickness."

After sahibs' dinner, Kalam Rassul and I went to that old woman's house. There had gathered many girls. All were sitting by wall in that room. Now that old woman said to us: "Among them, which is your choice, tell me." But there were no one so beautiful as Ladaki girls. But they were not bad. Now Kalam Rassul pointed out one girl. He said: "That one I like." I showed one; then all the other girls went to their homes. The two girls, which we chose, were brought before the mullah. There brought some breads, and, in a cup, salty water. These were kept in front of the mullah on a dastarkhan. Then the mullah read some words of Koran, then took a piece of bread, put it into that salty water, and gave to me and to that girl, and for Kalam Rassul made the same. Then we gave one tanga, each man, to the mullah. Before the mullah reading with girl, promise that twenty tanga to given the girl. (But the Khotan tanga is two tanga of Yarkand.)

Every day after breakfast, Mrs. Littledale and Mr. Littledale came with me to the sepoys' room and there waited, which I worked with the sepoys frozen feet. Now the sepoys let me do enough work on their feet, for the waiting sahibs. And, some days after, their feet got much better. Now this my work the Khotani people had seen and called me: "Doctor." But every one thought, very strange to tie the cloths on their feet. And many Khotani sick people were brought to me. I said: "We have no medicine, and I am not doctor." They did not believe it; said: "You must be doctor. If not, how are you making the sepoys' feet well?" Then I said: "Yes, I am doctor, but I have no medicine."

Three days after, I let go my cheap wife. I did not like to keep longer, and I gave her tangas twenty as that which we had promised. Beside that, I gave her a good hat, and some clothes. She was glad to get in three days all that things. From that day I do not like to have that kind of wife.

Work and Play in Khotan.

Mrs. Littledale made for us very good clothes of Russian cloth, and good hats. She liked very much to have for servants good clothes. We made some Ladaki clothes, that is same Chinese, and the hats were the same as a begh's. Now we were as beghs, and every one called us: "Begh."

Mr. Littledale said to me: "We will travel about six months in the desert. There we will not find any food. Therefore we need to carry all food from here, for about six of months. Therefore you find out how much food will want for eleven servants. You must look very careful, we don't be hungry there." I said: "Yes, sir." I made for each man one seer, for one day 11 seers for 11 men. Then I made for one month. This way I made six months account. I think there came about fifty maunds (about eighty pounds is one maund). I told

Mr. Littledale: "So much food we will need.'' Mr. Littledale said: "It is enough?" I said: "Yes." I said: "In this we will need rice, suttoo and flour." Mr. Littledale said: "You make a separate account: how much suttoo is wanted, how much rice and other things." I did that all, and showed to Mr. Littledale. He was much glad, and said to me: "Good head." That all thing brought Razak Akhun from bazaar.

And Mrs. Littledale wanted much cream, with which she made fresh butter, with her own hand. When she making butter, she showed me and let me do it. She liked very much my work, and called me: "Mr. Rassul" one time. And the sahibs called me: "Mr. Rassul" also, some time. Now we made much butter for the long journey, and put in tins, and shut the cover.

One day Mrs. Littledale said to all servants: "Make a good tamasha for you people." And ordered Razak Akhun to give money, as much as was need for the tamasha. Razak Akhun had arranged to make the tamasha at the house of French sahib's short-time wife.

After sahibs' dinner, we were ready to go to that tamasha, and there were two of ponies' loads of sugar which sahibs had brought from Russia. And for that tamasha, they said: "It is custom: when go to the tamasha, each man needs to take some sugar, every one to put on table." Now Razak Akhun and other servants took sugar from that bag, and they went ahead. Kalam Rassul and I left a little behind them, at the sahibs' dinner work. Now Kalam Rassul and I were ready to go. Kalam Rassul took a big piece of sugar from the bag, and several kinds of dry fruits. Now I needed sugar, and I took some sugar from the bag, as other servants. The Kalam Rassul did not let me take. He caught my hand. I thought he was joking me. But he truly he caught my hand, and only a little piece came in my hand. More he would not let me take. And he said: "I am bigger than you, and this things are in my charge. What power do you keep to put your hand in the sugar bag?" He with very bad face said to me this matter. I said to him: "Other servants took. I will take the same." He said: "It is in my power to give all the bag to them; but I will not give to you." Then we went for that tamasha. I was very sorry with merit of Kalam Rassul, because he was my friend.

Now we came that house of tamasha. There was a room, not very big, or very little. In that room were on ground all rugs of silks, and on all roof silks, and all wall were silks. That room was a silk room, and by that wall were sitting the begh, and Razak Akhun and our all men, and some other people; and, higher up than all men, were sitting two beautiful girls, who were all dressed in very good Chinese silk. The one was a little older. That, they said, is the French sahib's wife. She get very rich money from that sahib, and all that silk things of her room had made the sahib. The other girl was young and much beautiful. And in front them and Razak Akhun were few small tables. On them sugar, and many kinds of dry fruits, and wine, Chinese whiskey. And next side were some other women. Among them two women were in front. Each one carried a bundle of clothes. And next were the banjo musicians. There in front of one was a kind of banjo like a box, a little longer; on that were many wires. The banjo-maker take two iron things in his both hands, and make it sound very good. Some carried drums which, one side, was covered with goat-skin and around the edge were many rings of iron. That gave good noise. Now Kalam Rassul sat one side, high up. I sit on a lower place than Razak Akhun and Kalam Rassul. Now Kalam Rassul put his all food things, sugar and other things, on the table. They were much glad to bring so many things. Now poor me, I did not have things for table, only a little sugar. For that every one laughed. When they laughed, I said: "Half that Kalam Rassul put on the table is mine!"

Now those women and begh, Razak Akhun and Kalam Rassul, every one was drinking wine. Hussin and I did not drink. Now dance the begh and all men. There was an old man who spoke Ladaki. He told us all the custom with them. All dance, and we throw the pole from each other friends' heads to the banjo-men. That custom we knew before. There every one men danced, and some women danced also. But the two women did not dance. We much wanted them to dance. We said many times: "Please, show us your dance." They said: "We do not know the dance." The old man said to us, in Ladaki: "You people get up, and beg them. Then they will dance." We did that. Then they get up, with much blandishment. Then danced. The old man said: "Tell them to take off the outer clothes." We did that, as the old man told us, then they took off outer clothes. Now, under that clothes, thin silk clothes and outer very fine silk, surrounded by very good pieces silk. That look much beautiful and they dance very interesting. And then they danced theirself now, without our begging, and many times changed their clothes, from the bundles which were carried before them by two women: one take off; gave to the servants women, that put into the bundles, then wear next one. At that night we were much enjoyment in this tamasha. Afterwards we came to our camp, and every one praise to that woman's dance.

Now one evening, the amban of Khotan made dinner for Mrs. Littledale and for two sahibs. The sahib took me for interpreter with them. When we came the first gate, there shot some guns, for the honour of sahib. Then the amban came out one gate, then Mrs. Littledale and two sahibs take into his room. While there spoke. Then he took us in his dining-room. There was a large table, no cloth on, and looks that table very dirty. Now the amban gave one chair to Mrs. Littledale, then to Mr. Littledale, then one for Mr. Fletcher, then to some other Chinese men, the interpreter and I standing over against sahibs. Beginning, on the table were some seeds of melons. That eat. Then brought in food, few things, put them middle the table. And in front every one put a very small plate and two pieces wood. But for Mrs. Littledale there had a fork. And all the Chinese take the food; gave to Mrs. Littledale and to both sahibs; and the same of each one food amban tell to his interpreter into Chinese language: that interpreter said to me in Turki: I said that to sahibs in Hindustani; that same words sahib said to Mrs. Littledale in English. And there was some wine in very little cups. Now they one kind of food take, and bring next one, and said: "This thing have came from sea." And said: "Some came from China." Sahibs said: "It is very good." In taking dinner, they took a long time. And Mrs. Littledale cannot take all their food, and those thing could not come all into her small plate; put that all on the table. After all the food, they brought for each man each cup of rice. Then, in a basin, hot water and a dirty towel to wash their hands. Then done the dinner. Then we came back to our camp.

Now Razak Akhun made all the arrangement, the packing-saddles and other things. Some other things were not ready, Mr. Littledale bid me. I did them.

The sepoys were lying down by their frozen feet. Now the two sepoys got quite well, and they can work. And they said to me many thank, to making doctor on their feet. But the havildar's thumb was very bad and not got well.

Now Kalam Rassul and Razak Akhun bought some things for home, rugs and other things, and the other men wish to buy some things. I said to all them: "This things will not reach home. Why? We will travel very long time in desert. I do not knew what become there, and don't buy any things for home." Then all other took my advice, but Razak Akhun and

Kalam Rassul did not took my advice. They took some Khotani things for Leh.

Now we were at Khotan about a month, for all the arrangement. Then we said many salaam and goodbye, to the Khotani friends. Then we started from Khotan, with a party of ponies and mules, and with donkeys. But on the mules' and ponies' back no was loads. That was order of sahibs: until Cherchen no put loads on them. And our loads went with some carriage and some hire-ponies and donkeys.

Fight with Chinese.

When we came to a march, there were coming some Chinese men in carriage. They had come from Keriya and go to Khotan. There our men fight with them for some matter. The Razak Akhun and Kalam Rassul carried big knife-sword in their belt, and Razak Akhun keep bad temper. He took the big knife; the Chinese men took knife also. I was in a carriage. I get down from it, and beg before the Chinese, with the remember which I had got good Chinese beating at Udidlik at Major sahib time. When I begged the Chinese, then stopped the fight. But Razak Akhun got angry on me, and said: "Why you begged them?" I said to him: "You are a foolish man as a mad man. This matter will bring bad luck, and will be kill some men; then will bring a very bad name for sahibs. This is no good, anybody to fighting in next country." Razak Akhun said: "This is right matter."

The Written Bond in Keriya.

Now we arrived at Keriya, and camped there. At that night the amban of Keriya's all dry grass burning. There was much grass. The fire went high up. That looked us very good a tamasha. There we wait two or three days. The amban of Keriya was a young man.

He came to sahibs and said: "I got a order, that we not let go you by this way. Why? Beyond Cherchen are Tangut, bad people. Therefore our Government give no order to any European to go toward Tangut. There had killed the French sahib. For that, got much trouble to the Chinese government." Sahib said: "We will not go toward Tangut. We will go toward Lhasa, Tibet." The amban said: "There may kill you. Then that matter will come on the Chinese government." Sahib said: "I will never go back." The amban said: "I will not let go you." Now the interpreter I was. One time the amban went to his place, and there came a man from amban to call me. I went to amban. He said to me: "I will give you good money, if you take back this sahib." I said to the amban: "He will never go back. You don't think that." Then amban said to me: "If not, you tell sahibs give me written bond. In that, tell that: 'We will go to Tibet ourself. If there kill any one us and get any trouble, no any matter on the Chinese government.' If you as this a letter from sahibs bring, I will give you a present." I knew that sahibs wanted to give him that kind of a written bond, but I said: "This is difficult to get from sahib. Anyway, I will try for it." Amban said: "I will give you good present." I said: "We have getting enough money from sahib and not need any money from you." Then amban said: "What do you want? Tell me." I said: "I will tell to sahibs this matter. If they agreed, then you give us a good tamasha, and show us the dance of women." The amban was young. He like very much to give us the tamasha.

Then I came to sahib. I told this all story to sahibs. Mr. Littledale like very much to give the amban a written bond. And I sent the word to amban. Then the amban sent to our camp one sheep and some rice, and a good cook had sent to our camp, and one begh for that arrangement. I said to my friends the matter of tamasha, and how it get from amban. They were pleased for this. All that night we were in much enjoyment in dance and sing. The next morning we started from there, and our felt was heavy, to not get sleep at night.

THE SEPOYS AND THEIR SHOT.

After few days we arrived at Nia. There the havildar, his feet get more bad, and sahib said to him: "Will sent him back to Leh." And sahibs said to me: "If you can, then cut off his thumb of feet, which was black." I said: "Yes, sir. I can do it." Then sahib and Mrs. Littledale and Mr. Fletcher waited with me. I did cut his both feet thumbs, with a little difficult. Then sahib gave to the havildar money, from Nia until his home, and medicine, and pay. We said: "This sahibs gave good money to the havildar and are good sahibs." Then the havildar said to sahib: "Make Badullah havildar." Sahib said: "Yes." Then the havildar went back to Leh. We went toward Cherchen.

There left now three sepoys. They were very lazy in work. One day, on a rock plain, Mr. Littledale said to me: "The sepoys are lazy, but they are very good shooting men." I said: "Sir, this sepoy you have get from Government?" Sahib said: "Now, this were not in service of Government, but, before, they were soldiers of government. One sahib who sent them to me, he wrote me that they are good shooting. I have brought for our work also." I said: "Sir, where would we find a battle?" Sahib said: "We will not find any war, but maybe we will find the Tibeti some bad people." I said: "When get that kind of people, then we all are sepoys. We Ladaki men am not sepoy, but, bad-luck-time, must give sepoys' service, also." Sahib said: "No. The Tibetan look the sepoys' shooting. Then they will be afraid to us." I said to sahib: "Sir, we have not seen their shooting. We must need look their shot. Then we know. Let them shoot each man few cartridges." Sahib said: "Yes, we will do that."

That afternoon, after tea, sahib said to the sepoys: "We will shoot to-day some cartridge." There was a sand plain. There put a paper, middle it some black. Then Mr. Littledale shot two. It both hit. Then Mr. Fletcher two shot, that both hit also. Now the three sepoys, each man shot two. No one hit, and we did not see where went their shots. Now I like very much to shoot. I beg to sahib, to let me shoot. Sahib said: "You cannot shoot." But Mrs. Littledale said: "Let shoot Rassul." There was a small rifle. Mr. Littledale gave that one to me, and a cartridge. I shot very careful. By good luck, I hit that one. Then Mr. Littledale gave me a next cartridge. That one hit also. Sahib and Mrs. Littledale said me: "Very good," and they were much pleased.

And the sepoys were much ashamed. Because the sepoys, when we bid them a work, they said: "We cannot this kind of work, but we can shot very good. That is our work." Now, from that day, in shot, Ladaki got good. Now they said to me: "Our luck went down, your came up. Now you was good in shooting than we were. Now what order you people give us, we will do." And they were much ashamed. I said to them: "Does not matter, the not hitting to-day. The rifles were new for you people, and have no practise."

Razak Akhun.

Now the Razak Akhun was much angry man. If get him the tea cold, he threw cup, and if he be angry with a ponies or donkeys, he take off his sword, and said: "Kill them!" On men, if he be angry, he do as that, but very little after, his all angry stop. Quick got angry, quick stop. Razak Akhun and Kalam Rassul were both very good friend, but many time they fight each other. Now Razak Akhun and Kalam Rassul, inside, not were good on me, and inside me was enemy on them, also. But I not thinking that I will return their bad to them. I keep all my work, trust in God. Now Razak Akhun many time bid me unnecessary work, and to Kalam Rassul also. One morning matter: Kalam Rassul and I were in giving breakfast to sahibs, and other men were sitting for their breakfast. The Razak Akhun came, and said to Kalam Rassul and to me: "You people take the tent of Mr. Fletcher." I said: "We are giving breakfast. You see work in our hands. You tell about the tent to other men who are sitting without work." He said: "I must tell you people." I said: "We will take your order, but now you see, yourself, we are busy. How shall we go for other work?" Then he get angry and said to me: "I will cut off your head with the sword." I said: "You are a foolish man. You cannot cut our head in this matter." We fight a little for this matter, then I said: "If you do like this, you would not be a head-man, and I will come on your head."

Reaching to Cherchen.

Now we travelling for Cherchen. And in way we found many place jungle and sand, and some small well of water, that salty water. One day the sahibs and Razak Akhun were camped one place. They gave me a cup of tea, and when I drink it, it was much salty, and cannot drink. Now we gave to every one our men the cup tea. Cannot drink, and we joking each other. Now Mr. Littledale said: "Dig a next well." We did dig a next place, eight feet deep. By good luck, got very good sweet water.

Now the saddles of mules were not good, and the mules were fat. And were no loads on their backs, but the saddles fell down from their backs very many times in day. When fell it, then the servants make right, without opening the rings. In doing that, all mules got sore under their chest. That were very bad.

Now we crossed some jungle and plain and sand. We arrived near Cherchen. There came an old begh, and some other men, before sahib. We arrived at Cherchen that afternoon. There was a big house and a garden. Pitched sahib's tent in the garden.

The sahibs looked the sores of mules and sahibs were sorry. And every morning did doctor work for the mules, and it were very bad sore. And we washed them and put medicine, and there we got much work with this.

Making Me Head-Man on Foods.

And one day Mrs. Littledale and Mr. Littledale looked the sugar and butter. There one pony load of sugar is gone in two months, and one pony load is left. And at Khotan had made the butter for six months, that is gone in fourteen days. For this matter Mr. Littledale and Mrs. Littledale looked very strange, and said: "How shall we go in the desert if go our things this way?" And Mrs. Littledale said: "Now where shall we get sugar? The one load of sugar would not be enough for our way. At Cherchen could not find sugar." Now the arrangement of Razak Akhun not come good; all were bad. Mrs. Littledale and sahibs did not like at all the arrangement of Razak Akhun. Now Mr. Littledale said to me: "Razak Akhun is a good man, but his head is not good. You are a good man, and good head. Now from to-day you are caravan bashi, and hold all this work in your hands." I said to sahib: "Sir, I will not take the work of caravan bashi. It is Razak Akhun work. How shall I take? This matter will bring me a great shame at Ladaki, and every one say there: from Razak Akhun I took this work; and be my name bad among Ladaki friends." Sahib said: "We have given you this work. Why come shame to you? You must take this work." I said: "Sir, if you had given me this work at Kashgar, then does not come any shame. About two months Razak Akhun did caravan bashi. Now, if I take his work, it is deceitful." Sahib said: "If you not agree to this matter, then in our long journey we shall find bad luck. Then what shall we do?" I said: "I will look on the food; will not spend them wrong way. And the one pony load of sugar, that be enough for us. I will look over all food, but I will not take the caravan bashi work." Then sahib said: "I will think about this."

The next day sahib ordered to Razak Akhun: "You go to look the way up the Tokus Davan." Then Razak Akhun went to look that way. And Mr. Littledale said to me: "Now, until Razak Akhun be back, you look all our work." I said: "Yes, sir." Then I made all the mules' saddles new, and by sahibs' order, I bought ponies and donkeys, and bought much corn, and I did all the arrangement; and I keep all the rice, flour, butter, all thing into a room, and I gave for daily food enough for all men. And there Razak Akhun did not get back about a month. I did that all arrangement. The sahibs were pleased with my work, and large money came in my hand. Now my felt said: "Must take a little commission for the play. When I buy a thing, of ten rupees cost, for eight rupees, from it I keep one rupee commission for myself." This way I did, and sahib look all that my things very cheap and very good, and once more called me: "Mr. Rassul." But I said myself: "What means the Mr.?" I did ask the sahib: "What is the means of Mr.?" They said: "It is, in English, called to good men and big men, and you are a good man, therefore we called you Mr." I said: "I am not a Mr. I am a poor servant. Don't call me Mr."

Now many time we made tamasha, and the old begh made tamasha, and when we go for a tamasha, there got high up place to me to sit. Why? I was head-man. Therefore they gave me a high place to sit. But that does not like Kalam Rassul, and he go quick on my place, and sit himself high up. I nothing say to him.

I sit a low place. But the begh and villages people make all honour to me. If I sit a low place, does not matter. When they put tea, put it in front me, first, then give to Kalam Rassul. And pipe also. And all honour making to me. Many time did that. Kalam Rassul was ashamed. Then he let me sit on my high place.

The Quarrel of Sepoys.

Now the Badullah sepoy was a bad man, and now he was havildar on the other two sepoys. But the two sepoys said every time: "We do not want him on us havildar." The Badullah said to them: "I am havildar." And the Badullah was very bad.

One day Mrs. Littledale and two sahibs and I were at sahib's tent, and we making account of money. There came the three sepoys to sahib, and all three sepoys had hold of one rifle. We looked that very strange, and when they came to sahib, Badullah said to sahib: "Punginor take rifle to kill me, and Purdil caught him this rifle." Then sahib looked to the rifle. There found three cartridge in it. Sahib said to Punginor: "Why did you make this?" He said: "I put three cartridge, one for Badullah, the next for Purdil, and one for myself; but Purdil caught my hand." Then said sahib to him: "It is very bad matter. Why you did so?" He said: "We do not want Badullah on us havildar. If make him havildar, then I will kill him, and I will die, myself." Sahib looked this very strange matter. Sahib took their all rifles and cartridges, and said: "Now you people go, and I will think about this matter."

When the sepoys went to their room, sahib said to me: "What do you think about the sepoys? What be better, let tell me." I said to sahibs: "The other sepoys do not like Badullah to be havildar. I think it be better no one to keep havildar on them. All three sepoys is same, and you are sahib. You tell: on three sepoys, you are havildar." Sahib liked to do that, and called the sepoys and told them that matter. For this matter the other two sepoys liked very much, but Badullah said: "I got havildar. Now free my name from havildar, then I will kill myself." Then sahib said: "I will keep your name havildar, but on all three sepoys I am havildar."

Work and Play in Cherchen.

Now Mrs. Littledale said to me: "You must learn English words to speak with us." Then Mr. Fletcher said some words of English. I write them in Ladaki: "Hot water," "cold water," "bring," "take way." All that words I write, and I speak a little English with Mrs. Littledale. She said: "By and by, will you be better English."

Now we everybody play with the beautiful girl of our house-master. And she joking me very much, and many time I caught to her, she caught to me. Kalam Rassul had given me an oath that I not playing with that girl, but she play with me, I play with her. One day she caught to me, and we kissing. That see Mrs. Littledale. I was much ashamed, and run away. There Mrs. Littledale called to Mr. Littledale. I was much afraid for this matter. Sahib called to me. I went. There were Mrs. Littledale and sahib. They joking me, and said: "You have got very beautiful girl here. We are much glad for this." From that day, Mrs. Littledale bring to her tent that girl, and bid for some work.

Now there arrive back Razak Akhun from Tokus Davan, and, after welcome, he see all the things in charge in my hand, and Kalam Rassul told him much matter about me, and he does not like that all. He look enemy face to me. I said to Razak Akhun all true matter, and made oath before him, but he does not believe, and he thinking I did him deceitful.

Now we had ready all things, but for our way butter was not enough. Razak Akhun said it is enough, and not could get in Cherchen anyway. (Cherchen is a little village, about five hundred farmers. There is very difficult to get things. At that time there was no bazaar.)

Back-Biting of Sepoys.

Now we did gather from each our men two tangas for a tamasha. For that we bought a good sheep. I did give some rice from sahib's rice. That did not like the Badullah sepoy. He went to backbiting to sahib. Sahib did not understand his words. Sahib called to me for interpreter, because sepoy speak better Hindustani, therefore more difficult for sahib. We Ladaki speak with sahib some Hindustani, some Turki. And it was very different style, our Hindustani which we speak with Mr. Littledale. That cannot understand many people. Now Mr. Littledale and Mrs. Littledale both were outside their tents, Badullah was standing before them. Sahib said to me: "What Badullah said? Something about rice?" I did ask Badullah: "What is matter?" He said: "You stolen rice from sahib. That I want tell to sahibs." I said to sahib: "I have stolen rice from you. That matter Badullah wanted tell to you." There Mrs. Littledale said: "Why for?" I said: "For tamasha." Then Mrs. Littledale said: "There must need meat also." I said: "For meat we gathered tangas twenty, but I stolen your rice." Mrs. Littledale said: "No, no. It is not called stolen. And you must give back the tangas twenty to our men. You must give the tangas twenty from my money, and you put in bill." There the sepoy went to sahib, in the hope to make angry on me the sahibs, to make himself good before the sahibs. There sahibs no get angry on me, and beside that, the twenty tangas got, also, from sahib. For this matter I was please, but the sepoy was ashamed to backbite sahib. And at that night was much enjoyment at that tamasha.

Leaving Cherchen.

Now we were about one month more in Cherchen. And there had gave the apricots trees flowers.[1] That look to us summer.

Now we were all ready to leaving Cherchen. There all old people and young, and boys and girls, every one were our friends. They were much sorry. And we got some letters there from Leh, and we wrote some letters to Leh, and I told in my letters, that now will not get our letters a long time. And I was much glad to get letters from my good friend Sonam Wangdus.

One day we started from Cherchen and said to all our friends good-bye. They said to us many good-byes, and many Cherchen people cried when we started, and we were sorry to separate from them, and said many salaams to the Cherchen people.

Now we started from Cherchen. After several days on march every one servants were a little tired. Mrs. Littledale and the two sahibs had riding ponies. Mr. Littledale and Mr. Fletcher gave to all servants their riding ponies, for a half hour each man, and one hour. With that got a little rest, sahibs walking while we riding their ponies. There got very short time to ride each man, but every one felt glad to do the sahibs that, and looked kindness of sahibs.

The Sepoys and the Breads.

Now in my hands were charge all foods, and I was as a head-man, but for that Razak Akhun and Kalam Rassul does not like to have me such work. Now there had some dry breads in few sacks. We made tea, and I gave to each man one bread, to take with the tea.

[1] "On April 5 the apricot trees only showed faint indications of buds; two days later they were shedding their blossoms."—St. G. R. Littledale's *Geographical Journal*, May, 1896.

The sepoys opened the bag of breads themselves, and take out much bread, and eat them. I said to the sepoys: "My dear friends, you people must take my advice. All this breads had not brought to use such a place, where find wood for cook, and much time to cook, like to-day which we have got. These breads we will use to two place: one time when we come very late to a camp, next when we would not find firewood. Such a place we will use the bread."

The sepoys got angry, and Razak Akhun also, because Razak Akhun name was caravan bashi (but all the order on camp was mine). They said: "We will use the breads. We will not take your order." I said: "I not said to you people, by order. I said in friendly, which be better for us in the long journey." They said: "You do not let us take food, then how shall we work in the journey?" I said: "By kindness of God and sahibs, we have much rice and flour and suttoo. Cook them. Make full stomach. But every one must make careful with food. Why? Now we going into desert, which we not find foods." They said: "We will use the breads." I said: "I will not let you people take."

And I ordered to Hussin to shut the bag of breads, and the sepoy went to sahib to tell that: "Rassul does not let us take the breads." Sahib called to me and said: "What is the bread matter?" I told all that what happened with them about the breads.

Mr. Littledale said to the sepoys: "You people remember, that three of months butter made finish in fourteen days, and six months' sugar in two months. That all does not matter. There was village. We could get more. Now we will go in desert. If there finish, then we all men will die. Then, what shall we do? Therefore I had gave this all into Rassul hands. He is sahib on the food. Although we are sahibs, for food, what Rassul give us, we will take that. If we sahibs do that, then you people must need obey to Rassul." They said: "Yes."

Our Work.

Now in our travelling we got much trouble in falling the loads and donkeys and ponies in mud. When we camped at a place I looked some ponies' backs, and made clean the saddles of ponies and mules, and I said to all men in sweet matter: "Please, you look the back of ponies and donkeys; would not be sore."

Now we work. Some servants obeyed to me, some not obeyed to me; but in working, myself, then work every one. There were two of men order on servants; one, Razak Akhun, the next, mine. But what work be to do, I go in that work myself. Then I bid to other men also. When come to a water-cross; beginning, I take off my clothes, then going in water to help caravan. Then my part men come with me. The Razak Akhun part do as us. There in servants were two of parts: one part, of Razak Akhun, one part, of mine. But, by helping of God, more men were in mine. In Razak Akhun part was Kalam Rassul and the two sepoys.

Now with us were seven Ladaki men, three sepoys, all ten servants. Animals were: mules and ponies about thirty, and donkeys about eighty-five. Kalam Rassul was cook, I was stable-boy, other eight men were sais men (ponies men). The three sepoys were very lazy, but sepoy name Punginor was a little good to work. Now I work with the sais. Why? I was as a head-man. Kalam Rassul does not help. But when we put load and unload, at that time sahibs helping us. With that, every servants good worked. But there were more than one hundred animals, and there were not enough men for all animals. And, beside our animals, there were about a hundred hire-animals, pony and donkey, from the people of Cherchen, and with them were about fifteen men of Cherchen. Among them was a caravan bashi, name Mula Shah, on the Cherchen people. Now our camp was very big. It was made six of months provision.

SEARCHING THE AKKA TAGH.

Now we travelled by valley and plain many days. Now we reached a high place, more high and more high, day by days. And we do not know where is the Akka Tagh mountain. Abdurahman had travelled over Akka Tagh with French sahibs. And Abdurahman does not remember that way. We every one ask to Abdurahman: "Where is the Akka Tagh?" He said: "It is near." And he some time said another matter. And his telling not come right. And travelled many days; could not reach to that near place which Abdurahman told to us.

Now about twenty days we travelled after Cherchen. But I cannot tell all that, what kinds of place and valley were there. I am not remember so much which I have seen, but I have some remember, which I tell all that. Now we travel some time by valley, sometime came upon large plain, and up, and down.

About twenty days after from Cherchen, we saw far away a big black mountain, and snow over that mountain. Mr. Littledale said: "That mountain is Akka Tagh." After few days we reached under that mountain. Now Mr. Littledale said: "We will cross this mountain." But there could not got way over that pass. Now Mr. Littledale went one side to look a way, I went the next place. We both travelled a long time over that mountain, always saw many big and black rocks and steep rocks, no was there any hopes to be a way over it. We came back in hopeless. Now that country were high and cold, and much wind a place. Now the sahibs and Mrs. Littledale speaking, and counselled themselves about the way. I think at that time our way was toward south and east.

The next day we turned right side, and travelled by up and down; camped to a place at a valley. There was very little wood. We find some dungs of wild horse. The next day left that place, came to a little plain, where lay many large rocks. We turned left side, came into a valley, where were very much white rocks and gravel. Now we travelled up by that valley. Now we do not know where are we going. At last got in that valley very bad road. Many ponies fallen down. We packing their loads again. In doing that we tired, and that country seemed high. A little got sick our heads. And we said each other: "At this place would not be travel any human." Before evening we reach under a little pass. There was a little water but no any grass and firewood. There we camp. There we had a little wood with us, that was not enough. There break boxes and cook tea. At that place dead the black pony which I had bought at Cherchen. And my head was sick. But I did not let know the sahibs the sickness of mine. I was ashamed to tell the sahibs. The Abdurahman got very sick. That night seemed bad a night.

The next day crossed a pass and came in a valley. When came out that valley, view large plain surrounded by mountains, and running very clean water. And on that plain saw some place very green grass. We were every one glad to saw that place. There we camped under a little rock. There was a little good wood, and grass, and water. The Cherchen hire-men said every time to sahib: "Please, sir, let return to us. We came far way from Cherchen." Sahib said: "Will send you people back after few days."

At that place Abdurahman had been sick, and sahib send back some Cherchen men from there, and some hire-pony and donkeys, and Abdurahman send back with them. And sahib gave much money to Abdurahman and present. We each other said: "Look Abdurahman! In short time he got so much money, and we will travel long time with sahibs. We will find rich money from sahib." I said among them: "These sahibs are very big men. We must need do good work, and truth in everything. Because we have much work, this all do not think trouble. We will find good money, and beside that, sahib write our name in his book, and the Government be kind to us." And I said: "We must think Mrs. Littledale is as our mother, and Mr. Littledale as our father and we all their children. We must work from inside heart. That will bring us good name as this song." I sang this song. It is a Lhasa song. I sang it in this way:

"The Master is of gold mountain.
We am the servants, white plain, strong of men.
White plain, strong of men, have kept hope on the mountain of gold.

And we, youth and young, are the eggs of white hen.
Without broken any egg, we will work for our master.
Without broken egg, we will be back to our own country."

Razak Akhun said: "It is right matter." And we sang every one together this same song.

Then I said again: "We must needed never fight among us each other. And not tell: 'This is your work,' and 'My work.' We needed do all kinds of work, what kind of work come on our hands." Now every servants agreed to my matter and looked my friend.

At that place fell some snow. There lost some our ponies. Galam Mahmad, riding on a ponies, went to searching them. At evening he came back with ponies. He was dead, that pony, on which he was ridden. That place was very high. That man had went fast. Therefore dead the pony. I reported it to sahib. Sahib said: "Does not matter." We all men were sorry for that pony.

Now our thought were, that finish the pass. Mr. Littledale said: "It is not finish the pass of Akka Tagh." Mr. Littledale said to me: "Abdurahman went back.

We must need a man on his place. You get a man from the hire-men of Cherchen." Razak Akhun and I both counselled and we like to take Mula Shah. He was very hard-working man, but was difficult to make him agree. We said: "We shall be like your brothers. You come with us." At last he agree. We made his pay rupees 20 for a month. At that time the Turki people afraid to go such far journey. (After that time, Mula Shah many time travelled. And he travelled with Dr. Sven Hedin, no afraid.)

Now we travel by a long plain, surrounded by mountains; and which side our way was, there were more taller mountains. Was very cold and blowing much wind. Was one very tall black mountain, that shut our way. Mr. Littledale search, but could not get way over that mountain. Now what shall we do? Every one were in sorrow. We returned back, and travelling between two small mountains. Afterward came to an opening place very wide. South-west view very far way, but south-east was shut the same mountain. Mr. Littledale said: "We must need cross this mountain," and said: "This is the pass which called Akka Tagh. Now how shall we cross it?"

And at those place was very good bortsa wood. And seeing many place green land and rich grass for animals, but not good grass for animals, very hard grass. And on those land were flock of antelopes grazing. Both sahib shoot them, and we always got good meat.

Now at that place we wait several days, to searching way. And some men sent each different place to searching way. I said to Mr. Littledale: "Shall I go to searching way?" Mrs. Littledale did not let me go. She said: "You have much work at camp." She gave many clothes to wash to me, and she showed me how wash them. There were two iron boxes which kept the cooking pots in them. I making water hot in them, and in one put many clothes together and put soap, washing them as how Mrs. Littledale showed to me.

She like very much my washing her clothes, and sahib's.

Now came the people back who had went to searching way. They said: "Is not any way to crossing it. Always seen many tops of mountains." Now we were all in sorrow, and said: "Now where shall we go?"

Now Mr. Littledale went again to that place from which we came back, and Razak Akhun took with him, and said: "In four days will come."

When Mrs. Littledale and Mr. Littledale separated, at that time Mrs. Littledale much sorry. I was much sorry in looking at that their love on each other, and I remember my wife, and said myself: "I came so far away. Now my wife must be sorrow in my remember." Always every day, many time, I remember my wife and bring her face under my eyes, but at that place more remember. I said to Mrs. Littledale into my broken English: "Ma'am, you don't think sorry. Sahib will come soon." But she was all time sorry. Because I was room-boy, therefore I looked that all.

Now we lost four of our donkeys, which could not get them. And there was all ready to return some more of Cherchen men. They had robbed those donkeys and hidden them, but we do not know that. And the Mula Shah was a robber man. That we do not know. The Mula Shah's hope was that he will run, and he had got some money from sahib, his pay advance. One day he was robbed flour. That had seen Mr. Fletcher, and caught to him; then we knew Mula Shah is a robber man.

Now after four days Mr. Littledale and Razak Akhun got back and they said: "We got the way." We every one were glad to heard that news from them.

Crossing Akka Tagh.

After some days we got top the Akka Tagh. View to south a very big plain, and saw a small lake, and very far look next a black mountain. On that mountain one place like a saddle. Mr. Littledale said to us:

"By that little saddle is our way." That country was grey and black, no any green, but some blue lake.

Now we travel down from Akka Tagh, and camped[1] where was a little lake. But some our caravan had left behind, not reached with us at that night. Now at that place was much bad wind and much cold. That kind of wind and cold we did not found before as that night, and cannot pitch the tents with the bad wind. If there put stone on the pegs of tent, there were no stone. We did put on the tents' pegs the bags and flour, all heavy thing.

The next morning, arrived there the other part caravan, which left behind. Now from that place we returned all the Cherchen men. Now we had own donkeys and ponies only. And there were much things. We had not enough animals for our loads, and we could not got to a march at that day. We did about four miles, and camped to a plain; left some our donkeys in way with heavy things, and one or two ponies left there. Beside them lay some our loads in way.

Now every one seemed unlucky a journey. Mrs. Littledale and Mr. Fletcher counselled their selves in Mrs. Littledale's tent. We sent some men back, and brought those things, which left behind in way, upon their backs.

After a long time, Mr. Littledale come out his tent and called to me. He took to me outside our camp, a little far, and said to me: "Now our journey left far way to Lhasa; but where we will find people, to that place left forty days' journey from here. At that place we will get all thing what we need, ponies and foods. At that place live the Chang-pa people. But it look to me much difficult to get there. Why? Now beginning to get tired our animals. If tired like to-day, then how shall we get there?" And said: "I am much sorry, and it look unlucky for us. I afraid if die all ponies.

[1] Camp No. 23, 17,009 feet high.

Mrs. Littledale could not walk. What do you think? Let tell me."

I said: "Sir, I hope we not find such bad luck as you said. God will help us. If get that kind of bad luck, which die all ponies, we all servants will not let walk to Mrs. Littledale. We can carry her upon our backs in chair, but I hope will not be that kind of bad luck. Don't you take sorrow for this matter. Will not die more animals. I will tell what is my thought. We need every day make a short march, and after a week take one halt. With that will get rest the animals, and they will find time to feed grass. Then all the animals become better and will not be tired, and will not be tired men also. Then we can do well the journey. If is the Gagalinchin forty days' journey, we will go in eighty or one hundred days; does not matter. If we do hurry, then animals could not go."

Mr. Littledale, while thinking. Then answer to me, and said: "It will be better, but we have no so much food. If be finish our foods, that be more bad. I tell you, one time a sahibs had travel by this way. He had finished his food, then had much trouble. They had to eat boots."

I said: "No, sir. The all foods charge you had gave in my hands. Now we pass about one month and half. We had made the arrangement at Khotan for six months. Now I can give very good food for six months from to-day, may be seven months. We will be lighter loads every day."

Then Mr. Littledale said: "We will take short march, but before, I will weigh the food." I said: "Sir, if weigh or not weigh, does not matter. I can give food for six of months."

Now sahibs much glad with my matter. Mrs. Littledale said to me: "You seemed to me as my son." I thanked her for this matter and was myself much enjoyment to be pleased Mrs. Littledale and sahibs with me.

At that camp no was water. We digged a ground, there got water. After, we let gone ponies to grazing. They had found a lake behind our camp, and it was very good water.

Tying Mula Shah.

Now sahibs called me again, and said to me: "The Mula Shah is a bad man. He will run to-night. Why? His companions are near. We did return them to-day. You must be careful with Mula Shah. Three or four days must watch to him. After, he will not run." Sahib had a iron chain, which put on hands, and tied. Sahib said: "It will be better, your one hand and Mula Shah's one hand tie. Then he cannot run." I said: "Yes, sir."

I came to my tent. I said myself: "This order sahib give not right. I have so much work, more than all men, going on table, and washing all the things after dinner, and could not sleep at night. This was the lazy sepoys' work, but cannot help. If tell sahibs, it is ashamed; they think: 'This man not obey.' It is difficult, so many days."

Now, when I put dinner on the table, Mrs. Littledale said to sahibs: "With the punish, why give punish to Rassul? Rassul have many works. The sepoys have no work. Tie Mula Shah with a sepoy." Sahib agreed to do that. I said myself: "Mrs. Littledale is a wise lady."

The Oath of Happy Night.

Now I were in enjoyment in every matter. Here were the sahibs glad with me, and all servants were friends of mine. But Razak Akhun and Kalam Rassul did not like me and showed me enemy face, and they broken my order. Therefore I tried to bring them in my friends. At every night we everybody sang together very much and talked, making enjoyment each other. Awhile at such a time we have friendship; but when work, at that time, they broken my order. Now I said myself: "How shall I make clean their dirty thoughts which kept on me?" In my thought came: to ask at night, with sweet matters, why those people are angry with me.

At night, after all were done, we all men gather in talking. We took dinner, and talked after dinner. Our tent was big enough for us. Now I said among all men: "In this ocean sea of desert we have no father and mother and brother, but on the place of our father and mother are God to help us. After that, is Mrs. Littledale and Mr. Littledale. After them, we all are brother and relatives each other. Why? If we die, one among us, we will put him under a ground with our hands. If he be ill, we will look him. Without each other we have no any relatives and brothers." Razak Akhun said: "It is right." And other men said same. I said again: "If is that, then we do not need put enemy each other inside. That man who kept enemy among us, that is a bad man, in front God and in front us. We must need make clean our dirty thoughts, which I kept on you, which you kept on me. This is our Mohammedan custom: if fight each other, make friends again quickly. Now why do you be angry with me? Tell that all among us."

I had a part of Koran, which I read it. I carried on my hands that Koran and then I said: "I said nothing false, Razak Akhun, to sahib about you. And I did not told to sahibs: 'Give me head-man.' Sahibs told me I must do caravan bashi. I did never agreed. That matter I did told you people at Cherchen. Then sahib said: 'Razak Akhun must keep name caravan bashi, and he will give order, but the foods charge will come into your hands, and you look all work with Razak Akhun.' Then I did agreed, could not help. We are servants, must need take the order of sahib." Other men said: "This matter of Rassul is right." Razak

Akhun said: "You spoke false for me to sahib." I said: "Therefore I taken the Koran into my hand. I was not false to sahib for you."

Then we smoken tobacco. Then I said: "You must thinking out yourself to your fault. Because you was old servant of sahib, therefore sahib made you caravan bashi at Kashgar. You made finished six of months' sugar in two months, and six months' butter in fourteen days. Beside all that, the mules sore very bad from Khotan to Cherchen, although no were loads on them at that time. If were loads, does not matter to be sore. With this fault sahibs changed you, and gave to me your work. But I did not agree. Now you are caravan bashi."

Then Razak Akhun said to me: "It is right, but you told to me one day that: 'If you do like this, then I will ride on your neck.' That make me believe you did deceitful with me." There said Kalam Rassul: "It is right matter of Rassul. Razak Akhun, you was wrong in this matter. You said many times: will cut our head with your big knife. When you was angry with men and with animals, you take your knife and you told: will cut Rassul's head and mine. Then Rassul told: 'If you do that, then I will ride on your neck, and you will come under me.'" Now Galam Mahmad said to Razak Akhun: "Let go all this matter, and make friends we each other. I knew Rassul from young-time. He is good man. And with you he did not bad." Razak Akhun said: "Kalam Rassul made me false with you. But from this day I will not take Kalam Rassul's matter and we will make oath to not make enemy among us."

Then we took oath with Koran, and every one said, "Auspicious." Then I fill a cup tobacco and tea; gave to Razak Akhun; and said: "Until to-day what matter, bad or good, had been between us, let go them and pardon my fault." Then Razak Akhun did same me. Now Kalam Rassul said: "This all fault was of mine.

You both pardon my fault." Now every one said: "Auspicious" again, and laughed every one.

Now we sang together and were every one in enjoyment together at that night. Razak Akhun said: "When any man go a wrong way, then every one tell him: 'You are forgetting the oath of happy night.'" Then other men said: "We will give punish to that man who forget the oath." Now every one said: "We done very good this matter. Now is late. Go to bed." Some said: "Does not matter. A little sleeping is enough." Now, by helping of God, we all were very best friends each other.

SHOOTING ANTELOPE AND YAK.

Now we all travelling every day six miles, sometimes seven miles. We saw many times flocks of antelope. Humans seemed for them a tamasha. They never had seen any humans. Many of them came to look us. And when our smell hit them, then run a little and stopped again. We always found much meat of them, although we had with us about twenty-five sheeps from Cherchen. We kept them to use, necessary time, and use the antelope meat.

One time we saw two yak. Mr. Littledale shoot both them. I never had seen before any wild yak. It seemed to me as yak which people use for to carry loads, but it were very bigger than them. Razak Akhun made hallal to them. We took off the skin of yaks. For meat it was very hard to cut. Now Razak Akhun and I said: "We will cut the belly and take out the tallow fat." We cut it with much difficulty. There was in his belly about two maunds of grass. To take all that out took very long time. Then we worked to get tallow from the yak. It were not so fat. We got a little and took some meat. Mrs. Littledale said: "Take the tongue of yak, put into salt." We did that.

Then we travelling again, but I cannot tell about the place there we got in. Like an ocean of desert I can remember, that is all.

How we Work.

Now I tell how we work. We had two camps: one, donkeys, the next, ponies. With donkeys were Omar Shak head-man. Under him Galam Mahmad and three sepoys and Hussin, six men. With ponies, Razak Akhun and Mula Shah. Kalam Rassul was cook, I was table-boy, but we help for ponies.

Now morning, Razak Akhun and Mula Shah gather ponies in. Hussin gathered the donkeys, donkeys-men and ponies-men going together. When came all animals to camp, then donkey-men make clean donkeys' saddles and gave grain, ponies men work with ponies. Kalam Rassul and I help clean ponies' saddle and gave them grain, and then take our breakfast.

Then Kalam Rassul making ready a kettle boiling water and two pieces pig-meat. I gave to Mrs. Littledale and two sahibs hot water in their basin. Then take breakfast for sahib. Beginning, Mrs. Littledale gave me her tea-pot, which she put tea. I put hot water and put on table, and some bread, and take in hot plates the pigmeat, and honey.

While they take breakfast, we packing their beds. After breakfast taking things off table, washing them and put in box. The tea-pot made clean, then gave to Mrs. Littledale. She put it into her box. After that we put down the tents.

Then we put all things on back of ponies. Then starting from camp, and walking with caravan; Mrs. Littledale always going with caravan on a red pony. And when go any loads bad, she showed us. We do them. Mr. Littledale look his compass, and looked road, and going ahead. We follow to him.

Now, when we came on a camp, we, all men, unload very quickly; then pitch tent. That time sahibs help us. Then making beds. When we put clothes on bed, at that time, Mrs. Littledale, herself, making from the feet-side-end. After that we make other sahib's tent and bed. Then we pitch our tent. Then Kalam Rassul making for sahibs cook; we bringing wood. Now the Mrs. Littledale and sahibs for tiffin take cake of suji flour. Then Kalam Rassul cook a meat stew with onion and rice, and some potatoes,[1] and cooked some fruit, and boiling a kettle hot water. Now I make clean the cups and plates and forks and knives. When came dinner-time, I take three cups and a small tin of soup, then the kettle boiling water. After that, sahibs put some soups into their cup, and then put the hot water. Then I put, in two hot plates, rice for Mrs. Littledale and Mr. Fletcher, and in one hot plate potatoes for Mr. Littledale. Then I put the stew on table. Then that fruit in a wooden bowl. Sometimes cooked three pieces meat.

Then I washed all those things. Kalam Rassul washed his things. The other men sang in their tents. After that I gave for two sahibs and Mrs. Littledale water, hot, for baths. But not use much water, only little, but take every night baths. Then I gave hot water in a bag, which Mrs. Littledale kept in her bed to making warm. Then I said: "God-night."

Then I come into our tent; then take our dinner, in much talking and laughing. After dinner smoking tobacco. Then sang again the songs. When we walking, and when we working, and at night, is our much song time and talk time.

Beside this work, Kalam Rassul cooked bread for sahib, and cake, for three days at one time. I repair the broken clothes of sahibs and tents and shoes and gun-gloves. Besides that I wash many clothes, about two times a week. Mrs. Littledale kept always clean things for her and for both sahibs. But in doing this all I had more work than all men. And Kalam cooked

[1] Brought from Russia.

for sahibs. Sometimes Hussin cooked for us, sometimes Omar Shak, sometime Galam Mahmad. And when I washed clothes, sometimes fifty, sometimes one hundred, Punginor sepoy helped us, but he could not wash. And I looked at all the ponies' backs. Always sahibs look me in working every time, and when we walking, at that time I carried on my back the rifle of sahib. Mrs. Littledale said: "Many work you did, but we will not forget."

The Lost Sheeps.

Now we travelling other several days. One morning we were putting loads on ponies. There our sheeps went a little out camp. I bid Mula Shah bring them back, but Razak Akhun does not let him go. Razak Akhun said: "For a little time will not lost the sheeps. You work here, put loads." When we finish the work, we started. There could not get all the sheeps. Mrs. Littledale got much angry with me. She said: "Why you not give order to watch sheeps?"

Now Razak Akhun wait there, with the ponies, to searching them. We travelled from that place; camped in a valley, a pleased place. And there were as rocks the dry dungs of yaks. We were enjoy to got such a place, but were much sorry for sheeps. After, Razak Akhun we saw, a little far away, coming down from a sand hill; but were no any sheep with him. Now when he arrived at camp I asked him: "Where is the sheeps?" He said: "I found them near our camp into a small valley. All sheeps had been dead. I do not know how dead. Maybe kill them some bad animal. If tell that, there was no one would take any meat." And he had brought all the kidney in a handkerchief, and he said: "Mrs. Littledale like the kidney, therefore I brought it." When I heard that, fell myself in a river of sorrow. Now what shall I do?

And there Mrs. Littledale saw us and asked about sheep. Razak Akhun put all the kidney against Mrs.

Littledale. By unluck, she got very much angry with me. I was much sorry. Now Razak Akhun said to me: "It was my fault." I said: "Does not matter, your fault or mine, but you people must need obey to my matter. Now this matter is past. Future, you people must be careful." They said: "Yes."

Now that night we lost our enjoyment. The next day Mrs. Littledale said: "You people will not find meat." I said: "Yes, ma'am." After that we travelled many days. Several days was in sorry and shame for the sheep. Then Mrs. Littledale forget that angry of sheeps, and we forget also.

Our Enjoyment.

Here I will tell some our enjoyment. When we work, sang and talk. When walking, at that time, sang and talk. But the night had very best singing time. We every time spending the night in song and in telling, sleeping a very little time. Now we sang. Razak Akhun said: "I will sing in a sack in remember of my wife." Then he sang, beginning. Then we sang all together with him. When finish that song, said every one: "You sang good for your wife," and talked and laughed all. Then Kalam Rassul said: "I will sing, in remember Leh villages, and in remember my wife and friends." He beginning, then sang every one together. Then I sang. They said: "Yours is good, and are good wife." And Hussin had a friend girl at Leh, but he cannot sing. I sang for Hussin. They said: "No, not good." Galam Mahmad was very best singer-man, and he had a friend girl, for that he sang. We said: "This very good song." And laughed, and speaking very long time for friends of Leh. And said: "When we get to Leh, will do this and that." In all this talking we spend all the night. But we sleep very little. It was our custom and not seemed difficult. And I had that banjo which I had got at Kashgar, I making many itmes that banjo. But Kalam Rassul's banjo had broken.

Our Sorrow.

Now we this way travelling, very long time in that desert; not got to villages. Many time we view a far way some mountains ahead. We said: "After that mountain, must be a villages or human." After few days we getting on that mountains; view same desert. Now every one seemed a long journey. And each other said: "When would we pass this desert and get to a village?"

And Kalam Rassul said many time bad matter about the journey, which made tired the other men, and they fall into sorry. And he said: "This sahibs are come to die in this desert. When they die, then Government look very good to their children, but what shall we find?" The Kalam Rassul said every time bad matter. He making all men sorry (but he was jokeful man also). Now he said among us: "From where we are came, and where shall we go, and what kind of journey is this?" And he said: "It is no hope we to get Ladak again." Then fall all men in sorry and said: "We have so much work." And said: "The sepoys are very lazy men. They are more high pay than us." With this matter make more sorry.

By kindness God, I never tired in such matter. I said to Kalam Rassul: "Why do you spoke such foolish matter? I hope we will find villages, and must come to Ladak, by helping God, after some months. And will make many other journey after this. Then will tell this story: 'When we was with Mr. Littledale, was that and this.' But you are as a woman, not like man. We am men." I said to other men: "You people don't listen to Kalam Rassul matter. He is quite foolish man." Then other men said: "Yes, Rassul matter is right." I said: "If you people go in sorry, then must grow much sorry. Then will not get Ladak. We don't take sorry beside sorry. Must sing, and make enjoyment ourself. We know well Kalam Rassul is bad man, which he many times said bad matter for sahibs and to Mrs. Littledale, although eat sahibs' foods and wear sahibs' clothes." Kalam Rassul said: "I work for sahibs. Then this food I will thank to my work, and will not thank to sahibs." I said: "Must thank to sahibs. Whose food we eat and clothes we wear, must thank to them." Now a while I and Kalam Rassul fight for this matter. The other men said: "Does not matter. Let go this matter." And Razak Akhun sometime said my matter are right, sometime said Kalam Rassul matter is right. There broken the oath Razak Akhun and Kalam Rassul. But I had all the other men. By help of God, they obeyed to me. If Razak Akhun and Kalam Rassul deceit with me, they could not help.

The Cold Donkeys.

Now those place had been much wind and cold. Several donkeys dead with cold. There Hussin was head-man on donkey. He said to me: "The donkeys got cold by their forehead. If cover on their foreheads, then will save them." There we had a big numdah which spread into our tent. That we cut and put each donkey's forehead one piece. With that, help to donkey for cold. And we had many sacks, which was grain in them. When going empty we throw them. I told Hussin: "You don't throw them. Put on donkey head each bags." Hussin did that. The donkeys save. But Razak Akhun and Kalam Rassul both were angry for that numdah. They said: "Now no left numdah in tent." I said: "Does not matter. If die donkeys and ponies, then we will not find tent also." Mrs. Littledale looked at work with donkeys. She was much glad and said: "Wise boys."

One day Mr. Littledale took me for a little while to hunting. He said to me: "You are a more useful man than any man, and you carried upon your back my rifle also. Therefore from to-day is your pay rupees five more, per month." I thanked to sahib.

Throwing Things; and Badullah's Greed.

Now we travelling again many days; only saw desert, no other different country, although many time saw lakes. Now had been weak all the donkeys and ponies, and left behind some more donkeys and ponies. Were more weakness every day. We sure they will be tired and cannot go.

We camped one day to a place, where was a good water and no wind place. There Mr. Littledale said: "Now Gagalinchin is not far. But our animals are weak. Now we will throw some things here. Then will be light our loads. Then can go well all animals." I said: "Yes, sir." And sahib said: "All the servants, if have not-using thing, must throw them." I said: "Yes, sir, we will do that." I told to all servants.

Then Mrs. Littledale called to me. I went to her tent. She gave me a neck-thing and she said: "I have weaved this with my hands, and you put it on your neck." And she gave me a deer-skins, a cape, but there was no sleeve. I took my knife and made two holes for arm to that cape; then I wear. Mrs. Littledale laugh. Then called to Hussin and gave to him a black coat, very good one, and said: "Throw your old coat and wear this." He did that.

Now there throwing sahibs many things and washing soaps and candles. And we had brought some red cloth for present. Sahibs throw all them.

Then Mrs. Littledale and sahibs came to look at servants' things. Hussin, Galam Mahmad and Omar Shak and I had nothing, only I had my banjo. That Mrs. Littledale held in her hand, and said: "This we will not throw." And in Kalam Rassul's and Razak Akhun's bags were rugs and many other things, which they had brought from Khotan for their house. Sahibs said to them: "Throw this all things and we will pay the price." They told sahib the price of their things, and sahib wrote the price into his pocket-book.

Now the two sepoys no things had, but Badullah had some heavy cloth. Sahib said to him: "Throw that." He said: "I will not throw. I had brought this, if I die, then my body wrap in this coffin." Sahib said: "You will not die." At last he throw half that cloth. Then sahib said: "You cannot put on ponies and donkeys. If you carry it yourself, then can take it." He said: "I will carry it myself."

Now sahibs order to all servants that: throw old dress and wear new from the sahibs' throwing bundles. We all did that. At that night we spread the rugs in our tent, and middle the tent we put two boxes. Then we light a hundred candles on the boxes, and all men had new clothes. Now we talked each other, and ourself making like big munshi, and speaking like babu. And Kalam Rassul said many laugh-matter. Every one laugh very much and sang, and enjoyment ourself.

The one sepoy, Badullah, was very lazy a man. Beside lazy, was very greedy a man. Now, where we throw the things, there lay many things, sahibs' clothes and Mrs. Littledale's clothes. Badullah going many time to that place where lay the things. Next morning he had brought many red and blue cloths and other clothes. And he some tie on his head, like pugaree, and some he tie on his belt, and he some carried upon his back, and several he had weared on his body, which made very fat. Now he seemed us a tamasha, and Kalam Rassul joked him, then joked every one to him and laughed. But Badullah was a very foolish man. He said: "This is very fine thing. I must carry on my body, and will not put on donkey or ponies." I said: "If you take all this things on your body, then how shall you walk, and how shall you work?" He does not listen. (Now Razak Akhun and other sepoys said him: "You don't throw them.") Now we started from that place. Sahibs looked at Badullah and laughed, then said: "What did you do?" And said: "Let go this things." He said: "Sir, I will take."

Then sahibs nothing said. Now when he walk, can not walk, then he throw some things in way. Few days he took them, some he throw; some he put in his bag, but sahib and other men said: "Badullah is a very foolish a man."

Sahib kept in Badullah's pocket a like-watch, which show how many miles we travel in a day. Now in morning when all men working, Badullah hold that watch in his hand. If we bid him for a work, then he said: "Will break this thing." When sahib looked to him, nothing do, then sahib said: "Why, Badullah, do you not work?" He said: "Will break this." Sahib said: "Will not break." Then he work. Because Badullah was very tall man, therefore that measure-thing sahib kept in his pocket.

THE FIGHT ABOUT RICE.

Now we travelling by desert, and digging water from ground. And a many days after, we reached to good grass place and more good grass and more, by day by. Now many donkeys had dead, there left about forty donkey. But ponies and mule were not die much, only dead from Cherchen about six or seven. But every one animal was very weakness. At those place was very best grass and we saw several fire-place, which people had been there. Now Mr. Littledale said to me: "Now we came very near to Lhasa country, and, when we meet people, then must needed travel very fast. If not, they will shut us. Then could not get near Lhasa. But our animals are too weakness. What shall we do?" I said: "Sir, we must need halt, about a week, to a good grass place." Sahib said: "Yes, we will do that." But, first, sahib said: "We look the foods are enough or not." I said: "Sir, now we have about three months foods." Mr. Littledale not believe, and weigh all the foods. There found much food, but the rice had more than other things. Sahib said: "We have much food. We must halt a week, other side little pass, which were ahead for rest. But you needed now not use other foods, only use rice. I said: "Yes, sir."

The next day we crossed that pass. By good luck reached to a best pasture-grass, and lovely valley, but there was not much water, but was a stream, very poor water. In that valley we waited a week. Now we all men washed clothes and got bath. I washed many clothes for sahibs, and every one were enjoyment to got there. I had gaven the food, rice. We take in a day three times foods. I gaven rice the three times to all the men. Now a long time ago Razak Akhun wish to fight with me, and he said: "Give more butter in food than we have." I said: "Cannot give more. If we finish, where shall we get butter?" For this matter passed several days, every day we speak about it. Now at that half-place he said: "We will not take rice for three times. We must take flour and suttoo. I said: "This is order of sahibs, to use rice." He said: "Must not use rice." I said: "Razak Akhun, you think out yourself. At Khotan you bought more rice than other things, and Cherchen I told to sahibs the butter is not enough. At that time you said it is enough. Now is not enough. Now why do you gaven trouble to me?" Now we every time go in this matter, but no fight, and talked and sang also. One day we were in talk. Razak Akhun said some bad matter about me, and then said some very bad matter about my wife. I returned his abuse. We both fight there in talk. At last he said very bad matter which I got very angry, cannot stop myself. Then first I beat him with my hand, then he beat me, until other men caught to both us. But I got much angry at that day, to telling me so bad matter without my fault. I had carried many time their bad matter and said very sweet matter to them, but at that time was my fault more than Razak Akhun, because I caught him first. After that, I cannot stop the angry. Then went to sahibs' tent, but they had heard before. I told sahibs and Mrs. Littledale, and then they said: "Don't fight both. It is no good matter. But to use the rice it is my order," said to Razak Akhun. We both came back into tent. Now Razak Akhun and I not speaking. A little after, I finish my angry and was myself, much sorry and ashamed, with Mrs. Littledale and sahibs, and our camp looked very unhappy. Now Galam Mahmad and other men said: "We found this very bad time to fight you both men." In this talking I said: "It was not my fault. This is fault Razak Akhun and Kalam Rassul. They breaken their oath. I did not break promise of that happy night. That know you people." Now in this speaking we both got a little friendly outside. Then I put my cup full of tea against Razak Akhun, and said: "If be any fault from me, you pardon." Then every one said: "Rassul heart is clean." Then Razak Akhun gave his cup to me and said: "You must pardon my fault." Now we both got friends again. We said each other: "We both must go and tell sahibs we are friendship again." We both went to sahibs' tent and said: "Sir, we got friends again." Mrs. Littledale was very much glad to heard that. Now we were a best friend again, outside. In side, what is, do not know.

Signs of Human.

Now I lived at camp, in repair sahib's clothes and the gloves of guns, and washing clothes. Other men going out camp and they said to me the news. They said: "One time here must lived people. We found many tents-place." And in this speaking every one were glad.

We had wait at that place a week. The ponies and donkey got a little fresh, and then we leaving from that place and travelling south. On way, saw very good pasture, and many tents-places, and one place we found a tent-place that was taken at that day, and we found there fire. Now we said: "Here must be people very near." Mr. Littledale said: "We do not want any Tibetan look at us. If they see us, then they will report to the government of Lhasa. Then they will not let us come." Now we travelling, every time, by that way, which way show sahib's compass. Now we come high up a rocky hill. There north and west view a large opening country, and west side a big lake covered with ice. We travelling by that rocky hill, then came to a branch of the mountains. There was a small valley, very good water and enough grass. We camped there. Now sahib and Razak Akhun went up that hill to look way.

While after, they came back and said: "There are flocks of sheep and yaks and many tents." And sahib said: "Now we cannot go from here in day-time. Must need start at night." And sahib said: "You must be careful with our ponies and donkey. Don't let go out this valley to them." I said: "Sir, we will watch them at night and day." Sahib said: "It will be better, every two men, two of hours watch at night." I said to all men that matter. Every one like to do that. Then sahib gave me a clock to look time.

Now, at night, we two men watched ponies two hours. My companion was Galam Mahmad. We both going around the ponies. When they not run, we stopped one place and talked: all that of Ladak friends and of some girls. In this talking we not wanted to sleep, and after two hours we waked two others. In doing that, we passed that night. Next day waited there, in looking way. And we put sticks[1] in gloves of guns, and carried all servants upon backs as guns, and some had real guns. Now in looking, we were carried every one guns.

Now we started from that place at evening. At that night was no moon. Now we came to a very bad

[1] Theodolite-legs and tent-poles, etc.

mud-place. There we get no way, we searching way in that mud, and many ponies, mules and donkeys falling. We got much trouble. After very long time we finished that mud, but that mud was rather far way. There came on a rocky plain, there found much trouble in darkness, and no sleep. Now like very much to go sleep that night.

The early morning we camped in a valley. We unloads and pitch tents. There, by bad luck, there breaken the tent of Mrs. Littledale. She ordered to me to repair that. I did that. Every one went sleep. I repair the tent. I wanted very much go to sleep, but could not. When I ready repair the tent, there got up Mrs. Littledale and sahibs and all men. Mrs. Littledale said: "Bring breakfast." Then Mrs. Littledale said: "You are fixed the tent very good. Now you must sleep. If not sleep, then you will be ill." Then I sleeped for a time.

Next day we started from that place, and there was not any people, and no any tents in way. When we get top a pass, there was many rocks gathered, and had builded a like-chorten. On that hung some cloths. That was the offering-place, which came at Ladak over many pass. We all Ladaki were glad to saw that custom, same our own country. After that we came in a valley; saw two bear, which Mr. Littledale went to shooting them. They give no time to shoot; run away. Now we several days travelling, sometimes in valley and sometime on plain, but we got always good grass and wood. Several times we came on big road, but by good luck do not meet with any men.

We had food and all things very much, but was no butter, and in those days was for meat difficult, but sometime sahib got some animals. We had a yak tongue, which had keep in salt many day. When we cooked it, it did go more hard, never going soft. That tongue we cooked many days by order of Mrs. Littledale. We cooked, never got soft.

Now we reached upon a pass. There was a big road over it, and the stones-offering-place. Now from that pass view south-west a large lake, and other side that lake many mountains, and many covered-snow mountains. Now Mr. Littledale said to me: "We got good luck, got safely here. This lake, with other side snow mountains, is near Gagalinchin. Now we left until Lhasa eight days only, by through road. But we cannot go through road, there will meet with people."

Now we travelled from that place at night. Camped to a plain. Sahib was ahead. He had seen some yaks' caravan. We hidden from them. That yak caravan do not move, we found out in telescope. We found several place their track, and some salt fell in way, so we know they take salt to Lhasa. We do not want to halt, but they was on our way; therefore we halt.

The Water-Cross in Boat.

After two days they leaving that place. And sahib said: "I found out very near now we will find a big river." Then we travelling a little; reached to that river. It was a big river. There cannot cross. Now what shall we do?

Now Mr. Littledale said: "We will make a boat." Then we unloads. Then there took all these long poles of tents, and bed-woods, and there was a big water-proof, which used to put on ground in tent of Mrs. Littledale. Now made a boat of that water-proof and those tents-poles. To making that there lost a long time. We all Ladaki do not believe that we can cross by that boat.

Now at last got done that boat. Then made a long rope. Then one man, riding on a strong pony, crossed that river, and took that rope one end; next end we hold from this side. Then we did put the boat on water, and tied that rope from side to side. Now sahib said: "Go in that boat" to Mrs. Littledale. I not believe to can cross in that boat, and afraid, beginning, to let go Mrs. Littledale in that danger place. I said: "Sir, beginning, we put two bags of grain. If go that, then go Mrs. Littledale." Sahib like that. Those bags of grain went without difficult. Next time went some men; after that, Mr. Fletcher and Mrs. Littledale. We go in water until half-river, to push boat and pull.

And all men said to me: "We am hungry, must give suttoo." I said: "Yes, it is time to take suttoo." Now some men said: "It is very much trouble. If get rupees one thousand of pay, that is not enough for this day's trouble." I was very much tired, but I was ashamed to show to sahibs the tired face. I showed the good face, and said to other men in Ladaki language: "This day is among all the days of journey a courage-making day. If a man go tired in such work, that man is without bravery. Singing-time is this." Every one said: "It is right."

Now, little before evening, our all things got out that river well, with all men. And ponies and donkeys swam that river without load. Now we put loads on ponies' backs. There got evening, and some our clothes are got wet, and there fell our smoking-thing in water.

Now near that river we camped, every one tired very much. Why? The last three nights was not sleep in watching ponies, and that night was no happy in lost our smoking-thing. And we said: "Until we take food, let go ponies find some feed." By bad luck, there lost one mule. Now we were not sorry for that mule, but we were afraid the mule give witness, among that yak-caravan, that here are reached sahibs, in looking at the saddle of mule. Now the next morning, Omar Shak went to search that mule. By good luck he got that mule near the yaks-men, but yaks-men had not seen.

Losing Ponies in Watching.

Now we started from that place, came on big road. We let go that big road, travelling by no-road way. Then camped to a place, where was a sheeps-camp. There the next day was big road again. We let it go again, and, travelling behind a mountains, camped in a valley. Other side that hill had people. We do not know that, but we knew it at night. The other side that hill, dogs barking we heard at that night. After three days, we came to a rocky plain. From east had come a tall mountains, round south and toward west. And under the both mountains were grazing flocks of sheep and yaks, and were many tents of Tibetan. Now we have no way; all side shut our way.

Mr. Littledale said to us: "Now if we could, we must cross this high mountains. Maybe other side will not be people." We said: "Yes, sir, what you like, do that." Then we travel toward that mountain. There came in a very bad rock valley and steep; no got way. No got any way. Now we was hopeless there, to get way by east. We turned south, in not liking that way. Then we came near a big pasture; came more near people. Then we turned east again. There was a valley. We went in that valley for camp. From a little hill some boys and girls called to us: "Come this side. We are here." We nothing said to them. We said ourself: "This boys and girls called us, in hoping we be their companions."

At night we watched ponies, every man two hours. My watch was second. There came the first watcher and waked us. Galam Mahmad and I went, and they charge to us the ponies and the donkeys. We did watched two hours. Then we waked Omar Shak and one sepoys. We charge them, and we came our tent and sleeped. After about two or three hours the Omar Shak came and waked me again. I was in sweet sleeping. I said: "What matter is?" He said: "We got no ponies." He lied, and said: "You did not charge in our hands." I said: "Omar Shak, you must afraid to God, to tell so big lie. I gave into your hands, and counted. Now you sleeping. You did not watch ponies, and lost them. I will not get up. You must get them. Why did you sleep in such place? Now lost all that good work, which we did from Khotan to here. Now what shall I do?" I said myself: "I am as a head-man. Must needed to search them myself with the lazy men. If not, how shall I show my face to sahibs?" Then I got up, and went with the men to searching ponies.

There were much rocks and darkness and the rain made mud. We got full unluck at that night.

Now I said to those lie-men: "Please tell true, how lost the ponies." They said: "You had charge in our hands. We went a little sleep. Then we looked to ponies, and we lost that place, at what place the ponies had grazing. Therefore we waked you." Now there were many up and down place. Where was that place I could not get. Now from the midnight, in searching ponies, very much got tired and wanted sleep, but at that time lost the sleep in sorrow. I said: "Each man must go separate place to search." They said: "We will got to camp, and wake them also." I said: "No, why give trouble to all men with us? Our own unluck is enough." We searched from midnight until morning, which came up a little light. Now I said: "Must look very careful for tracks." By good luck, there got tracks, and followed tracks. By good luck, got all animals, in little valley, near camp. We had travelled wrong way the half-night.

Now we leaving that valley in morning, and came out on green land. A longer after we came to a badly mud place. There many horses' loads falled, and mules and ponies' feets felled down in mud. It was like a war with the caravan in that mud. No get a minute for rest, and that mud came more and more; never finish. Now we make long march from seven o'clock of morning to five o'clock of evening. If God like to given a man happy, then join from all sides happy. If God like to given a man trouble, then join all bad luck. It is the power of God.

Meeting with People.

Now there met with a man, which weared dirty clothes, long dress, and hat like English hat (a little bigger than English hat), and very dirty man. Now sahib said: "You ask to this man, what name is this pass?" I said: "Sir, what shall we tell to these people if ask us: where do you people come from?" Sahib said: "Tell: we am trader, and we come from Tashilumpo, and will go Lhasa." Now I said to that man: "You are well?" He said: "I am well." Then I said: "What is name of this pass?" He said: "It is called Gylu La to the pass."

Then we walking up by that valley. There was a big road. There were five tents on the road. When they saw our coming, all men run up the hills. When we came at the first tent, there were three women taked milk from yaks in bull yaks' horns. Mrs. Littledale said to me: "I wanted some milk." I said to those women: "Are you well?" They said: "Yes. Are you people well?" I said: "Yes." They were middle-age women. Then they said: "From where do you people come, and where do you people going from here?" I said: "We am Ladaki traders and came at Tashilumpo; there sold some goods. Now we will go to Lhasa." Then one woman said: "Who is this lady?" I said: "She is a big lady of Ladak, and she had come to see Dalai Lama." Then they said: "She is a good lady, coming from Ladak to see Dalai Lama." Then I said we wanted some sheep and butter and some milk. There brought one woman a yak-horn full of milk. Then Mrs. Littledale said: "Give some money." We gave one rupee. They were much glad. Then to the next tent Razak Akhun bought some butter and one sheep. Then we asked them: "How far is from here to Lhasa?" They said: "We have not been." I said: "How far, in hearing from people?" They said: "We heard: a week road from here to Lhasa." Then we said goodbye to them, and travelled again.

Now I tired; no left any might; no any manful also. All the caravan went ahead, I left behind. I rest a little, then walking again. After two or three yards, rest again. I said myself: "Than this work, why I not did coolies' work at Leh? I will not reach Leh again. If tired so much here, how can I make the long journey?" Then I remember my mother and wife, and then I weep myself. In all this telling myself, walking alone, after three yards taking a rest, came on a high place. From that place, about a mile up, looked our camp. My felt much better, but that one mile place seemed as five miles far at that time.

At last arrived camp, before sun go down. There sahib tent was not pitch. Why? There were some boys grazing yaks, and sahib said to me: "We will not pitch tents until night. These boys see our tents; then will tell to their family all interesting tent matter." I said: "Yes, sir." I had no might; cannot speak with sahibs. That all my happened the sahibs do not know, but I showed them good face, which like I have not tired. Then I came to servants' camp. There was ready tea and suttoo. I got a little fresh again. Now the boys came near our tent for tamasha. We gave them some suttoo and tea. When sun went down the boys went to their tent; but we do not know where is their tents. When got darkness, we pitch our tents under a little hill.

Next morning, when we loaded, there came five men from the hill, down toward us. They had carried all armours, and each man upon their backs carried guns, and on each gun hung piece red cloth, and each man had spear, and in each man belt carried sword, big knife, and each man had pony to ride. And their dress was long until foots, of sheeps-skins, and belt of red cloth, and their hats were of grass, covered with white cloth and looked like English hat, but theirs are a little bigger. Their shoes looked like Chinese.

Sahibs said to me: "This people came to stop us. You tell: 'We am traders,' and give present each man one rupee." I said: "Sir, the rupee-given is no good. Then they will think sure English. There are no custom of traders to given present without any work." Sahib said: "What you think better, do that. How we can, we will go near Lhasa." I said: "Yes, sir." Sahibs said: "Don't speak all men with them. You and Razak Akhun speak, and does not matter lie-matter, and make their head bad in speaking."

Now the five men met with us and said: "Where do you people going and from where do you people come? And of what country are you people?" I reply all that trader matter. They said: "Any trader not had been by this way. How do you people come here?" We crossed in this speaking a little hill. Other side that hilll were about thirty men on our going-road, waiting for us. And they were all same armour of that five men. And there was a tharspond, had carried upon his back many arrows. He is high rank. And there were the head-men of villages. They said same matter those five men. We reply that we am traders. They said: "Please, you people must let us know right." I said: "We have no more matter to tell." And we travelling fast. Now our ponies and donkey were strong enough. That one week waiting for their rest, that help us. Sahib said: "We needed take very long march, therefore for two servants take one ponies to ride with. Then will not be tired any servants." Then we made empty five ponies for servants, and travelled, the Tibetan people following us.

Now they said: "Among you people which one is big man?" We said: "We each man are head-men of own goods." They do not knew which is sahib. And said about Mrs. Littledale. We said: "She is very big a lady of Ladak, and had come to see Dalai Lama." They said: "We got the doubt to coming by this road. If you people are sure Ladak traders, then we will show very near road to Lhasa. If be other kinds of men, then the Deva Jung will cut head to us." In this speaking we crossed that pass, and top that pass was big plain. We travelling over that, and one place were several tents, and there they said to us: "Please take sit here. We will give you people sheeps and butter and wood." We said: "We will not stop here, and don't wanted sheep." Then they asked us in a tent for tea. I said: "I do not wanted tea," and no one went in their tent, but Kalam Rassul and Galam Mahmad went into that tent. There was a woman who had been Ladak with a big lama. She had been brought from a place a far away all that night, to make know if these people are surely Ladaki. And that woman knew, in looking Mrs. Littledale, that it is an English woman.

Now those people said: "You people are surely Ladaki, but we think here must be some English. If be any English, then the government of Tibet will cut our heads." I said: "Here are not any English." Now, in this speaking, we came to a down-way, very bad rocks. After that came to a very good camp-place. They said: "Please stop here. We will report to Lhasa." I said: "Why do you people report for Ladaki men?"

Now every time the people gathered more and more. Before sun go down, we stopped and pitch tents. Then the Tibetan know which is sahibs, and which is servants. At that night we heard the noise of many people coming, and stopping with us. Next morning, when we got up and looked, there were about three hundred people joined. I went into sahib's tent, and reported that here are gathered so many men. Sahib said: "I wanted to go until Tengri Nor. You look very careful. Must try to get to Tengri Nor. If find such bad luck as French sahibs, then we not need to go Lhasa, and we can stop soon. We will not throw our life. Talking does not matter, but fighting is bad. You make with some men friend, and get matter from them, and what they thinking us." I said: "Sir, I will find out all matter, and I can find their temper."

Now there was lama, weared yellow dress. He knows some Ladaki traders, name of Lapchak, which go from Leh every two years from Maharaja side to Lhasa. And I written an "om mani padme hom" on the sahib's honey-tin. That lama said to me: "You are a lama." I said: "Yes, I am a lama; you are lama." He said: "What is your master? Tell true." I said: "I must tell you true, and should you tell true what will I ask to you, we both are friend. Between us have the "om mani padme hom" He said: "Yes." There we got friend. Now we loaded and was near to start from that place. I said to that man: "These two are English sahib, and other one are very big lady, relative of queen of English." With this matter I got more friend with that lama.

Now they wanted speak with sahib. I said to sahib: "It be better, we will tell: 'We am big men, will not speak with you, little rank, and if come from Lhasa same rank of mine, then will speak with that.' " Sahib like very much this matter.

Bribe to Sahib.

Then I said to the Tibetan that, and started from that place, and they travelling with us. It was very best tamasha for us. I said to that lama friend of mine: "You tell me what order you people have from Lhasa government, to make a sahib stop." He said with sweet matter: "To returned sahib we have order from Dalai Lama. If could not that, then Deva Jung (mean 'Government') will take from us the fine: one rupee for each yard footstep." And he said: "We will give bribe." I said: "Wanted no bribe, and I tell you people, he will not stop and speak until he find his same rank of man. It is custom of English." That lama said: "We can gather three thousand rupees in one night, and that give to sahibs. Then he will go back." I said: "It is no custom of English government to taken a bribe." And many they asked about our rifles. We said: "This is for one thousand men killing, our one rifle be enough." And they said: "What is in the boxes?" We said: "In these boxes we have enemy-killing thing. If put fire to a box, then burn all men of country." They are jungly men, believe to that matter.

(Now there were about three hundred people following us, all riding on ponies, and every one had gun, and big knife, and spear, and some red dress, some of blue, and some yellow. Now their food each men had carried behind their saddles, a shoulder of sheep-meat, some two shoulders. That meat cut with knife, and eat without any cooking. And several men bring one pot, which cook tea in that, and take some suttoo. And many of them cannot take suttoo. They said, with suttoo and flour make sick their belly. Now the our three sepoys looked that, without cooking taking meat, and their hairs very long tail. The sepoys said: "These people surely are jungly people." And they said: "How do you people know their language?" We said: "We had learned it." The sepoys said: "You people are brave men which know this kinds of language.")

TENGRI-NOR.

Now after three days we crossed a small pass, and got on that pass view many mountains, covered snow Those were glaciers, and a big lake, very blue water, and good grass-land. That lake Tengri Nor lake. Now, down from that pass, came on a very big road. Now one place there was a beautiful place and several beautiful tents and some big black dogs. There had camped a big lama, and with him were many other lamas. We asked to some men: "Who are this?" They said: "We is a big lama came from Lhasa to see holy lake of Tengri Nor, and will go around it. Then their sin is clean."

Now that evening when pitch our tent, and drank some tea, there came some men, and quickly pitch a tent. And they said: "Here will came the wazir of Senja." Sahib said: "Now by good luck we see the Tengri Nor Lake, but, if get way, must go more far. For that you look." I said: "Yes, sir." And sahib said: "What you think? What shall we tell to this big man?" I said: "We must show the thumb and fingers of hand and ask to him: 'Which rank do you keep?' He must show us a finger. Then we tell: 'Sahib's rank is so high like a thumb. If came like thumb from Lhasa, can speak with such men only.'" (I forgot to tell, up; there are custom always, show thumb and finger for ranks.)

Bribe to Men.

Now there reached the Jung. He was a young man, and came with him about fifty mounted men, and the Jung had very good clothes. We did that thumb-matter. Then he said: "We will write Lhasa. Until come that big man, you stop here." Sahib said: "I cannot stop."

Then sahib went into his tent, that big man to his tent. Now that lama, my friend, said: "If you tell the sahibs, they will stop." I said: "I am servant of sahib. What he like, that he do. How I tell him stop?" Now that Jung said to me, with oath: "If you people make stop the sahib, we will give rupees three thousand. That money is very easy for us, but we cannot take that punish of Deva Jung. Any other sahib had not reached so near as you people are came. And their men had took money, therefore did not came so near. Please you all Ladaki make counsel. If wanted more money than rupees three thousand we will give. Must make stop here, till come reply for our report from Lhasa. We will give butter and sheep, milk. We Ladaki and Tibetan is same, no difference." I said: "We have much money; no needed your money; and cannot make stop."

Now our men were in greed of money. They said to me: "Sahib said many time to you: look very careful. If you tell sahibs, now we cannot go, the sahib will stop. This time God gave us good earning-time. We must take money." I said to them: "Don't tell this matter. If we look for money, then bring shame to English Government." They said: "Which other men took money with the last sahibs, no came any ashamed. Now how we bring ashamed?" And more said Kalam Rassul and Razak Akhun. They said: "Englishmen, when finish their work, then will not look behind. They are unfaithful men. Never remember our good work and bad. Now we get this money, it is very best for us. You said many time: Government will know our work. That is quite wrong thinking." I said: "We must need go right way. Which matter be useful for our sahib we must do that. If sahib not look, God will look." They said: "It is matter for a big fakir, not among us. Now we will never get such a money-getting time. It is very foolish: if money came in hands, that let gone." Now all that night we were in the speaking.

Now, the next morning, that lama came to us again from the young Jung, and said again all that matter.

And he said: "Will come now the Zong our big man of this countries to see Sahib." I said: "Him yes he may come." Sahib was at that time in his tent. I went to sahib and said: "Sir, the Zong big man of this place will come to see you now." Sahib said to me: "What matter to be better for us you tell him." I said: "Yes sir, when he come, you tell me something, then I will ask him his rank.

I will show him my five fingers and will tell which rank you are from it. He must show a between one finger. Then I will tell him sahib rank is very big same the thumb. You are a little rank than Sahib," said I: "Will not speak with you. Must come a big man from Lhassa same the rank of Sahib have, then sahib will speak with him not with you." Sahib said to me: "Yes, you tell that, and said, we must wanted go to before, if not be any trouble. If be any trouble you must tell me we will stop, if no trouble what do you like tell that." I said: "Sir, by your kindly there not be any trouble, I will look very carefully." Now the big man Zong came to Sahib, he was a young man, (his rank is as Tehsildar) when he came, Sahib come out from his tent. The Zong said salaam to Sahib, and then he said to Sahib: "Why do you come here?" I was interpreter. Sahib said same the above matter. Then I showed him my right hands five fingers and said: "Which rank are you from these?" He showed a between one finger. Then I showed him my thumb and said: "Sahib rank is as the thumb, very big man. And he do not like to speak with a little man as you. Sahib want high rank man same his rank then he will speak with him." When the Zong heard this matter he nothing said. I know in his face he got nothing to say for us again then he went back to his tent. Then we took off our tents and loaded on animals and travelled to south. The Tibetan with the Zong big man travelled behind us, and they never show us right way. And they said: "You people must stop, there are two big rivers very strong water, cannot cross them." The two rivers came from west go east in to Zingmur lake. We said: "When we came there, we will see, no more we will talk with you people." That afternoon we came to that river, it was surely strong river very hard to cross. Now some our men went up the river to look water cross, some went down, one place we got the way where there the river devides in two Division that place was a little good to cross, and the weather was cold enough. We all servants there took off our clothes and made a line in the river by holding each others hands and we led our animals in front of us. The Tibetans watched all our doings and crossing the river etcetra and they got much amazed. The next river was not so hard as the first one. We lost much time in crossing the rivers, but by the grace of God we crossed both the river easily. In the evening we arrived where there was a meadow and there we camped, but there was no wood only dung. Every one felt very cold by crossing the river. The Tibetan, in that evening camped a far way from our camp. These were three vallies, we did not know which valley is our way, Sahib said to me: "I think Rassul, our way is the left side valley, as Ramsinghs book, any way you find the road." I said to Sahib: "The Tibetan every day send letter to Lhassa we will look that man which way he goes." Now one mounted man started from their camp and he went toward the far way valley west south. We got hopeless when the mounted man went that way. But they made this trick to show us and to deceive us that we may go wrong way, I said to Sahib: "We will send our one man toward the left side vallies, because there the two vallies were very near to each other. We will find the right road. If there find big road and Mani on the way that will surely be the right road." Sahib said: "Yes send our one man to look the road," as that I ordered to Usman Sheikh and I showed him a foot of mountain and said to him: "You must go there," he said: "Yes," and he rode towards that valley and a while after, he came back to camp and he said, "There is a great road and there are some Mani also," now we were glad to get our way. I give the road getting news to Sahib, he also glad with the news. Now we looked from our camp to the Tibetan army and they looked us, now they know that we sent man up to looking the road, and find the road but we did not know that. Every one of us felt cold by crossing the river, so we took our supper, and let our ponies lose for grazing, then we all went to our bed.

The next morning, there was no one man at the Tibeti army camp, and we do not knew which side they went, and why they went. When sahibs came out their tent, they looked it very strange, to lost the great party of army in that night. And sahib said: "Maybe, they will meet us up the valley."

Making Ready the War with Thirteen Men.

We travelling up that valley. Under a rocky hill there was a little flat place. There was coming a mounted man toward us. We knew him, from a little far away, with his yellow dress, which he was a lama among the army. When he came near us, he nothing said to us; and he went back up again. We travelled behind him.

When we came under the rocky hill, there came a great noise. When that noise we heard, we looked up the hill. There were all the army sitting round us, and were holding all their guns toward us.

When I saw that whole army, I was afraid.[1] (While after, felt better.) And sahib said: "We make ready our rifle." And he did that, but I had no rifle of my own. I bear a rifle on my back, that took Mr. Littledale. And Mr. Littledale said to me: "What do you think?" I said: "They cannot kill us. Only, they make us afraid."

While we were in the speaking, there coming down toward us the little big man and some other men with him. Sahib said to me: "You must look very careful. If we find bad luck, then we will go back from here." Now the big man and other coming to sahib; and they looked back to their army, and said: "Don't shoot. Don't shoot, now, until we speak." We said: "You people cannot shoot us this way." Now the big man and other met with sahib, and the big man said to sahib

[1] Littledale testifies that the sepoys, on this occasion, showed complete readiness to back their sahib against what must have seemed to them hopeless odds.

that: "These people are very bad. And their wish is to kill you people. And I did stop them." Now Mr. Littledale keep the passport of Chinese on his chest, and said: "If you people shoot, then shoot on this passport. We have come here, by this passport order. But we have not come for a battle. If you people wanted to make war with us, does not matter. Here we have thirteen men only, but our Kingdom of India is a great place. You people must consider over this matter." I was interpreter.

With this matter the Tibetan afraid a little; that we knew into their speaking, and into their face. And we said to them: "Now we will never go back, until you people kill us."

Now Razak Akhun and Kalam Rassul, beside sahib, said ourself to the Tibetan: "Why for you people made ready the war with thirteen men? When we started from home, we had given off our head. We are not sorrow to die. If we die, the full justice of English Government will look our family future, and will take Lhasa under our government. But without your people's fault, our government cannot take the Tibet country. You people must kill us." We said the words of Kissar Ghapas: "Are much grass on the hills. If need cut, a small knife is enough to cut."

With all these matter they afraid, and said: "We will not kill you people, but we beg to you people, you people must wait here few days till we get answer from the Deva Jung."

We said: "If was this matter, then why you people made ready your army for a war? Now we will not stop. We must go to Lhasa."

And sahib said me: "You tell all that matter which make better for us. In this, lie or true does not matter. What you like, tell them. I want very much to go other side this pass."

I said: "Yes, sir. We will go other side this pass, but now we must tell we must go to Lhasa." I said to the Tibetan: "This sahib is bad. He said: now will go to Lhasa. He said yesterday he will wait in Goring valley. Now he got angry with you people to got ready your army at a battle." And I said: "I am you people's friendship. Why? Ladaki and Tibetan are all same relation, but I could not help. And you people don't keep any hope to our waiting here." Now they afraid, and a little believe to my matter. And they said: "Only three or four days wait here. We will give sheep, milk, butter, all thing what you people need." I said: "Will never stop here, but maybe stop other side pass, same we promise yesterday."

THE BOND.

And they said: "That be good for you people. But for wait other side pass, must please give us a written bond: will not go toward Lhasa."

Sahib said: "Yes." And sahib wrote such a bond in English. They said: "We do not know English. We want it in Tibeti." Sahib said: "Will you want in Ladaki?" Sahib said to me: "You write a written bond." I said: "Yes, sir," and I took the pen and paper. When I wrote it, the Tibetan laughed at my writing. I felt ashamed. Why? My writing was not so good. It was broken Ladaki, as this which now I use the broken English. When I wrote it, they said: "The words is good in your written."

After, the young head-man said to sahib: "Now show us some interesting thing for tamasha." Sahib showed them some telescope-glasses, knife and other thing. But Mrs. Littledale weared her dress of waterproof. She carried water in front her dress. The Tibetan looked that much interesting, to bear water into her dress. And there Mrs. Littledale and Mr. Littledale showed them their young time pictures, which showed in the pictures Mr. Littledale and Mrs. Littledale were both much beautiful. That seemed the Tibetan much interesting.

THE BAD PASS AND RAINING TROUBLE.

Now the time was late afternoon. The Tibetan people said to us: "You cannot go over the pass to-day. Why? It is late and the pass is a very bad pass. There will be very cold and will not get any wood. There will find much trouble." And said: "We said for the lady. It be much better to-day will stop here. To-morrow early starting will be better." For this matter we believed, but sahib did not believe.

Any way we started from that place, late afternoon. That pass was enough high.[1] Now we came to narrow place. There was bad road. There fell some our mules. With them left some men behind us. There we came over ice and snow. There fell some donkeys. There left some more men. Now Mrs. Littledale and Mr. Littledale and Mr. Fletcher and Razak Akhun and some other men and I came, at that evening, top the pass. There found some ropes; on those ropes hanging many kinds of cloths red, blue, yellow and white. All that seemed beautiful. And top of the pass had made lhatoo (a bundle of twigs). On that hung many cloths and some white silk cloths, which called khatangs, and on that were some arrows.

Now view from the pass other side deep valley, and there were clouds; could not view well. Mr. Littledale said to me: "Now we are come very near to Lhasa." And then we went down over glacier, and was much snow. Then came to much rock place, and there was much water on road. And there got night. In dark cannot see road, and many place felled down among the rocks. Beside all that trouble, there raining much.

Now the trouble of cold, and on road water, and felled among rocks, and the dark, and with the raining, we got much trouble. And our clothes had been wet, and where is the camping-place we do not know. And Mrs. Littledale cried. With that I was much sorry.

[1] 19,587 feet.

At last got a little place among rocks. There pitched tents. There was no any hope to get any wood, and we no have any fire. And the sahibs had soup in tins. Those tins can make hot. Hot-making things were with the tins. And we all servants had some dry biscuit. Now we eat that biscuit with cold water.

That night was very cold. That night passed with much trouble. The next morning, not anything to eat, besides that biscuit and cold water.

Now we started from that place, and going down a big valley among much big rocks and gravel and there raining much. Now we were inside cold with the cold water, outside cold with the rain. Now we were very weakness as that which nearly to die.

Then finished the bad road, and came on flat place. There was the valley much beautiful and very good grass. All sides were green. Now we travelled by the lovely valley down, in the raining-trouble. A little after, by good luck, the rain stopped, and we stopped one place a little for rest. There the sun was a little warm. And there could not get any firewood. There were some dung, which had been wet with the rain, and there were some bush-wood. All was green. Cannot use for fire. Now we must need some hot tea. What shall we do? There was in that camp an old saddle of donkey. That we broken and made a little tea. With that we got a little fresh. After that, there raining again. We leaving from that place, in the hope we get a good camp to stop. A little down was much good grass, and was the bush-wood all wet. Now the rain was very hard, and we cannot travel, and there we stop. Now our some men and donkey and some mules were left behind.

True Matter from Lama.

Now there was coming up a lama from Lhasa. I did ask him: "From where are you come, and where do you go?" He said: "I have come from Lhasa, and going round to holy Tengri Nor Lake." And he said: "You are a Ladaki?" I said: "Yes." He said: "I am a Ladaki. My home is at Tikste village, and I have been here a long time. I am come from Ladak in my young time. Then I said to him: "You are welcome for us, our country-man." Then I did ask him: "How far is Lhasa from here?" He said: "Two days from here. If go on good ponies, then can go in one day to Lhasa." Then I said: "How far is to a villages which have fields?" He showed me down a valley, and he said: "Out this valley you will get village." I told this matter to Mr. Littledale. Sahib said: "It is right matter. If go to Lhasa easily can go, but it would not be good, because we have gave to the Tibetan our written bond. That will make bad, and lie in government law. Therefore we cannot go." And sahib gave to the lama one rupees present to telling true matter. And the lama went to Tengri Nor.

Making Bashful.[1]

Now we camped at a place. The rain was very hard. There was no hope to get any firewood. At that night the sahib taked those tins things; we took again, with cold water, the biscuits. The next morning every one were sleeping. I thinking out, and said myself: "It had been about three days; only got a little tea, beside that cold water and biscuit. Now what shall I do? Every one not trying for fuel. It is shameless, and I will show to this people *bashfulness*." This all said myself.

And I said: "If be a little fire, then can burn the wet green bush, but must need a little dry wood." In my thinking, this matter came out. Now the Omar Shak was a *bashful* man. I waked him up, and then I said

[1] Editor—I have not been able to decide just what word Rassul seeks in "bashful." A dictionary may have confused him as to the distinction between "ingenious" and "ingenuous."

to him that: "In men must need *bashful*, but we not got any, which not got any warm food in two days. To-day have three days, and all the men are shameless, but you and I both have some *bashful*. We must try to-day to get some fire and will cook some thing.

He said: "It is much difficult. What *bashful* shall we do?" I said to him what was in my mind. Omar Shak liked to do that, and he got a stick and a little other wood in camp, although the rain was very hard. Then, on a rock, Omar put a bag's end, and put on it stones. The next end Omar held on his head, and he making the fire with tinder and flint which we had one with us. I brought from all side small wood, but it were all wet. By good luck, at last, there got a little fire. And Omar Shak said: "What put on fire?" I said: "We will put the kettle." Now, after long while, kettle boiling; we both men drinking boiling water. In that got little warm.

Now sahib and all men were sleeping, hopeless to not get breakfast. And I went to Mrs. Littledale's tent, and I said to Mrs. Littledale from that tent-door: "Shall Mrs. Littledale want tea?" Sahib and Mrs. Littledale said: "Want very much, but how get it?" With this matter Mrs. Littledale was much glad and said: "Bring it quickly." I did give the tea, and I said: "Shall you want other things?" Mrs. Littledale said: "If you can, then bring me two pieces pig meat." I made ready and gave to Mrs. Littledale, and she was much thankful on my *bashful*.

Now we put on the fire a pot full of water, and made much good fire, can burn the wet wood also. Then we put in the pot rice, and made boil, and put salty in. Then we both men drinking much rice-soup, now got much strong and enough warm; but the our men were sleeping, they do not know this. Now we put water again in the pot, and got ready the rice-soup for all men. Now we waked to all men, and said: "Take soup." They never believe, and said from their bed to us: "Don't joking in the good sleeping-time." We said: "We do not joked. We made *bashful*, made ready." They not believe, and not get up from their bed. Then we fill their cups with the soup, and gave each man on their bed. Then they believe, and said: "Wonderful. How you people did it?" I said: "With *bashful*. You people are shameless. If had tried, we must got dinner last night." They were much glad and said: "Truly you people made *bashful*." I said: "Any man must needed *bashful* in a journey."

Down the Goring Valley.

Now the rain did not stop. We every one sleep in tents. By good luck, stop the rain and God gave good sun. And we had waited, because some our men left behind us. There not was any Tibeti. Now that afternoon, all men and animals reach there. They were half die. The big party of Tibetan army and the big men left other side the Goring pass.

Next morning, we travelling, there came other one jung and with him were about 50 Tibeti. And that jung was a very clever man. When he met with us, he said: "Welcome, How do you people come to this country?" We ask him: "What rank do you keep?" He said: "I am not a very big man, but on my villages I am big man." Sahib said: "My rank is bigger than you. I will not speak till come a big man as me." Jung said: "You people made promise to stop here in this valley. If we let you people go, then Deva Jung will cut our heads. Beside that, will take for one yard step one rupees fine. You think about it, how much money shall we give fine to the Deva Jung. And the law of Deva Jung is very hard." They said very much sweet matter and they said: "We are poor men. If we get punish from Deva Jung, that is on you people."

We did not stop. Mr. Littledale said to me many

times: "You must look very careful, don't be bad luck." I said: "Yes, sir."

Now we came much down the valley, very nearly to get out that valley. Then would come the Lhasa villages; therefore they begged so much. Now one time the jung said to his men, with bad face (but not said to us): "Some good shot men are sent ahead to foot of mountain. Must shoot this people. In one day I was born in the world, and one day to die. Now it look to me same, Deva Jung kill me, or English kill me; therefore, why not kill these people?" Now we knew in his face, that he show us bad luck. That I did ask to other our men. They said it seemed bad in their face. Then I said to sahib: "Now looked us bad." And I told that all matter of the jung. Sahib said: "Then must stop." I said: "Yes." Now I said to the jung: "Sahibs say you are a good man, and we will take your advice, and will wait here till come a big man from Lhasa. After that, we must go to Lhasa. How long we wait there, you need to supply us all things we need to this camp." Jung said: "What you people need, we will supply. For that we will not take prices."

Now we camp there for a long time.[1] Now the Goring valley was very beautiful, both sides tall mountains, and many of the mountain-tops covered with beautiful glacier and snow, and in the lovely valley very good pasture, good grass and little jungle of bushwood. That all sides look green, and in that valley run very clean water stream down.

Much Speaking with Lamas.

Now after few days there came a big lama and a big layman. They came from Lhasa to speak us, and were with them several little lamas. They said: From each monastery temple came a man, to look what the big man speak with sahibs. And there were several man

[1] At 16,600 feet.

with red silk hats, said they are the chaprassi of the big men. Now they pitch their tents at the same place. Now there were many tents and many people. Now the valley was a little town. Now the big lama, and the next big man, and the chaprassis and the little lamas which were come from each monastery temple, all came to see sahib. And there brought about three maunds of flour in a leather bag for sahibs. And they put the flour against sahibs, and said: "Welcome from the long way." Sahibs said to them: "Yes, we came all right. You people are well?" They said: "Yes." Then the lama said to sahibs: "I wanted to bring more things to you, but the Deva Jung gave not time to do all that arrangement. Why? The Deva Jung ordered us very hard, to go quickly to see you, and thought you were coming from far away and would be gone your provision." Sahib said: "I thank you for your wise thinking. And we had come from far away, but we had made enough arrangement for our provision." Then sahib showed them me, and said: "He is in charge on the provision. Ask him." I said: "We have three months' provision more from to-day, but we thank to your wise thought."

Now the lama said to sahib: "I think your mind would be to come to other country, not come to Lhasa; but you would be lost your way." Sahib said to him: "We did not lost our way, and with the mind we had come to go Lhasa, and will see the Dalai Lama. Why? Mrs. Littledale wanted to see the Dalai Lama. Therefore we have come from so far away." The lama answered to sahibs, and said: "You cannot go to Lhasa, and you could not meet with Dalai Lama. The mind of your are wrong." And he said: "Maybe you did not know this matter. If you knew, then you never be come here. Some year ago, at Darjeeling-side, we were a little battle; and at that time we had made a promise, that any Englishmen will not coming toward Tibet. For that you people had give a written bond. Then why did you come here now?" Sahib said: "Yes, I knew that matter. There were a little battle. And that battle had been for a little man, and it is quite lie-matter; we had not given any written bond to you people for to not coming toward Lhasa." And sahib said: "You think over that matter. Because that battle had been for a little man. Now we are very big men of London, and Mrs. Littledale is a relation of Victoria, and Victoria sent to her own relation, the Mrs. Littledale to see Dalai Lama and Lhasa. Why? Here many Englishmen had come before, but you people had not given way. Now the Victoria sent her own relation in the hope you people will let us come. In this hope we have come so far way. Now if you give us trouble, then would be a greater battle than that last battle. That battle was for little men. We am big men." The Tibetan said: "We will not said you are not big men. You are big men. And we will not make any battle also. But we will never let you go to Lhasa, with the order of Deva Jung, and it is quite wrong mind of your to kept the hope to go Lhasa, and to see the Dalai Lama. It will never be. It would be better for you, and for us, that you make ready to go back toward that way, from which you are come. And in this shall you want any help from us, we shall help you. I am much sorry, but I am servant of Dalai Lama and what can I do?" Sahib said: "I will never go back. Than our going back, it is much better for us to die here. If you people kill us, then the India is near. They will take our wreak from you people." The lama said: "The Deva Jung did not send us to kill you, but order is to return you from here." Sahib said: "We have some matter of big men, that we will tell to Dalai Lama. Your rank is not so big as our rank, and we will not tell you all that matter." The lama said: "I will write to Dalai Lama."

And that lama speaking very quickly, which I could not understand so much his words, and I said: "Sir, you tell me slowly." Then he said: "I will bring a good interpreter from Lhasa." Then they went to their tents. Now at night we sing in our tents. Some the Tibetan chaprassi were young as we were. They came into our tent and sat with us, but they not take any food from our hands.

The Coming of Big Man with Vahapjoo.

Now after few days there come other big man from Lhasa. His rank call Mirpundtungaur, and were with him a lot people, and he had brought with him an interpreter Mohammedan, named Vahapjoo. And the big man was an old man, and some other lamas, and big men were with him. The big old man was not lama. Now we all Ladaki were very glad to come the Vahapjoo. We said to him: "Welcome." And he said to us: "Welcome." And we made dinner ready for him. And he said: "I will ask big man, if he order. Then I will come for dinner." At that evening he come for dinner. We made him very much honor. Why? He is a little old man, and a long before he had come Ladak, and he was in Ladak three or four years, so I had seen him at Leh, when I was young. And we looked him a very good man, but we do not know at that time, what kind of a man is he. Now he asked us many news about his Ladaki friends, and about Hadi Nassar-Shah. Then he asked to us: "You, who are?" to each man. We told him that all. He knew to our fathers. Then he said: "The sahib, why for he came here?" I said to him with some lie-matter and some true matter, and he searching matter from us, and I wanted some matter from him, to tell sahib. And I said to him: "How far left Lhasa from here?" He said: "Now left about eight march." That matter was lie of his. Now, after dinner, he went to his tent. The Ladaki said each other: "This man is very clever man." I said our men: 'We must be very careful this man. Don't tell him our matter. But we need make him honor when he come to us."

Next day the old big man, and other came to see sahibs. The Vahapjoo speak good Hindustani. For this he made interpreter, but sahib cannot understand his Hindustani. Then I made interpreter to sahibs, with the our style Hindustani. That seemed Vahapjoo much interesting. Now after some days that big man said to sahib: "We had wrote to Dalai Lama. He says what your matter is, tell to us. And is this order to us: return you toward your coming way." Sahib said: "Lhasa is near to India, and is with our government neighbourhood. It is our neighbourhood. Then why did you people hold next king in your friendship? Dalai Lama must need to make friendship with us. Why? We are near. If the Dalai Lama get any trouble, we will help him." The Tibetan said: "We have not made any other king friendship, and we do not want to make friendship with your government also." Sahib said: "We heard that you people are making friend with Russian government. If is that, then they will make bad with India. Therefore we afraid. Therefore our Victoria sent us here to tell this matter to Dalai Lama." The Tibetan said: "We have not friend with Russia, and we don't want your friend. Beside that, if we like, we will make friends or not. In this, what is entering of your government? What we like, that we will do." Sahib said: "If you people go in Russian friendship, they will make bad to you and to us. Therefore we keep entering in this matter." They said: "We are not friend of Russian, and others, and of your. And in any kind would we get of trouble, we will carry them ourselves. We don't need any help from you, and from others. You people don't take sorry for this matter."

Now every day we spoke this kind of matter, and the Tibetan sent their daily report to Dalai Lama. And in that valley were the trouble there raining every time very bad rain. At one night fell snow. Midnight I heard that Mr. Fletcher call to me. When I get up, there saw on all green place had been white of snow, and Mr. Fletcher tent-pole was broken. It was nearly to kill him. Then we could not make that tent, sahib sleeping in servants' tent. And in under our tent run water. The cold was as winter.

There at every night we sing, in Ladaki and Tibeti. And those young chaprassi, every time, come in our tent, and sitting with us, and look our enjoyment and our sing, but no one take food from our hands. (But there was that old man. He had come one time at Leh. That old man eat from our hand.) And there were some lama and munshi of Tibetan; we going into their tent, they coming our tent, we joking them, they joking us. And every Tibetan called me: "Rassul Huzur." This name got me this way: when sahib called to me, said: "Rassul!" I said: "Huzur." Therefore the Tibetan called me Rassul Huzur.

Now the Tibetan said to me: "You all Ladaki are good men, but you yourself are more good man. But you are bad, doing the servants of Englishmen. Why? They are bad men." I said among them: "You people are in dark shine of Tibet. We are in light shine of English government. Why? Our king is justful king." They said: "That is a woman." I said: "Yes, she is a woman queen, but her justice liked God, and given her the emperor of world. We have the justful in our government, which not beating stealing-men, and not any tyrannical under kingdom." Some believed this matter, some not. I said: "The dark law is in your country, which if beat to a stealing-man three hundred whips beating is nothing matter. This kind of bad justice not is in our government." And I went many times into their tents at night. They had no candles-light. I said: "Look at us! We have good food and good light in our camp." They said: "All are for you people good, but the servants-making of Englishmen are not good." I said: "This all enjoyment are from our justful and lighted government."

THE ILLNESS OF MRS. LITTLEDALE.

Now, by bad luck, there got ill Mrs. Littledale. Tibetan said: "We got order again from Deva Jung, that to return you people, toward that side, from which side you had come." Now sahib said to them: "Now we don't want to go to Lhasa. Now we beg to you people; kindly let us go Darjeeling. Mrs. Littledale got ill." The Tibetan said: "You cannot go by that way." Sahib said: "You must let us go for the illness of Mrs. Littledale." Tibetan said: "If Europeans travel on our place, there come bad luck, and would be dry the grass." Mrs. Littledale said: "You write again to Dalai Lama." The Tibetan said: "We were written many times to Dalai Lama. There got angry on us. It would be better you turn back." Then Mrs. Littledale gave the rifle in the big man's hand, and said: "If you people will not give us the Darjeeling way, then kill us with this rifle." The Tibetan said: "We will not kill you, but we will not let you go by Darjeeling. Anyway I will write one time again to Dalai Lama."

After few days, the Tibetans come to sahib, and said: "We got reply to that letter. Dalai Lama said you must return by that same way." Now sahib said to them: "We are much compulsion. Why? Mrs. Littledale got ill. And we will not look at your any place. Therefore you people tie cloths on our eyes; shut our eyes. For this you write again to Dalai Lama." The Tibetan said: "Now, how much shall we write? There got every time angry the Dalai Lama on us. Now we cannot write." Now we said many good matter. They not give us the Darjeeling way.

STARTING TOWARD DARJEELING.

And Mrs. Littledale got more ill and more. Now what shall we do? And now they will not write to the Dalai Lama again. Now we counselled. Come out this mind: to make ready to start toward Darjeeling.

And made ready our caravan. There came the Tibetans and said: "It very good, your going back, and we will help you." We said: "We are going Darjeeling." They said: "Cannot." Then sahib said: "Write again Dalai Lama. We must need the Darjeeling way for Mrs. Littledale illness, and we will give you yumbas twenty. If you do not write, then we will write a letter to Dalai Lama, and we will send that letter with our own man." Then sahib said to me: "You write a letter to Dalai Lama from my side with this contents: tell very much salaams from Mrs. Littledale, and she got very ill here, therefore she beg you kindly to let go by Darjeeling way, and we will give yumbas twenty present." I said: "Sir, we will tell we will give yumbas twenty for tea for lamas, and for lights for the monastery temples." And I said: "Dalai Lama is a big man. My writing is not so good." Sahib said: "Does not matter."

Then I did write a letter to Dalai Lama, with the contents which are up. Then the sahib put on the letter five seals, and gave the matter to Razak Akhun and said: "You carry this letter to Dalai Lama."

And Razak Akhun carried a rifle on his back, and he hung a sword on his belt, and rode on a pony, and he started from the camp. When he started, there caught him the Tibetan and said: "We will not let you go." When caught Razak Akhun, he said to me: "I will take my sword and shall I kill some men?" He said to me in Turki this word. I said to him: "You don't be foolish. If you do anything to them, then would be kill all us." Then the sahib took pictures at Razak Akhun, middle the Tibetan people. Then the Tibetan said to sahib: "You cannot send your letter to Dalai Lama, and cannot go to Lhasa. We will send a letter again, and we will look what reply come that letter."

Sahib hold that letter back which he send to Dalai Lama, and said to me: "We will take this letter to London, and will show to Victoria, and will give your name to Victoria, about to write this letter." I was much glad at this word, which before Victoria be my name, and said myself a lucky man.

Kalam Rassul Bad Matter.

Now the Kalam Rassul every day gave the breakfast very late to sahib. At that morning, he did same late. Therefore came Mr. Fletcher to Kalam Rassul and said him: "Why you do so late?" Kalam Rassul returned some bad words to sahib before Tibetan, and that saw Mrs. Littledale and Mr. Littledale from their tent. We thought that very bad matter. Razak Akhun, and other Ladaki, and I abuse to Kalam Rassul, and we said: "We all men will beat you for this, which you made unhonor to our sahib before Tibetan." He begged pardon to us for this matter. Now Mrs. Littledale said to me: "Kalam Rassul is a bad man, a very lazy man, which he did this bad thing. Now we take from him the cooking and keep him on donkey-work, and give the cook-work to Hussin." And from that day Hussin was cook for sahibs.

Tibetan. Black Heart

Now, after few days, the Tibetan said to sahib: "We got reply from Dalai Lama to that letter." And they showed that letter which let me read. There said: "Will not give the way of Darjeeling. Must go by that way, which side came." Now we got hopeless to going Darjeeling. The Tibetan said to us: "Go to Ladak, but outside our country." Now in this matter we speaking much. The Tibetan gave us very much trouble and they never thinking out about the illness of Mrs. Littledale. I never seen like the Tibetan bad merit. (Ladaki kept one word, means: "Tibetan black heart.") We all servants said: "We must do some lie matter with Tibetan, and we will take our road through Rudok. That we will fix on way. Here cannot do anything."

Wise Dog Tanny.

Now Mrs. Littledale got more illness, and more, by day by. And there were two dogs; one was named Tanny.[1] That one was very wise dog, and was like a son of Mrs. Littledale. I had gave him food from my hand about ten months. And sahibs and Mrs. Littledale ordered that dog; he making much play. If I tell him for some play, then he got angry, and he show me that: "You are a servant of our." That dog was small one. The next dog we had brought from Cherchen. His name was Gikim. That dog all night making much noise, very bad, in that illness time of Mrs. Littledale. That dog made much trouble. We take him afar; there he did not stop. All night gave us much trouble.

Arrangement for Going to Ladak.

Now we fixed the arrangement for Ladak. There in the Goring valley was one kind of grass with big leaves. That grass is a poison for Yarkandi ponies and mules. We dead there with grass several ours ponies and mules and some donkeys. And there we bought some ponies from the Tibetan. And rice, flour, suttoo, and all things what we needed, the Tibetan supply us. And Mrs. Littledale and Mr. Littledale wanted some Tibetan things. The Tibetan did not sell to sahib. Sahib showed me that some men ear-thing and necklace and other thing. I said to the Tibetan that I wanted for myself. Why? My relation have Buddhist at Ladak, I will take for them. Then they sell to me as cheap. Now the Dalai Lama gave to all people as sacred things, red pill,[2] and some silk things. We wanted those things for way, to make lie-matter. I

[1] Tanny, a remarkable fox-terrier, accompanied Mr. and Mrs. Littledale on all their journey until his death. The Royal Geographical Society made him a member, and gave him a silver collar.

[2] This sacred pill the British call "potted lama" as it is made from the powdered bones of lamas.

said to some lamas, that I wanted some sacred pill of Dalai Lama, for my relation, for present of Lhasa. They brought of that things enough for me. And then we bought some puttoo cloth, brown colors as lamas. That use very much Ladak. I bought one coat of Tibetan for rupees twenty. Now in these thing the Vahapjoo took from us much price. And he gave a bill to sahib. We knew in that his bill he was very lie a man.

Now we make a chair for Mrs. Littledale, and we were ready to start back. And the young chaprassis of Tibetan came many times to our tent at night, and they take some foods from us, but by hidden from the Tibetan. Now the chaprassis, two men, said to us: "If make journey with you people, would not be tired." And they wished to come with us, and they cried, and said: "We will run at night, and come with you people." We said: "We cannot take you people."

Now we Ladaki make some words as sing. We said:

"English are hat of sky,
English are peak of rocks.
English come from North:
Tibetan cried, every one,
And English turned back:
Tibetan laughed, every one.
If be long life, will hold Tibetan under the hat of sky."

I sent some salaam to Hadji Nassar Shah's son who live at Lhasa. Sahib sent for Dalai Lama some telescope-glasses, and to other big men make present also.

Starting Back.

The next day we crossed the Goring pass again. There was snow over the pass. I written on the snow some reproacher-words for Tibetan. And there was a little big man with us as a jamadar. The Tibetan big man had sent him with us. Now we carry Mrs. Littledale's chair on back of mules. (After few days, mules learn better to carry that chair.) And we cross those two rivers again, and that time got good water-crossing place. That time Tibetan show us good road.

Now Mr. Littledale wanted go Ladak very quickly. Season was late. They afraid for Zoji La. We always take a long march, we all servants walking. Now we could not walk so long a march. We said each other: "We must buy each man ponies to ride." Hussin and Galam Mahmad bought ponies, and went to sahib for money. They said to sahib: "Please, sir, give us some months our wages." Sahib said: "Why you people want money?" We all servants said: "Now we could not walk. Therefore we wanted each man ponies for ourself." Sahib said: "We will give you people ponies from to-day." Now from that day we got riding-ponies. At that day we crossed the pass which called Gylu La, which we had come by that pass. After several days, we arrived at that river where made boat, coming-time. There the Tibetan showed us very good water-cross; do not need there any boat. Until that place was a jamadar man of Lhasa. With him were some Tibetan army. After that place, they all went back. The Tibetan little man said to us that: "This is the river Tsacha Chu. Now you go from here to Ladak outside the border of Tibetan."

Now south was a big lake (Zilling Chu), north was our last road which we came from Cherchen. Now we travelled western, because there was not any Tibetan with us.

The Tibetan Watcher-Men.

There come two men behind us. I said to them: "Welcome." They said: "We am the Senja Jung men, and we come to go with you people, by the order of Deva Jung, and we watch to you people, and will not let go in our border." I said to them: "It would not be any change to that matter, which, with the Tibetan big men, sahibs made promise at Goring valley. That promise is, that we will go toward western. In that, if come in border does not matter." I brought them in our tent and gave tea and suttoo, and I asked them: "You people will smoke pipe?" They said: "Yes."

(Next day we travelled. There were no any people, beside these two men. Before get at camp, there was a large plain. There, north was a tall mountain, beautiful rock, and far away, south, the lake. There Mr. Littledale showed me that north side mountain, and said: "From here to Ladak is two hundred miles by through way. Must try to get us the through way." We were in the speaking. There rise a deep wind, very hard, and there felled snow; we every one felt much cold. We got very little fire. There were dung for fuel. All that get wet. Next morning Mrs. Littledale get angry on me for fuel. She said: "Why for you not carry one ponies load dung with us?" I said: "I will take every time one ponies' load dung from to-day." Mrs. Littledale said: "This evening, you must go yourself for dung. It is the punish to you for not carry dung." At that evening I went for dung, same the order of Mrs. Littledale, and I got good dung. Mrs. Littledale laughed at my bringing dung. From that day I every time carried one or two ponies' load of dung. That get useful for the future in many journeys.)

Now Mr. Littledale said to me: "If get about forty hire-yaks, so save our ponies, we can go very quickly Ladak. For that you make arrangements." Now those two men had been our very good friend, although they were a watcher. In making friends they help us. Now I said to them we wanted forty hire-yaks. They said: "To-morrow will find." They arrange for forty hire-yaks. After that, we travelling among people, which we met many tents in way. The two friends said: "It was not order of Deva Jung, but we did all this for friends. If not take through way, and among people, then will not get any yaks." I said to them: "Dear friends, who will tell the Deva Jung this matter? Beside that, the Deva Jung had promise to us to go through western. You people don't be sorry for this matter." Now we paid the hire of many yaks to that two men, but they were greedy men, kept those money for themselves. I look this very careful, and put in my head this matter.

Now Mr. Littledale wanted the name, all that, of place. If we ask them, they never give us the right name. Now when we see a tent from far away, I go quickly, then ask them the name of place. They tell right. (I am much sorry about the names of place. How shall I give all the names of place in my book, and the date? Because, at that travelling time, at those place, no was any mind of mine to make a book. Therefore cannot give so right name of place, and how high and low were those place. But those place were much high: that will find in Mr. Littledale's book, who want look. Will not find in this poor man book.)

Now we always travelled western, and pass many small pass, and hill, and lakes, and cross several streams and plain, some up and down, and I gave many place-name to sahib. Sahib said: "By this place-name found out, that there had been the Nain Singh."

Lie-Matter with Tibetans.

Now about ten days those two men travelled with us. Then they said to us: "Now finish our border of the Senja Jung. We will go back." Then sahib gave them some present. Now we all Ladaki men said to those two men: "You people were a very good friends for us. Now we much sorry to separate. Now we wanted for a few days the yaks. For that, you people tell the village people: the yaks-giving are order of Deva Jung." They said: "Yes, we will tell." Now there is a custom, the yaks change in one march several times.

One village take about three miles, then take next village about three miles. Now that two men said many good-bye to us, and went back.

Now we put our things on yaks; start on our way. After little way, the yaks changed and got other forty yaks. Now Razak Akhun and Kalam Rassul and I said: "We must make a deceitful with the bad Tibetan." Our dress were brown colour as lamas, but our heads were no tails, as lama. Now Razak Akhun and Kalam Rassul made a lama. I made a lama servant of sahib. Now we said, to every one Tibetan, all that lie-matter. We said, we came from China to Lhasa, and we had brought from China many mules of load good silks, for the present for Dalai Lama, and the Big Lady is young sister of Victoria, had sent to see Dalai Lama, to make friendship between English and Tibetan. The holy lama, Dalai Lama, made much honor to the Big Lady, and gave good place to her to live in Lhasa, and we were about a month at Lhasa. And we present all that silk, and gave a great tea for all monastery temple lamas. And Dalai Lama gave us as a present all this ponies, and all our food, and, until Tsacha Chu, had sent a very big man to help us. And sahib sent him back, and the one lama is until Ladak to help us. Razak Akhun said: "I have come from Lhasa, to help these sahibs by the order of Dalai Lama. It is order to given forty yaks, and must watch the ponies, and kept ready firewood on every camp." And Kalam Rassul said: "I have come from China to help the sahibs." And I gave to the Tibetan those sacred pill of Dalai Lama. With that they believe to us. And we said: "Now the English government and Tibetan get very good friends. Therefore we came through way. If not, cannot come any English in border of Lhasa." By good luck the jungly people very much believe at us. Now we said: "Our big lady got sick, therefore we wanted go quickly to Ladak, by Rudok." But they do not know Rudok where is. They were as animals.

Now we come to a lake. There Mr. Littledale said to me: "Rassul, now we don't need so much hire-yaks." I said: "Sir, we have made a great lie-matter with the Tibetan. Therefore they gave the yaks without hire-money, and now which side you wanted go, that side we can go, inside the border of Tibetan. And the Tibetan will help us very good, until we meet a next jung." Sahib said: "I do not believe." I said: "You look. Until Rudok we will go by a great order. After, I cannot tell. There we will do same work."

Now we travelling every day; got yaks and guides. Beside that all, at every camping-place were ready firewood, and gathered many people to help for us. And I gave to them a little sacred pill of Dalai Lama's. And for next camp we sent order. This way, in process, our order went on Tibetan as a great Lhasa man. This way came through Bhangba, Ghirsa and Senkor. They are very badly robber, but they help us very good. Mr. Littledale seemed this our lie-matter help very much, and was very glad. And said to me: "Rassul, we am lucky people, always got prosperity. One, we got near Lhasa. Not had reached any sahib so near as we reached. The next, all these places not had seen any sahib."

Now we were very glad the bad Tibetan to believe our lie-matter. But we were in much sorrow for the illness of Mrs. Littledale. And said each other: "If Mrs. Littledale die in way, what shall we do, and how shall we go to Ladak? Then we will lost our all happy of getting at own home." For that we every one prayer for save of Mrs. Littledale.

More Trouble with Sepoys.

Now we had always rich foods, and breakfast and dinner take every one servants together, but for tiffin every one take flour, and making own bread, each man. There I saw many time they making much bread, which they could not eat, throw them. I said to all servants: "How much bread you people need, so much flour take, and don't take any more." For this I told to Hussin: "You give to each man one wooden bowl flour." Hussin did that, but one sepoy, named Purdil, does not like. That sepoy said to me: "I will not take food from you and Hussin hand." For this matter he does not take three days any food. I begged him every time and said: "You must take food." He said: "I will not take food, while you in charge." I said: "This not belong me. This food belong sahib." How much I told him sweet matter, so much he abuse me. I report sahib every evening, that Purdil does not take food. Sahib said to me: "If he does not take food, does not matter." Now in three days, does not take any food, and sahib called all servants to his tent, and said to Purdil: "Why for you not take food?" Purdil said: "I will not take food in giving Rassul. My food must give you." Sahib said: "Rassul is a head man on food. If you not want order of Rassul, then you go out my service. I will give you ponies, and all your wages pay." Now the sepoy said: "Sir, I not go out your service. I must take food from Rassul. I took some men advice." Sahib said: "From to-day don't you take other men's advice."

FOOLISHNESS OF TIBETAN PONIES AND MEN.

Now we were many pony of Tibetan. We gave them grain, never eat they. And gave suttoo. They do not eat it. The Tibetan never had seen any kind of grain, therefore they not eat, and in the long journey they go weakness, by day by. And with us were some sheeps for meat, and some goats for milk for Mrs. Littledale. Those goats had been very weak in the long journey. Now we gave two goats to the Tibetan, and take one goat from them.

Now there, every time, we use all that our lie-matter with the Tibetan, and gave them the sacred pill of Dalai

Lama. When gave it, the Tibetan put their heads on ground for it, and said: "This sacred are of Dalai Lama, not any doubt."

And we had very much suttoo and flour. We gave suttoo to all them who watched our ponies and who make fire. When they wanted suttoo, we put bag of suttoo before them, and said: "How much you people could, so much you eat. But you people cannot take for your home." They said: "You people put the suttoo in our cups. We cannot take any suttoo from the bag ourselves." We said: "In giving little suttoo with hands, that are the Tibetan customs, not our English government custom. Our English government custom are so light as sun, and who work, must give them full stomach; must keep bags before working men." The Tibetan never had seen such rich suttoo and food. The Tibetan said: "Surely are English government as light of sun."

Now, in doing this, we reached near Ladak. We came at a place which called Jangpa. There that border yaks-man and helping-man had not come. The people who were come with us from next march, they put a white cloth before Razak Akhun, and one before us, and said: "Here are not come this border of men to help you people. And you big people cannot wait here. Therefore we will take you people for next march. This pasture-grass belong them. Now they not come here to help so great men as you people, now this pasture come under us in our custom. For that, you people order to us, to possess this place. For that you people give a letter." Now we said each other in Turki: "How shall we tell: take this people this place? If not tell, then this people will think us lie-men and no-power-men." Now we said: "We came so far in lie-matter. That all will know Tibetan after. If look this, does not matter." There I wrote a letter. I said: "Jangpa people; when we reached here, you people was not ready. Therefore we gave this pasture to the people, who help us on your border, same the custom of your." And on it made as the sign of a lama's name. Razak Akhun did that. But this all matter sahibs do not knew, how we doing all this lie-matter with Tibetan countries.

GETTING NEAR LADAK.

There came a large gravel plain. On that saw many mines of gold. And there come many Ladaki traders, but at that time no one was there. And Galam Mahmad had been there, for trader-work, with his mother's brother. Now we every one were much pleased to reached there, and every one said each other: "Now we get near Ladak." Because every one servants were tired, in the long journey, and every one wanted home, and wanted to see own wives. Every time tired some donkeys and ponies with the trouble of long journey. When they get tired and cannot walk, we made them present to the Tibetan. Now Galam Mahmad was as a guide for those places. He always travelled with the chair of Mrs. Littledale, and he was very hard-working boy. On him were sahibs and Mrs. Littledale pleased. And sahib said to me: "At Kashgar, we looked this boy very young, therefore we do not like him, but you told us he is good man. It is right matter. All your work is right." And Mrs. Littledale said to me: "Rassul are table-boy, and shikari, and caravan bashi, interpreter and clerk, and, with telling lie, bringing good luck for ourself, and are doctor and tailor."

Now they said, there are a long valley. In that valley will not find water. We carried a ponies' load of ice, and camped in that valley. The next day we arrived at Ra-bang. That place-name we had heard at Ladak many times. There came many Ladaki traders, but at that time there no was one. There was a small lake, and good grass pasture, and some small manipadme. In summer at that place joined many traders, Tibetan, Ladaki, and Lahaul. Their goods-selling and buying-place was that place.

Going by Rudok.

Now next morning we were ready to start. Mr. Fletcher go little ahead. Now we were nearly to start. There come some Tibetan, and there pitch the tent of Tibetan very quickly. A little after, there coming back Mr. Fletcher to camp, and there coming behind him some Tibetan. Mr. Littledale called me for interpreter.

There came from Rudok a head-man, and some other little big men of Rudok were with him. Now they said to sahib: "Why for you people come by through way? It was not order of Deva Jung. Your coming-way was outside the border of Tibetan, but you people travelled inside our border. Beside that, you people order on our Tibetan people as your own country. All that was not in the order of Deva Jung." We said: "We came right way, as that promise which we did with big man of Tibetan, that we go by western. In this, if came in your border, does not matter." Now the Tibetan said: "Until to-day you people reached here. Does not matter. Kindly you people turn back from here. We will show to you people other a road. You people go by that road Ladak." Sahib said: "We will not go by that road. Will go by Rudok." Now after very much talking, we started from that place. They could not make stop to us. Now there among the Tibetan was an old man, named Thago-cha. He said to me: "We will show you people a near road to Ladak. If you take the sahib by that way and not go by Rudok, then we will give present to each Ladaki rupees three hundred." I said to him: "We do not need any present of your. We getting good wages from sahib. But I will help you without your present. We are near home, each other. Therefore will help. Sahib never take my matter." Sahib said: "Must go Rudok, and in temple of Rudok will wait two days, then go Ladak." That old man said to me: "It will be very bad for us. Then the Dalai

Lama will cut off our heads." I said: "Does not matter." And I said: "This sahibs could not get any matter to make a war with Tibetans. This sahib and his lady have come to die in this Tibetan country, but are not kill the sahib there. Now came here. If you people have power to kill them, sahib like very much to die in your border. If kill this sahib, then on this matter will make the English government a great war with Tibetan." They afraid with this matter, I knew in their face. Now we travelling by lovely valley, down by a stream. In that valley we travelling two three days. Reached at Roksum. There sahib went ahead. There quickly coming Galam Mahmad toward me; said to me: "Sahib wanted you very quickly. There are joined many Tibetan and shut to sahib." I went quick. The Tibetan had brought a long written letter before sahib, which the order of Deva Jung. Sahib said to me: "You read this letter and tell me." I read it. I could not understand so much, but I understand the words: "Don't let come sahibs a footstep in the Tibetan border." Sahib said to me: "You make a copy of that letter." I made a copy of that letter and gave to sahib. For this matter, to not coming Rudok, we speaking there very much.

They said, if go Rudok, not given yaks. Therefore we throw many things, not needed yaks; start toward Rudok. At that night-camp, coming and going many people. Next morning were gathered about three hundred. That old man said to me: "Look these people. This all want to fight. Now what shall we do?" I said: "You people let us go Rudok and tell to sahib: 'Don't stop in Rudok temple.' And you people help us same before with yaks." And I said to them: "We left yesterday many things at Roksum, but, for all those things, will take the English Government much money from you, one time." They said: "That all things will bring behind you." Now they afraid, and said to me: "You tell to sahib, that now we let go to you people to Rudok, and don't stop there." I said: "I tell sahib, but I not know surely if sahib agree or not," I tell sahib, and he agree. And we give written bonds, both sides, but the old man joked at my broken written. I felt ashamed. Now we got as friends.

Galam Mahmad had some Tibetan friends there. He had heard from them, that at Rudok there had come some Ladaki traders. We every one Ladaki wanted to see them, and wanted to ask them the long news of Ladak of one year. We heard, they lived at Rudok near the temple. I said to the Tibetan head-man that: "Now sahib will not go in Rudok town. But we are Ladaki, we can go in Rudok town, and we will meet with the Ladaki there, and ask them the long news of Ladak. The head-man said: "You cannot go, because you are Englishmen. I will send words to them. They will come on your going-way. There you can meet with them."

The Long News of Ladak; and Report of Our Coming.

Now we start from that place, and cross that stream, and cross a very little hill. There seen a large plain, and on a hill-top the temple of Rudok, and on it many house of lamas. That all we saw from far away. Now we came very near the Rudok temple. There we saw our Ladaki friends waiting for us, on our coming-road. When we saw to them from a far away, we running our ponies. That seemed very far way, until we met to them. When we met with them, we said to them: "Welcome." They said to us: "Welcome." Then Razak Akhun put on a handerchief, some biscuit and some dried fruit of Khotan before them, and asked to them all the Ladaki news. They gave us very good news of our family and friends. They said one our good friend was wazir of Ladak. Therefore we all glad. Now we said to Omar Malik: "Must come to our camp at evening. Must talk some more."

Now we left Rudok and came at a village. There was a house and some cultivated, and some trees. There we camped, and we look very many time behind for Omar Malik, but he does not come. We were very sorry to his not coming, but he had afraid at the Tibetan Now I wrote a report to the wazir of Ladak. In that report I said: "Mr. Littledale and Mrs. Littledale and Mr. Fletcher and many ponies and donkeys have with us" (and each man name I gave in this report), and I said: "Mrs. Littledale get ill." All what happened from Goring, all that news. I wrote to wazir, and then I wrote a letter to my friend Sonam Wangdus with full news of our coming. And I wrote next a letter to all numbardar and khardar in all villages from Shushal to Ladak. In that I gave the date our coming and said: "Keep all thing for our camp ready, on our arrival-date." I told sahib: "I have sent a letter that every one border people take, in night and day, to wazir of Ladak." Now I put a piece red cloth on it, and told Tibetan: "Bring a mounted man. Take to Shushal." I said to him: "You must take this letter to our Ladaki border and bring receipt from Shushal numbardar." Now we made present two bags of rice to the head-man and start from that place.

Kalam Rassul's One Joke.

Now our order were on Tibetan, same before. What we bid them, they obeyed us. And what our things left behind at Roksum, brought them to us. There several men and some women come with the yaks. They always looked interesting our things, and what tell them, they believe to us. The Kalam Rassul was much joking man. I will tell his one joke. There at a camp a sepoy got ill, and he weep. The women ask to Kalam Rassul: "Why for the sepoy weep?" Kalam Rassul said to them: "The sepoy are very strong for a battle, and one man can kill many thousand people.

And the sepoy will not die with guns or hitting swords, but they will die, if fall snow from sky. Now the sahib told the sepoy: 'To-morrow will fall snow, and you will die.' Therefore weep the sepoy." The Tibetan believe to Kalam Rassul matter.

Sorry and Happy in Getting near Home.

Now we travelled three days. From that place was one march to Shushal, is the border of Ladak. Now we all Ladaki were much glad to get so near Ladak, but every one servants get sorry there. That is this: until that place, the money of sahibs, and other many things kept into my hands. From that place, all the money and other things holded up under Mr. Fletcher. We were all in sorry for that. We said each other: "Look at the sahibs! From Kashgar, all the things and money had been spend from our hands. Now we come near our home. Sahibs hold all things under themselves. Why? They thinking now we will rob their money. If we would rob the sahibs, then we had rob at Khotan and Cherchen." And Razak Akhun and Kalam Rassul said among us that: "We told before, Englishmen are good friends until be done their work. After their work, then will never look them, if be any faithful men." And then they said: "This all fault belong of Rassul, which he believe at Englishmen, and try to be honest before sahib. Now see the merit of Englishmen! It was much better, if we taken the three thousand rupees from Tibetan at Tengri Nor Lake. Rassul stopped that, also. And we reached near Lhasa with our honest work, which not got there any Englishmen. Every one, if come from home for journey, must try to got money, but here Rassul showed his honest to sahib. We lost our great money." Now they put all matter on my head. Now I said to them: "For true matter, always get good from God." They said: "Now where we search that God? We did long journey with this sahibs in desert. And three of sepoys' work we did one man. That knew sahib well. Now the sahib will not give so much present as the pay of sepoys to us, and will not get to us any name from Government. That all are wrong hope." And they said: "After this journey, we will not travel with Rassul. Why? He always helps the sahibs." And they said: "We will look for Rassul. What good luck will he find from sahib for his good work?" This all matter made my felt very sorry. At that night every one were in sorry, and no one sing.

Now the next day we reached to Shushal. Returned the yaks and men of Tibetan. Now in four days arrived Durga. Every our camping-place were all things ready for us, and gathered much people for help to us, same my order. And Mrs. Littledale said to me many times before that day: "Rassul, you must go to Kashmir with us. Now, after one month of your marriage, you came with us fifteen months. Now will wait home one day with your wife. After one day, go Kashmir. Your wife will weep. After Kashmir, then you can live with your wife a long time. Your wife must bring to meet me." I said: "Yes, Ma'am." But I wanted very much look my wife, and do not want to go down Kashmir, after so long journey. I said myself: "Mrs. Littledale have been ill; therefore must need go. If not go, then sahibs and Mrs. Littledale think me unfaithful a man, and will lose all the good work of mine before sahibs."

Now at that night we camped at Durga. Now we like very much to make there a tamasha, in pleased to arrived own country. At that night in one house joined many women and men, and the banjo-men, and make very good tamasha, and ourselves dance very much, and sing. Now we all servants were carelessness, in dancing and singing there. We forget our ponies. At evening had gave grass to all ponies, not watched to ponies any one. There had rob all the grass of ponies at that night. We do not know it. The next morning we travelling up the pass. Now the ponies tired there. We left there several ponies, because the ponies were all very weakness, without that grass.

Then came an old man from Leh before sahib. The wazir was got that my letter, which I sent. Now we ask that old man many news of Ladak. Now in way met many Ladaki men. Now Leh left one march only. And Razak Akhun said: "To-morrow we will reach home. Therefore must cook for each man one cake. That we take in our tiffin-bag, and when our wives find in our tiffin-bags cake, then they thinking: 'Our the husband are getting good tiffin in this journey.' And they will be very kind and will give us good food." We did bake cakes, but all get out bad.

Now, at that night, did not get sleep, in the pleased to come to-morrow at home. The next morning we changed our dirty dress, and started from that village.

Now come near Leh. At that time pleased, how shall I write? Every one traveller know this happy; after long journey, reaching at home. Sometime felled in sorrow and said myself: "Maybe my wife be die. Maybe mother be die. These people not give me that bad news. Cannot believe till see with own eyes."

My One Night and Day at Home.

Now, with help of God, we reach in bazaar of Leh. Now my home was near bazaar, and I went very quickly at my home. There got all well. I said salaam to my mother; and my wife, when see me, laughed, and said: "Welcome." I said: "By help of God, and with your right prayer, I came well."

Now there came many friends of mine to see me. Now that night was a very happy night. Was so pleased I cannot tell all that happy. But were the sorry to going Kashmir so soon. Now my wife said: "I was always in your remember," and sometime cried, and sometime laughed. Now my wife said: "Why do you go Kashmir now, if you are love me? We don't need so much money. You did enough long journey." I said: "My dear wife, I will not go for money, but Mrs. Littledale are big lady. Sahibs are all very glad on my work, with your prayer. Mrs. Littledale is ill." She said: "I heard the pass for Kashmir be shut, and how could you get back at Leh for this winter?" I said: "I will not wait in Kashmir. How bad the road be, must come for you." We passed that night this way, half in sorry, half in happy.

I said my wife: "You go see Mrs. Littledale." My wife said: "I am much shamed, but I will go with you." I said: "Yes, I will take you with myself." This matter heard other friends, that my wife will go see Mrs. Littledale. They made ready their wives to go see Mrs. Littledale. Now when my wife and mother and I went to see Mrs. Littledale, there came other servants' wives also, and the wife of Ramzan Ali. When Mrs. Littledale see them, she does not like their coming to see her. Then Mrs. Littledale said: "How are you?" My wife said: "I am well." Then Mrs. Littledale said: "You are young and much beautiful." Sahib and I were interpreter for my wife and Mrs. Littledale. My wife laughed at Mrs. Littledale telling. Mrs. Littledale said: "After Kashmir, Rassul will live with you long time." My wife not answer with shamed; laughed only. Then Mrs. Littledale made present. Then my wife said many thank to Mrs. Littledale, and said many salaam, and went to home, and other servants' wives went to their home.

Now in the morning when I came at dak bungalow, there all the saddles, bags, ropes, and other small things were taken all the servants to their house, each one at night. I did not get any things; and I did not look to those things, only was happy to get home. Now Mr. Littledale paid all the servants the wages, and gave to each servants two ponies. The ponies were all very weak. I got two ponies. One dead at that evening.

Now wazir said to all servants: "Sahibs is much pleased on your work. I will make for you people a dinner and a big tamasha, but I will wait until Rassul be back from Kashmir."

FROM LEH TO KASHMIR; AND PARTING WITH SAHIBS AND SEPOYS.

The next day we started from Leh to Kashmir, but my felt are not liked, to go to Kashmir, in love of my wife and friends. Hussin and I had much work on that journey, and the sepoys were no help to us, but we nothing said. Why? It was left a short-time journey. Now every day we did two marches. We came every day at night at camp. And in cooking passed much time: get up at early morning in darkness-time: had no time to sleep. Now one camp, Mrs. Littledale wanted some hot milk. I went to a Kashmiri, in house, and said: "Please, give some milk. We will give money." That Kashmiri not want give us milk. That house was the head-man's house. Then I took a stick to beat the head-man. There gave quickly milk. Now were raining much. All clothes and things got wet. I said to Hussin: "This one day's trouble is nothing. To-morrow will be finish all trouble." Hussin said: "Does not matter. Because we were borned in the world for trouble."

Now I speak with the Kashmiri the language of Kashmiri. The Pathan sepoys said: "Rassul, we are not Pathan. We are coolies before you. You are Pathan and brave man, which you can speak all languages. Therefore we said you are Pathan, and we are coolies."

Now after many days we reach Kashmir, and Mrs. Littledale went into bungalow. We took all the luggage into the bungalow. There was much mud with the rain. When we take the things in room, we take off our shoes. The one sepoy, Badullah, he was a very foolish man. He went into the room with his shoes. There made all the room dirty with mud. For this Mr. Littledale got much angry, and said to me: "Let him go to serai, and live with mules."

Now, the next day, Mr. Littledale gave our pay and present, and the expense for Ladak, for Hussin and to me, on the door of B.J.C. bungalow. And Mr. Littledale said: "We am much pleased on your work. We looked you as our sons." I said: "Thank you for this matter." And I said: "We will tell goodbye to Mrs. Littledale." Sahib said: "There are no order of doctor sahib to see any men to Mrs. Littledale. Why? She is ill. The ill was from Goring valley." Then we came to serai. And we said: "If the sahibs had good justice, they must needed give us more money than the sepoys. We were long time with Mrs. Littledale, and she was as our mother. To-day not let us tell goodbye to her, and not let us see her, and gaven the pay on door." Now Hussin and I were much sorry with that matter. (But after-time Mrs. Littledale writing: "Rassul was as my own son," and she much sorry, to doctor not letting say goodbye us.)

Now the sepoys said to me: "Rassul, you help us very much. And you good worked with our frozen foots. But we gave you some trouble in this journey. All that we did with telling of Razak Akhun and Kalam Rassul. Now you must pardon all our fault." And they caught my foots. And I said to them: "Does not matter. In long journey, be sometime angry among each other, and sometime pleased. You people don't look over my fault. You must pardon." They said: "We always got good help from you," and thanked to us. Then we said goodbye to the sepoys and other men, and started for Leh.

[The journey back to Leh was made rather heroically. A visit to the fakir on the way, gave courage, by which they crossed a pass, declared impossible at the season, a feat by which Rassul kept his vow to his wife, and achieved considerable reputation for pluck and hardiness. His next journey was with Mr. Church after big game. That was followed by a succession of journeys with various sahibs, among them, Mr. Martyen, Professor Roland Dixon of Harvard, and Dr. Fillipo Fillipi, covering a period of several years. I have chosen, for the closing chapters of the book, the drama of the first months of his two years' journey with my husband, "the very poor longbeard sahib."]

Testing the Sahibs

PERSONS OF THE DRAMA.

(In the order of their appearance on the stage).

MYSELF, RASSUL.
MY WIFE AND SWEET LITTLE TWO DAUGHTERS.
THE B.J.C.
LORD SAHIB.
THE VERY POOR LONG-BEARD SAHIB.
THE YOUNGER SAHIB (clothes a little good).
MOHAMMED ISA.
MY MOTHER, an old Wise Woman.
DR. SHAW.
THE KIRGHIZ.
THE VERY POOR DUCK.
THE TIRED MULE.
THE SANJU BEGH.
CHORUS OF SERVANTS: Ramzan, Ahmad, Abdurhmen, Ibrahim, Jam Yung, and that old cook.
CHORUS OF VILLAGES PEOPLE.

ACT I.

SCENE 1. *Leh : The Home and Shop.*
SCENE 2. *The Road.*
SCENE 3. *Kashmir : The Camp of Servants.*
The Room of B.J.C.
A Plane-tree Garden.

ACT II.

SCENE 1. *The Road.*
SCENE 2. *Leh : A Garden.*
My Mother's Separate House.
Dr. Shaw's Bungalow.

ACT III.

SCENE 1. *Up to and over the Chang la.*
SCENE 2. *Up to and over the Karakorum Pass.*
SCENE 3. *Up to and over the Sanju Pass.*

ACT IV.

SCENE 1. *From Desert to Desert.*
SCENE 2. *A Serai under a Rock-Hill.*
SCENE 3. *From Hills to Hills.*
SCENE 4. *A Village : My First Dream.*
SCENE 5. *Villages and Hill :*
Darkness and Crooked Ground.
My Next Dream.

ACT V.

SCENE 1. *Poski : Beside the Stream.*
SCENE 2. *In Camp.*

Testing the Sahibs

Act I. *Scene* 1.

[*Enter Rassul and his Family.*]

Now, I was a little rich than before. My wife and I both spoked and said: "We don't want any journey any more now. God have gave us enough money. Now we can open a shop." I was opened a shop. In that shop I selled some cloth, and tea, etc. At day I lived on the shop; for food, coming home at night. At that time my wife and my felt were both very happy, and there were the sweet little two daughters. All that seemed very happy.

One day I got a register letter from B.J.C. of Ladak. He said in that letter: "One Lord sahib and one Major sahib want to travel toward Chinese Turkistan. They want you for head-man on the whole work of their. If you agree for this service, you write me soon."

When got me that letter, I said myself: "It rise my luck again. One time I was with a captain sahib same this journey. There, in my returning-time, alone, I made trader-work, got rich money. Now is same journey." I did agree for this service. As that I told to my wife, she does not like at all. I said to her with sweet matter, and said: "We will be more rich in this one journey." With my telling, my wife agreed a little. Then I replied to the B.J.C. as that: "I am agreed for this service."

After about twenty days, there get me a next letter and telegraph from the B.J.C. And he said: "You bring with you three other men, with a cook." And said: "You must be ready in Kashmir on the twenty-second of February." Now I said myself: "Three men are not enough. There must need six men." I choosed six good men, and gave money to them myself. And made all the arrangement for the journey from Leh to Kashmir. It was a bad season for a journey.

Scene 2.

Now we six men started from Leh. I said many salaam to my wife, and to my friends, and mother. Now we travelled at night and day. Always was a very deep snow and cold. Many people said to me: "You people cannot cross the Zoji La in this season." I said to them: "God will help me." At Dras we got some coolies. When we started, the mail runners came with us. With much difficult we crossed the Zoji La. Then God gave us road.

Scene 3. [*Enter B.J.C.*]

When we arrived Kashmir, all Kashmir was white. When we reached Srinagar, B.J.C. and some other sahibs were walking. It was twenty-third February, a days late. We said: "Salaam." The B.J.C. said: "You people are very strong men, which came in such time on the same date." And he said: "Now is not arrived the Lord sahib." And said: "You wait here."

In Kashmir were some Ladaki in the service of B.J.C. We made camp with them. Now we waited there about twenty days. Not get Lord sahib. Now I finish my money in the expense. I lose in the expense from Leh about rupees two hundred. Now I said to B.J.C.: "For expense there got only rupees twenty-five left." [*Enter Mohammed Isa.*] There came Mohammed Isa from Lhasa. My hope was, that he will help me in the bad-luck-time, because I was helped him before, when he was poor, and beside that he had taked a debt money to me, rupees thirty. But he does not help to me, when I said to him my poor-getting in Kashmir, and, when I speaked about my debt-money, he said: "I am not remember." With that matter my felt much angry. Anyway he gave to me, for rupees thirty, rupees ten, only.

Now my name was a little good: therefore the traveller-sahibs called me from Leh to Kashmir. That does not like the Kashmiri shikari, and all the servants of sahibs. They all joined as enemy, to push me down. I do not know all this matter, and I do not know when Lord sahib will reach Kashmir. But the Kashmiri known well his arrival. Then one Kashmiri servant went down to Rawal Pindi and met with Lord sahib. And he did tell Lord sahib: "Rassul Galwan is a bad man." And he had told many lie-matter about me, and Lord sahib was believe to the Kashmiri.

[*Enter Lord Sahib.*]

One day Lord sahib arrived to Srinagar. He come to see B.J.C. There called to me. I went and said salaam to both sahibs. The B.J.C. said to me: "This sahib do not want you as head-man. If you work under Kashmiri, then he will take you." I said: "Sir, I will not work under Kashmiri. I will work myself with my men. In that matter I am responsible for every work of Sahib." Sahib said: "I must want Kashmiri. If you not work under them, then I not want you." Then I said to the B.J.C.: "Sir, I have come from Leh to here, with your order. If sahib not want us, then please pay us our two months of pay for three men." The B.J.C. said: "You will get rupees twenty-five only. And here will come two sahibs. I will give you their service." I said: "Please sir, you must justice in this matter. I lost rupees two hundred. Where shall I get them?" B.J.C. said: "Will not get them." And then gave me rupees twenty-five, and said: "Finish this work." I said many sweet matter to the B.J.C. He does not help me. I felt much sorry, but to whom shall I tell? I came among our men, and told them all the story of sorry. They felled into sorrow.

[*Enter the Two Poor Sahibs.*]

The next day I was walked near the Club. There were two poor sahibs. One was with very poor clothes, with long beard. One was young. His clothes was a little good. I looked to them. They looked to me.

The next day the B.J.C. called me in his room. I went to him and said: "Salaam." B.J.C. give me a letter and then said: "You take this letter to Chenar Bagh. There, in a boat, lives a long-beard sahib. You give this letter to him. And I will give you and your men to him."

Then I took Ramzan and other one or two my men. Went to Chenar Bagh. There, when I went, the poor long-beard sahib came out boat. I said salaam, and then I gave that letter to him. He read that letter, and then said to me: "You can speak English?" I said: "Yes, sir, I can speak a little." And then sahib said: "You can speak Turki?" I said: "Yes, sir." Then sahib called to the young sahib. He came out boat, and then he asked to me into Turki: "You can speak Turki?" And then we speaked some Turki. The poor sahib was very glad. I know that in his face. Then the poor sahib asked me about the other men. Then the poor sahib said: "You come with me. We will walk a little." Then we walked outside the garden. The poor sahib said to me: "I like you very much, and you will get good luck with me." I said: "Yes, sir." And then I said all the story of Lord sahib, what trouble I got from him, that all. Sahib said: "Now you will get good luck." And said: "We must want a good cook." And said: "I will travel about two years, and I must want you in that journey." And said about Ramzan: "Who are that man?" I said: "He is a good friendship of mine." The poor sahib said: "I am sure from his face he will not be your friend. You remember this matter." And sahib said: "We both will be a good friend." I said: "Yes, sir." And then the sahib asked me about buying ponies. I said: "Sir, these all arrangements we will do at Ladak." I said myself: "This sahib is a good man, but I sure in his clothes he is a poor sahib."

[*Chorus of Servants.*]

And then we came back. There was waited Ramzan and other my men. There the poor sahib showed to us his interesting tents, which was very light to carry, and inside fire-place. Those tent I like very much, but Ramzan not like them. I said: "Sir, these tents are very good, but the tent's pole are not good, and needed lining for these tents." Sahib said: "Yes, we will make all this well."

Now I said: "Sir, I will go. To-morrow I will come to you again." Sahib said: "Yes." Then I said good-bye, and came at our camp. There joined all Ladaki and then we talked each other for the poor sahib. There was an old man. He was a cook. He said: "I did asked the Kashmiri cook about sahib's food. The Kashmiri cook said to me, that their food was very poor food, corn breads and dall. That sahib eat poor man's food." And he said: "I sure these sahibs are quite poor. Now, if they take poor foods and wear poor clothes themselves, then what shall they give us? We am his servants." For this matter other men said: "Yes, it is right." I said: "Anyway, we must need to travel with them a while. Then we will know him." And there was Mohammed Isa with us. He said to us: "Maybe, this sahib will come a very rich man and very good. Now, no one can tell," Now we were all night and all day in this speaking. And we laughed on the hat of the poor sahib and on his clothes. And we said: "Look to the Kashmiri servants. They never came to the sahib for service. They sure that these sahibs are poor." I said: "God is very rich. If God help us, these poor sahibs become rich for us. If God not help, then from rich sahib we get unluck. Beside God, no one can help." They said: "Yes, it is right matter."

Next day we went to the poor sahib. Now I said: "Sir, we needed all the arrangements make before B.J.C." (The sahib cannot understand well, that all my telling in the breaking English.) He said: "Yes, we will go before the B.J.C." There the B.J.C. was very angry on poor me. He said to me in to Ladaki language: "Why did you told to this sahib to not get money from Lord sahib, that matter?" I said: "Sir, what was true matter, I told him." At that time the poor sahib was there, also, and he had brought much money in note. Now the B.J.C. said to me: "What do you want?" I said: "Sir, you are given me to this sahib, though I do not want any service. We will go until Khotan. After Khotan we cannot tell we go or not. For that we want written promise make before you." The B.J.C. said that all to the poor sahib. He said: "Yes. If they not like, I will send them back from Khotan." Now there wrote the written promise before, B.J.C., and there made the our pay. The B.J.C. made my pay rupees forty for month, Ramzan cook rupees twenty, Ibrahim rupees fifteen, Ahmad rupees fifteen, Abdurman rupees fifteen, Jam Yung rupees ten. There were six men. But sahib not want that old cook.

At that afternoon B.J.C. called to me, and I went to him. There on table were many papers and B.J.C. said to me, with very nice face: "Rassul, Government was wrote to Resident for a good man for this sahib. Resident wrote to me for good man. Those all paper are these orders. You are a good man. Therefore, I want give you to him, with the government paper. Now you do good work with these sahibs. Then you will get a good name." I said: "Yes, sir." Then the B.J.C. puts all those papers into a big envelope. Then he wrote one separate letter to the poor sahib, and he gave to me those envelopes and said: "These papers go to Kashgar, to Mr. Macartney. Now you belong to this sahib from to-day." I said: "Yes, sir."

And then I came to the poor sahib and gave the letters, and he was glad in reading them, and then said to me: "Rassul, you are my man." I said: "Yes, sir. I am your man." And, before that day, was raining much. That day was very fine day. The poor sahib said: "Rassul, yesterday was raining. To-day got fine day. As this you will get good luck with me. As that raining you get bad luck with Lord sahib. With me you will get good luck as this fine day." I said: "Yes, sir."

Now we made the tents-poles and lining for the tents, and other arrangements for our journey, and very good clothes got for all servants.

ACT II. *Scene* 1.

One day in April, midnight, we started in boats. In early morning came to bridge. There was noise. We look out. There said: "Moved the ground." But we not known into boat. At that evening camped in boat. Now at night we all Ladaki servants talked each other a long time. One time Ahmad and I came out the boat. There under a tree, a long white thing we saw. We said: "What is this?" There answer the poor sahib. He said: "Rassul, I am here." I had never seen his sleeping until that day. [*Chorus of Servants.*] Now servant said each other: "With these poor sahibs what trouble shall we get? Look at his food for himself, and look at his sleeping! With how trouble he are sleeping himself, and look at his bed! What kind of trouble become to us with him?" I felled down into sorrow.

One place we lived in bungalow. But was very cold. And the water was very cold. The poor sahib taked bath there, in cold water, and outside room. We looked that very interesting, and said: "This sahib are taking much trouble on his own body."

One place the poor sahib taked me to climb a mountain. There was much deep of snow, and travelled by hillside. There not was any road. One time we felled in snow, and get no way. We turned back, came on a flat place. There we saw some foot-tracks, which walked with snow-shoes. The poor sahib said: "These shoes are very good to travel on snow. Must find these." We went by those tracks, sometimes come up and down, in falling in deep snow. We saw a small house. There was a man and some sheeps and goats. He know me a little, but he said: "Here is no road. Why come you people? Maybe come by mistake." I said: "No, this sahib like such place." And then I said him: "We wanted some shoes for snow." He gave us two pairs, and I said: "I will give back your things to Dras." And then he shows us for road.

The sahib told to me: after long walking, washing foot is good. From that day I learned the foots-washing. It was useful.

Next day the poor sahib showed to me a tall mountain to the right side bank. Over it was covered deep of snow. He said to me: "We will go over it." I felt: do not like at all to travel over it. I showed good face, and went with the sahib to that mountain. There we crossed a bridge, and then went up that mountain. It was very difficult to go up. It was more steep and difficult than yesterday's mountain. We cutting off the freezing snow with stick, and went up one place. Near the top was more difficult, but we reached top the mountain. The view from the top was very beautiful. All the hills and earth were white. One side was village under snow; next side was more high mountains, all white. The poor sahib taken many pictures, from side to side, and he written many things. After that, lying down, top the mountain. That seemed me very interesting, to sleep at such a place, but I cannot tell him anythings. After all that doing, no was road, was very steep. Sahib holded me, I holded him, made as one man, throwing ourself down. It seemed very beautiful. Coming below one place, there was next one pass to go below. I felt very much like to do that. Now the sahib waited at a place for picture. I like very much to throw myself below. When I throwing below myself, it was nearly to lost my life. I got to a end of bad rock. God save me from that danger-place. If I was fell next one yard, there was no doubt I was dead. (I have been like this two of time. One time when young, and was going after bush in the mountains. In helping God, get safe at this place.) While after, sahib came. I showed him that danger-place. After that, we get below. There were houses. There was a pattas maker. Sahib wanted many questions from him, I making interpreter. After, came big road, and travelled down at small village. I said all the story of that days to our men. [*Chorus of Servants and Villages People.*] They and the villages people said to me: "One day this sahib will kill you, in taken from mountain to mountain in such danger-place." And they said: "For rupees forty pay you wanted kill yourself." I said: "If God not kill, then will not die."

Now there was the young sahib. We thinking both sahibs same master on us, but I had been a doubt: that on everythings, boxes and on other things, saw only the name of the poor sahib. Therefore I thinking: than the young sahib the poor sahib is a bigger man.

Now was ponies' road. Now always we rode on ponies.

Scene 2.

In several days reached at Leh, and we camped in a garden, which was near my home. [*Chorus of Villages People.*] Now every one men said to me: "This year you got a poor sahib." I said: "Yes."

[*Enter my Mother.*]

At that time my mother lived separate house. One time mother came to see sahib. After that mother went home. I went to mother. She was an old, wise woman. Mother said to me that: "My son, you must take my advice. This sahib are not a poor sahib. You don't think him poor. He must be a big man, which he are making himself as a little man. I sure into his face he is a big man. I hope you will get good luck with him. And you don't look him as little sahib. You must honour to him in every matter." Mother telling that, I felt much better.

Now from Kashmir I never had asked to the sahib for money. Now at Leh I wanted much money. One day I told to sahib: "Sir, before, I have been with many rich sahibs. That known every one Ladaki. Now know every one Ladaki that Rassul are got a poor sahib. And I was spend large money of their." Sahib said to me: "Rassul, you will spend a large money of mine at Khotan also." Then I said: "Sir, please let me have rupees one thousand for the arrangements now." There the poor sahib was carried a small bag inside his clothes. From that bag he took out a paper of note. It was of rupees one thousand, and he gave that to me, and said: "You can spend this money." And said: "You buy ponies." Now I changed that note into rupees, and brought them before the sahib, and then I bought ponies. I buyed the ponies from my friends, and good ponies, which I knew strong ponies, I bought them. And the sahib said to me: "You must make ready all the arrangement in fifteen days." I said: "Yes, sir."

Now we got all good ponies and there were most white ponies. Therefore sahib said to me:" Rassul, we am good luck men. Look at our all ponies are white!" I said: "Yes, sir, we are lucky."

Now in the helping of God, all the arrangements were ready in the fifteen days, as sahib order. But we wanted some advance-money from our pay. Sahib said: "If Dr. Shaw will be responsible, then I will give you people advance-pay." Then we went to the bungalow of Dr. Shaw—[*Enter Dr. Shaw*]—, and Dr. Shaw said that: "I am responsible." Then the sahib paid us, before Dr. Shaw, each man four months' advance pay. There was an old man whom I had taked to Kashmir, for a cook for Lord sahib. He has not get any pay from both side, and he was a very poor man. Therefore I gave him rupees thirteen from my pay, and the other servants gave him rupees five, each man, and sahib gave him rupees ten also. Now the poor old man was glad with us, to got him some money from us.

Now my mother was lived at a separate house. I gave her rupees one hundred. She was very glad for that and the rest money I gave to my wife. Now I and my wife felled into a great sorrow. I do not like at all to go so far a journey. So my wife was not liked to let me go, but could not help. Beside that journey, I could not live. But I said to my wife: "I will come as soon as possible, for your sake." And in telling that, we both cried very much each other, at night and at day.

Act III. *Scene* 1.

Now we started from Leh. I said many goodbye to my mother and my wife and to all friends of Ladak and many joo to all the Ladaki people. Then we started from Leh to Khotan, by Shyok way. It was about fifteenth May of month.

The poor sahib was pleased with my arranged, which I did at Leh, and he was pleased with our packing mules and ponies. But he not like Yarkandi saddles for loads. He like more Lhasa saddles. Now the poor sahib have no any table and chair and bed, as other sahibs. But the young sahib had a small table and chair, and we all servants were more good beds than the poor sahib.

We camped at Chimrai. [*Chorus of Villages People.*] There the villages people said to me, that over the Chang La is much deep snow, and said: "You can not go over it, with the caravan, in this time." I said to them: "We will go over it. You people know I had come one time from Yarkand, with a great caravan. At that time I passed over it, and that time was more early than this season."

I sent up to pass to look the snow Ibrahim and Ahmad. At evening, they got back at our camp and said: "We have been top the pass. There is much difficult in deep of snow, but will not stop us." Next day, in very early morning, we started, and travelled up toward the pass. It was a big fight with snow, and got much trouble in felling ponies and mules in soft snow. And there was a mule weak. He felled at many places. I was with that mule behind, and the rest went ahead. A long time after, I got top the pass, and, a little down from pass were waited every one. They said to me: "Here is no road." It was a hot sun. Sahibs and other men were tried much, but the ponies felling in deep snow, cannot go. Sahib and men had spread on ground numdahs and water-proof, but could. not go. That day were not any hope to get down from pass, but for next morning was hope for to get hard the snow. The poor sahib said: "We will wait here for morning." I agreed to do that. Then the sahib opened his small tent which were with his bed. A little he sleeped. Now there were about forty men, and on ponies' backs were no loads. The all loads were on men's backs. [*Chorus of Servants.*] Now those men said: "This is not a waiting-place. If we wait here all night, then will die all men and animals, and will frozen every one hands and foots. It will be better if we go back to last village." I said: "Why go back? Why we will not try to go on down, to Tagshalltakpo?" They said: "It be more better, but there cannot go." I said: "We never go back, but will try to go on." I said all that to sahib, and he said: "What you like, do that." Now I said to the people: "I will take a ponies, and go ahead. You people follow me." They said: "Yes." I bleed a ponies, and said myself: "God, you help us and give the road." I prayed, then trust in God, and I went ahead. Many time I felled, and ponies' foot going down in snow. I searched the good road; coming behind me other rest people, with mules and ponies. They felled at many places, and got every one very much trouble in pulling and pushing in deep snow. At last, by helping of God, we arrived at Tagshalltakpo that evening. There was all world white with snow; only on some hilltops were no snow in throwing by wind. We camped on a little hilltop.

For next day was left a little fight of snow, but most

bad snow we had done. Soon we had got in happy at Tagnakpo. There were come three men from Durga. And they had brought us milk, wood, and grass. We waited there a little for rest, and there we gave some grass for animals, and we drink some tea. Then we travelled again down, and safely arrived at Durga all animals and men.

Now we had sent ahead from Leh, a chaprassi for grain and ten hire-ponies. We met with that chaprassi at Durga. All his arrangement are not ready, and we wanted wait, rest for two or three days. The animals very tired, passed blood.

Now I speaked very much with sahibs into my breaking English. Now the villages people said to me: "You were every time coming with rich sahibs. Now this sahibs are poor, but keep good temper." I said to them: "By kindly of God, this sahibs will come a good sahib for me."

Now we paid for all the things what we took at Durga, and sahib made some presents to the head-men of villages and made present to the chaprassi. All were pleased to get presents from poor sahib, and they were thankful to sahibs, and on me also.

Scene 2.

From Durga we went Shyok village, and crossed several times the Shyok river, and at Chang Jungle there camped. There, at evening, the poor sahib took off all his clothes, and made himself naked, and he rising before his fire and lying down, he doing many things before the fire. That looked every one very strange doing; but I looked interesting; because we were seen many his interesting doing from Kashmir to Leh, but we never had seen to making naked himself. [*Chorus of Servants.*] There Abdurhman and Ramzan said to me: "That this sahib is a bad sahib. He make himself naked before us. He caught our blessing." I said to them: "It will not be so as your telling. Because it will be a useful for his own body, therefore he making all this tamasha." They said: "Maybe is your right." But I seemed it a little bad, to making sahib himself naked.

For servants were no so much work with sahibs' camp as other sahibs: as pitching tents, beds, and chairs and table: no was that kind of any trouble. Now the poor sahib said to me, he will put his own saddle on his riding ponies. And there was a white numdah. That numdah he did put under his saddle, and at night he used to put under him that numdah. Now we looked all that doing of the sahib as a very poor man. [*Chorus of Servants.*] Ramzan said: "The elder sahib is a poor man, which he not forget his own poor custom, though he would get a rich money from Government for this journey." And they said: "The young sahib look a big man son, and all his doing are like big men, which he used chair and bed and table. He must be more big than elder sahib. His custom is all rich man custom." I said to them: "The elder sahib must be a big man. So look to me on his face." They said: "Will not be so." We looked both sahibs same, because we had travelled several times with two sahibs. But the other servants always looked the younger sahib the big man. Me seemed the elder sahib the big man. The elder sahib had not sleeping in tent. Sometime he sleeping on a hillstops, sometimes other places, and when he sleep he put for his pillow his shoes, and under him put that numdah, and many times he put under him his trous, and he put on him a long black numdah coat. We all servants were more good bedding than he have. Sometimes I said myself: "This sahib must be a poor man." Sometimes said: "He is a big man, because he liked to do himself a poor." In this matter I was sometime in sorry, sometimes in happy. But I remember the advice of my mother, which she had told me: "This sahib is a big man and good man." So she got out in his face. Now our servants said: "We will find a bad luck with this sahib." I said: "Why be bad luck? Like this sahib we have never seen, which he gave, for every one servants, riding-ponies, and good foods, and good clothing, and not any angry inside." Ramzan said: "The sahibs kept good temper, and gave good foods and clothes and riding-ponies, but the sahibs are poor. They making on every thing kind with us; but these sahibs look me, that they have come for a hard journey, and they will die, and we will die with them." I said: "Any men and sahibs do not like to kill own life. This is quite wrong. Every one wants own life. Maybe they go hard place. Does not matter. We can go. The sahibs are good men, and I have spoke with the sahib about his journey. He will go to China. That I told you people at Kashmir, and I had made promise with sahib. I will go." They said: "If you think good and you go, why not we go? We will come with you." I was pleased with their matter; and the both sahibs were very good temper, and never abused to any servants. We all servants were good ponies to ride and good saddles. For that, every one servants were thankful.

Now what we do, all that looked the poor sahib, and how we cooked, and how we eating, and he writing many things in his pocket-book. That matter not liked at all Abdurhman and Ramzan. [*Chorus of Servants.*] They said: "This sahib is a poor, and inside bad, and sweet-speaken man. So he looks at what we cook, and what we eat, and what we doing." I said to them: "Will not be that matter as your telling, and he will never thinking that we eat much. He like to look our interesting doing all." They said: "Maybe." Now I washed my face and hands for prayer. On all that he looked very careful. And he had not any basin. He washed, as me, on brook-stream, his face and hands.

Now poor sahib's travelling was much interesting. He going in many valleys, and on tops of hills, and he write many things, and taking many pictures. Sometimes I travelled with him, sometimes I travelled with caravan. One day he said to me, that show him the place of bortsa. I said: "Yes, sir. I will show you." Now the young sahib was with me, the elder sahib was left behind. We came at bortsa place; there not camped. Now sahib's order was: me to show him that place. Now how shall I show him? If wait, it will take a long time. I building there some stones, and then I wrote on a paper, in my breaking English the words: "Bortsa is this place." Then I went ahead with caravan. After long time, the sahib arrived at camping-place, and he was much glad on that my writing, and he said to me: "I get out the bortsa-place from your writing." And said: "I understand better." And said: "You are a wise man. I will teach you English." I was much pleased with all that telling to me the poor sahib.

Next day we passed the Depsang plain, and came near Karakorum. We got a very much trouble over that pass. Many places felled loads and animals in snow. Now we were all glad to got over that pass, and there were on several place some loads of traders. And a little down the pass, was a loads that was broken, and that load was of date. In that load was sit a rabbit, and eating the date. We was thirsty, and a little hungry, and every one took some of it. God must pardon for that fault.

Now we cross Fotash.[1]

Scene 3.

Now we travelling toward Shahidula. Now the young sahib was very good friends with all servants, and with me was more good and speaking very much, and the elder sahib was very good with me. I used to tell him all the trouble of my happened. One time he said to me: "Rassul, you are not caravan bashi. Your work are more high than caravan bashi. Why the B.J.C. made your pay rupees forty only? Your pay is from this day rupees fifty. For rupees one hundred you are

[1] I have omitted the account of attempting to cross the Hindutash.—ED.

cheap a man." I said: "Sir, they help at sahibs. They will not help on poor men." Sahib said: "You surely will get good luck with me."

Now I had about two hundred rupees' things, which I had brought from home, to sell in Chinese Turkistan. I said myself: "This things will be a money one time. Then sahib look much money in my hand. Then sahib will think all that money I stolen from him." Then I took the things and put before the sahib all my things. There was some saffron and turquoise, and other things, which make good money in Chinese Turkistan. Now I said: "Sir, this things I have brought from home to sell, about two hundred rupees' things. Beside this, I no have any money. If you see more money than this in my hands, then you must think I stolen from you." The sahib said: "I believe on you. You are a true man." Now the sahib like me very much. I very much like him. There were all servants hard-working men. Ramzan cooked, for sahibs and for all servants; Ahmad was very good for ponies' work, and he put best horse-shoes; and Abdurhman was good for horse-shoes, and Ibrahim. Jam Yung can put saddles alone man and loads also. For all this matter the poor sahib was pleased.

[*Enter the Kirghiz.*]

Now after few days we arrived at Suget Kurgan. There met with some Kirghiz. They said to us: "While ago was come here the amban of Guma to look a murderer man. And we get an order from him to help to this sahib. And what wanted sahibs, we will give them, and want no price." I said that to sahib. Sahib said: "Nothing wanted." And the young sahib said Turki, but the Kirghiz cannot understand the words of the young sahib. [*Chorus of Servants.*] I said to our men: "This sahib must be a big man. If not, why the amban give order to help?" Ramzan said: "It is for that Lord sahib. These Kirghiz helping us by mistake, wrong." I said: "No, the amban said surely for our sahib." Ramzan said: "The elder sahib is a wild jungly man. All the help would not be for this sahib." I said many times: "This sahib is a big man."

Now we arrived Ulbok. And we servants always making a fire, and round the fire we sit, and always look his interesting, all that doing tamasha. And he had an old hat. That hat he making many kinds of hats. And his poor clothes sometimes half wear, half not wear. In hot sun on march taked clothes off. Now he came out tent, and he weared that long numdah black coat, and he had put his hand's glove in the sleeve of his coat, and the glove was tied with string. Now he walked. The glove walked behind him on the floor. I said: "Sir, the glove felling." The other servants said: "Don't tell." Then I not told. At last I told. Sahib said to us that: "I am a fool man, which I not see my own glove, and you people are bad, which you don't tell me."

Now the young sahib said to me: "We will go to a very bad place, and there have lived wild men and there never have been any men, and we will go there." I believe him, and I like very much to go in such place. I said to him: "I have never heard of that place. If be so, then we must go there, and we will find out what kind of people they are." But it was: he joked me, and I believe him.

Now we came to the stream of Tagrachu. It is a well known bad stream in Yarkand way, but by good luck at that time was not so difficult. The Kirghiz had brought there camels for help us. I said to our men, that the water is low, not need camels. (At that time the elder sahib was behind us.) The young sahib said to me: "The four black boxes must put on camels' back to cross stream." I said: "Sir, it is no so bad stream. We not need to put the boxes on camels' back." He said: "No, no. You must put them on camels." When he said that matter, he made a little bad face before me. I not like that, and I said to all servants that: "Put the four black boxes on camels." They did that. Then I said to the young sahib: "Sir, you said we will go to many bad places. At those places, where shall we get camels? If no have camels, how shall we cross bad streams on ponies?" This matter made the young sahib a little ashamed before me.

[*Enter the Very Poor Duck.*]

Now in that stream we saw a duck, and she had carried her several childs up on her back. We saw that, a very poor duck, and she came near us.

Now we camped. The elder sahib brought into camp that poor duck, which we had seen into that stream. When I saw it, I was much sorry about that duck, and I said to sahib: "Sir, you have done a sin, which you have killed the poor mother of small ducks." Sahib said: "I did not see the childs of duck. If I have seen them, then I had never kill their mother." And sahib was in much sorry about that duck. Now the young sahib and all our men said, that this sahib's justice is bad, which he killed the poor mother of duck. I said to them, that he killed it by mistake: he have not seen the childs of duck. They not believe me.

The next day we halted there for hire-yaks for the Sanju pass. There dead an old Kirghiz. We all men went there for prayer for that dead man. After, we got three yaks, and other things which we wanted.

[*Enter the Tired Mule.*]

After two days, we arrived at under the pass. There get a little tired our one mule from the mules I bought in Leh, and at that place was very poor grass. I went in a valley, to look grass. We waited there for that day, and ponies sent a little down for grass. The next day we started up toward the pass. The Sanju is a well-known bad pass. There was much bad ice, but for us get good luck over it, by kindly of snow. Now the mule, which tired before day, get more tired there, and the other mules and ponies were going ahead, he left behind them. That mule called to his companions. He do as that: "I have been weak. Wait you." We were much sorry for that mule, in his call to his companions. Now that mule stop. He could not go up over the pass. Now what shall we do? If take him down, he could go a little way. Now that mule not go a yard place up. We believe to his tired, and there cannot wait all the caravan for him. I said to the young sahib: "It is the custom, if not go, let him stop here. He cannot go up." He said: "Yes. Let him stop." And that mule left there.

We crossed the pass. The elder sahib was ahead, and we arrived other side the pass safely. He said to me: "How are you?" I said: "Sir, all came safely, but left a mule." He said: "Why left? Must bring him here." I said: "Sir, he cannot come here." Sahib said: "Must bring him." I came to our men, and said that the sahib said: "Bring the mule." They said: "This sahib is a bad man. How shall we bring the tired mule?" And we fixed the matter, and made ready Ahmad to go for that mule. And sahib said: will wait there for two days.

[*Chorus of Servants.*]

At that night, I and all servants were in sorry and angry, to gaven the sahib trouble about the tired mule, and to sending a man again over the bad pass. Now some men said: "The sahib get doubt on us. Why? The Kirghiz are our friends. Sahib thought we gave the mule to them. Therefore he send our man back. Now here get left only one mule. He gave us so much trouble. Now we don't know in a long journey, how many ponies and mules would be tired. How shall we travel with this sahib in a long journey?" At that night, I was very sorry and angry on sahib to not believe at me.

The next morning Ahmad went toward the pass, and sahib went up to look the country. We wait at camp. At that evening Ahmad get back from pass, and he said: "I tried very much at that mule. He cannot come here." And he was hopeless to coming of that mule. Now came sahib. I said: "Sir, the mule cannot come here." Sahib said: "If he not come, then kill him with rifle." And said: "Send a man again." I get much angry, to give trouble again to my men about that mule. I came among servants and told them. They every one get angry. [*Chorus of Servants.*] And at that night we speaked about it, and in our council came out: that this sahib is a bad man. He killed the poor mother of ducks and he not believe to us about the mule, and he gave us trouble again about the mule. And Ramzan said: "Look at your good sahib, which you praise him all the time! By and by what luck come on us?" I believe at him, and we fixed matter that we must not go with this sahib from Khotan, and we will take a debt-money from a trader, and will return the money, which we got in advance at Leh.

Now Ahmad was ready to go again after the mule, and he took a rifle, and Ramzan said to Ahmad: "When will you kill the mule, you must bring his tail and ear. Maybe this sahib will not believe us to killing the mule. Then we can show him the tail and ear." I said: "Yes, bring them with you." And next morning Ahmad went up the pass again, for that mule, and sahibs went up mountains for pictures. At that evening Ahmad got back. And he had killed that mule, and have brought the tail and ear to show to sahib. And he put the tail and ear before sahibs, and sahib said: "Good, for killing the mule."

Now we paid for the hire of yaks to Kirghiz, and made some present to the head-men, and we started from that place, and we were always in talking about this matter. [*Chorus of Servants.*] Ramzan said: "The sahib looked how much we eat his foods, and in his travelling are not sure. Everywhere he like, there he go. One day we will die with him. And for the mule he gave us so much trouble. Two times he returned Ahmad over the Sanju pass. We have been with many sahibs, and many their ponies left. They not gave us like this trouble; and those sahibs were believe at Rassul." With this matter my felt much sorry. I said: "For foods, the sahib had told me: what we wanted, take us. For that, he is not a bad sahib. But for the mule he gave us trouble. If he do like this always, he is a bad sahib. We will test him till Khotan. If he get bad, we will return his money and go back Leh." They agreed to this matter.

Now we travelled down by that valley. At that day the elder sahib ordered me to travel with him. I did that. And his custom had, that he never travel by straight way. He travel everywhere he like, in valleys and on hills, and he crossed very bad streams. That day he did same that trouble. My felt was tired. There I get more tired, and before that evening we arrived at camp.

Next day, the elder sahib went alone on hills and valley. All us halt there. Now the young sahib was very good friends with all us. [*Chorus of Servants.*] Now every one men said to me: "You tell to him, that we will not go from Khotan." And we tell him all the story, to returning about the tired mule, and to our changing idea to not going after Khotan. The young sahib said to us: "Yes, you people are good men all. But the elder sahib are not so good, which now he gave to you people so much trouble about the mule. After, surely he give more trouble. And his travelling are quite difficult than any sahib. And in own country cannot travel any man with him. I must tell to you people he is not good sahib. You people must not go with him from Khotan. If go, then you will get much trouble with him." And he said: "You people must not go from Khotan. And I do not want go with him.

I have been tired with his work. He is a bad man in own country. You people must go back from Khotan to Leh, and meet with own family." And he said: "It is by friendship, my advice, because you people are my friends all." Now we every one believe the young sahib, and said each other: "He is a sahib. Ne never tell lie. Because he is a good sahib, therefore he told us true matter." Now every one surely do not like the elder sahib at all, and myself also.

At that evening the elder sahib said to me: "Rassul, let the caravan go to Poski. You and I will go through by the Sanju valley." I said: "Yes, sir." But there we had heard many times, from the Kirghiz, that valley is bad, and there said the Kirghiz, that valley is a flood-joined valley, and in it will be a high flood. Now Ramzan and all men were very good friends with me. [*Chorus of Servants.*] Now they said: "Rassul, you don't go with this sahib alone, by this bad valley. You tell: 'I will not go.' Now we don't need his service." I said: "No, it is very ashamed. I must go with him, and until Khotan, what he bids me, I must obey him. After Khotan, then, we will not go with him." And I said: "I will trust to God, and will not afraid to the water. God will help me."

At that place we heard that the Guma amban are sent his son before sahib. Now, all that night we were in speaking very much for go back Ladak. I thinking about all this matter;—[*Chorus of Servants*]—and then I said among servants: "I do not know sure. From Kashmir until here, the elder sahib was good man, but he did two things bad. One, killing the mother of ducks. Next, given the trouble about the mule. But for duck, he told he killed her by mistake. Maybe he come a good sahib. I must test him again." They said: "If he not bad, why the young sahib tell us all this matter?" I said: "Yes, I am believe to him, but when we told all the story to the young sahib, I found out in his face he was pleased to hear our not going. That time, at the stream-crossing place, when young sahib made us all that trouble about putting the black boxes on camels' backs, elder sahib told to me: 'That young sahib are very young sahib, and you know all works better than him. Must be patient with him.' Sahib not be angry, if lost all our things that time. Sahib said that not be our fault. Maybe the both sahibs would not be good, inside themselves. But I will look until Khotan." They said: "Maybe will be that. Now we stop to nothing telling until Khotan, and all that what sahib bids us till Khotan, must do."

Act IV. *Scene* 1.

Next day we started from that place, but they said every one men: "You must take one man with you. He will help you." There agreed Ahmad to come with me. Now sahib said to me: "You go ahead down. I will meet with you in way." I went ahead with caravan. Down there is a Chinese fort. There sahib met with me.

Then we said goodbye to all our men, for a week. We went ahead. Af first Ahmad came with us. We had only each riding-ponies, and had no any bedding, and any foods. Now we came on a narrow valley. There was a bad road. On that place was no hope to go any ponies, but our ponies were very wise on that bad road. Went same men. Sahib very pleased on the ponies, and praise to the ponies. Then there was a water-cross, very bad. There sahib went ahead. He felled down with ponies in deep water. God helped him. He get out again safely. Our ponies were very wise to go in water. Ahmad and I get a little down, get easily out. After that travelled down that valley, crossed many times that same stream. At one place sahib returned Ahmad. I was much sorry, but I cannot say anything.

Now sahib and I many times crossed that same stream, from side to side. Sometime the water came near saddle, sometimes down of saddle. I get tired in all that doing, because my felt was tired before that. Sahib does not know. Now, a very long time after, that valley get opened, and there were all the water-cross a little wide. Then we came on a plains. There we met with a man. I asked him: "There are more water-cross?" He said: "Now is all done." And then sahib said to me: "You ask him, how long left is the villages." I asked him. He said: "Now is near." I was much glad to heard that villages is near. And said myself: "There will get some foods and rest."

Now the time was nearly late afternoon. Now there was west side a big valley. Sahib went toward that valley. A while I went behind him, but I not like to go in that valley.

There sahib said to me: "You take both the ponies down to village and fed them, and yourself wait there for this night." And said: "I will wait in this valley for this night. You send me some breads and khatik." I said: "Yes, sir." And travelled down myself with the two ponies, and then I said myself: "Bad luck. What kind of sahib I got? In his travelling are no sure. Everywhere he like, there he stop."

Scene 2.

And then I came to a village. There under a rock-hill was a serai. I went into that serai. There was an old woman and a girl. When they saw me, an interesting man, they afraid to me, I sure in their face. Then I spoke Turki. They felt better. Then they asked to me: "Where do you come from, and who are you?" I told them all our story. They get more better. Now I said to them: "Call to a man. I will send some breads for my master." They brought a man, and came some other men. [*Chorus of Villages People.*] I told them what I needs. They made ready. Then I sent some khatik and breads for sahib, and I showed him, that in which valley sahib was. I made him understand in very careful, and then myself waited in serai for that night.

The village people supply to me foods, and they brought some numdah and other things for my bedding. Now my hope was, that to-morrow in early morning sahib will come here, then will go quickly at Sanju village, and there will get happy in everything.

The next morning that man get back, with whom I had sent bread, and he brought a pieces letter for me from sahib. And that letter he had written separate words, and like my breaking English which I used. That I understand well, and he said: send him some more breads and khatik. I did send them as his order.

[*Chorus of Villages People.*]

Now there came some head-men of that village to see sahib, and to help. They said: "Where is sahib?" I told them: "He is in that valley." They seemed that interesting and then they said: "Why he lived in that desert?" I said: "His felt are liked." They said: "What kind of sahib he is, which he like desert more than village?"

Now two days sahib lived in that valley, and I do not know, beside that valley, where he been.

Scene 3.

Now came order to me to bring up ponies. I did that, and met with sahib. He said: "Are you well?" I said: "Yes, sir." Then we travelled down, and met with the head-men and with other people, who were come to help sahibs. They said salaam to sahib, and said: "There at Sanju are come the son of Guma amban to see you." I made interpreter. Sahib said: "Yes." They said: "Shall you go Sanju to-day?" Sahib said to them: "I do not know, myself, where will I go."

Now we travelling down, passed some villages, and crossed a stream. Towards east were some rocky mountains. He get down from ponies and climbed up them. Now he taked off his clothes, only kept his trous, and always he had many things to carrying on his back, some long thing and short thing and round thing. And he had a long beard. Now sahib travelled on hills. [*Chorus of Villages People.*] We travelled by way. We looked him as a tiger, which going on hills. Sometime the Turki people and I laughed. Most time I was sorry.

Now at last there saw east side a big valley. Sahib went into that valley a while. I went with him. Then sahib ordered me, that I send some bread and khatik, for night, up that valley, and said: "You wait at village." I said: "Yes, sir." I felt more tired. Why? After long desert every one wanted village; he travelling from desert to desert.

Scene 4.

Now I came in a house, and made ready some bread and khatik, sent them up; and I lived for the night in that house. [*Chorus of Villages People.*] There the head-man and others spoke each other and said: "What kind of sahib is this one?" I spoke with them, and some time I laughed among them, and felt much sorry. I said to myself: "Rassul, you have been with many sahibs, very hard-working. Who helped you from them? Only got present, not get any name and rank at all. Now you get this sahib. He must be a big man, but for me God more big than any sahib. Now will take with this sahib so much trouble. Let go this idea to going with him for long journey." And I was much sorry for my wife. She was ill. I said, must go back and meet with her. And said: "What will this sahib help me for future? Nothing." (But he was my faithful master for many years, only I not know at that time.)

Now, next day, came back that man whom I had sent with bread. The next day and night, sahib did not come from valley. I was angry, and other men were angry with all that his doing. We did not send him any breads. Sorry sahib left hungry at that night.

Now at that night I sleeped. Saw a dream. The

dream was: I rode on the ponies of the young sahib, and a few trees' branches were in my hand. The ponies running very fast, and took me among much trees. I was afraid will hit me the trees, and kill me. There fell the trees' branches which were in my hand. I waked from sleep. I said myself: "This dream is interesting. Maybe the advice is not right of the young sahib. I must look for this matter." Because when I met with my fakir, his advice was that: keep own body clean. When I did that, many dream of mine came quite right.

Scene 5.

Now, the next morning, sahib came at that village where I was. And then he said to me: "You kept me hungry yesterday," and nothing said. I felt much ashamed with this matter. There he took some bread, and then we started again. Now Sanju village was very near. My hope was that now we must go Sanju. There, near Sanju, crossed the stream, and there toward west was a plains. Sahib went there, I going behind him. I do not like at all to travel in such place. Could not help. In that plain have been very hot sun, and no any water. A long after we came on a rocky hill-top. There sahib took some pictures. And there came the amban man for passport.

After that, we moved north and travelled by same desert plain. That afternoon we came under a hill. There sahib said to me: "You measure that hill." He showed me how to measure it. That I did. And there came the Sanju begh. [*Enter the Sanju Begh.*] He said salaam, and said: "You must come at village. Why you are travelling from desert to desert?" Sahib said: "I will come to villages, but not now." And then said to the begh: "You go back." Then the begh and his men went back to Sanju. Then we went over that hill, and I measure it, same how sahib told me.

Now we came top that hill. There sahib showed me one place, and said: "I will wait that place for this night.

You go to the village, and leave the riding-ponies there, and bring up four or five donkeys, and some bread and khatik and water." And said: "You come back at night." I said: "Yes, sir."

Then I came down to the Sanju village with our two ponies. There I met with the begh, and then I told them about the donkeys, and the breads and khatik. [*Chorus of Villages People.*] They said to me: "You wait here for this night. To-morrow we will make ready all things." I said: "It is no order of sahib. I must go back at this night." They said: "There would be a bad road. You will not get way in darkness." I said: "I must go at night. Please, you people make ready all them what we wanted." They said: "Yes." And the begh brought dastarkhan for me. Awhile I felt happy with that. After that the begh made ready the donkeys and breads and two men.

There got evening. Now which side I came down to Sanju, by that way was no road. Next side was road. That I had seen before, from the hill, from what place sahib returned me. That place I made remember. That evening I started from Sanju, and then get much darkness which could not see way. There, in darkness, get many up and down, and felled down in many crooked ground. At that night, I get much trouble. I said myself: "Surely will not travel with this sahib." Now where sahib is, get no sure in the darkness. By bad luck, there was no moon. Now after very much trouble, came on a hill in felling down, and felt afraid, in that thinking: "May fall down, and die myself."

Now by good luck, from that hill, near, I saw a little fire. There I made a noise. There answer sahib. My felt better; and then came sahib and said: "Got you all things?" I said: "Yes, sir." And sahib was glad to get me back that night It was near midnight. Now we sleeped.

The next morning one man we sent back to Sanju. Now the poor sahib, one Sanju man, and I, and four donkeys, we travelling from hill to hill. At last we come in a sea of desert of plain and there was hot sun. Now the Sanju man get tired to travel with us that day. One place we wait for rest in hot sun and there took some breads and khatik and then travelled again by big plain. Now the thirst and the hot sun and the body tired and the feeling tired are joined. That one day seemed as a month.

Now before that evening arrive on a sand hill; there we camped for that night. There was not any water beside that water which was with us. I made clean my hand and face with sand and prayed there. At that night I sleep wonderful because I have not good sleep the last night. Now at that night I saw a next dream. I was on the ponies of the elder sahib. That ponies rise up, and take me on his head, and put me high up on a beautiful rock. There opened, middle the rock, a gate. On that gate was the elder sahib. He took my hand, and took me into that gate with him.

I waked from sleep. That dream made my felt better. I got sure, in both dreams: the young sahib's telling was not right, and I got hope the elder sahib will come good.

After few days we came to Sanju. The Sanju begh made ready a house for us. We not waited there. We came through to Poski. And sahib said: "The ambans making all the helping-trouble for us, it be the work of Government. But I do not like all these."

Act V. *Scene* 1.

Now we arrived at Poski. There was pitched our camp under some beautiful trees. My felt got happy. And there we met with the young sahib and all our men. We said each other welcome. And the both sahibs speaked themselves.

Now that evening the poor sahib taked me beside the stream, and said to me: "Rassul, you told before the young sahib, that you people will not go with me after Khotan." I said: "Yes, sir." And then I told all the story, of mule and duck, and the interesting travelling, all that. Sahib said to me: "If you not like to come with me in desert, then you don't come. When you like, you come with me. And I not thinking so much bad about the mule. If be tired all the caravan, that was not your fault." And then sahib said to me: "If not go any men with me, I do not want them, but I must wanted you." And said: "The young sahib is a servant of mine, as you. I have brought him for my work. But I get you more good man than him, and good friend than him. I like you very more than him. If he not want to come with me, I not want, but I must want you. And I will give you for your pay rupees one hundred. You must come with me." And sahib that time all money taked from young sahib's hand, and gave into my hand. Now I thinking myself for that two nights' two dreams, and the telling of the sahib came same. I felt much better and like to travel with sahib. And then I said: "Yes, sir. If I go with you, then all the servants must come with me." Sahib said: "You will get good luck with me." (That all come right. I got much good luck, but I am sorry I not helped him so much.) Now I get much happy.

Scene 2.

Then we came at camp; I told the story to all servants. They were all pleased, but the young sahib was not so happy. Now I wanted test to the sahibs. I sit with them one place, same them.[1] But in doing that, the young sahib get angry, the elder sahib not get angry.

[*Chorus of Servants.*]

Now were all servants agreed to go with the poor sahib for the long journey.

[1] For purposes of the test only. Rassul was, all through the journey, impeccable as to etiquette.

EPILOGUE.

The story was interrupted at this point by the war.

When the writer takes up his pen again, after that long interval, he seems to have lost his art. "I am not much remember where was much happy. All that not remember. The difficult and hard place are good remember. And the youth-time remember were very good. In the old-time is not good remember as youth. Anyway I am written with very careful."

His material grew progressively more and more interesting up to an intensely dramatic climax in the Tsaidam, but his treatment of it is so wholly inadequate, that I have thought best to cut short the book at this point.

The unhappy young sahib (he was *very* young!) soon parted company with his embarrassingly unconventional employer, and the latter's expedition went forward peacefully for a time.

The most interesting events of this period are barely touched on, while there are long chapters, telling proudly of high honour paid, in cities, and in lonely mountain districts far off the beaten trail, by everyone, from beggars to ambans, to his sahib "who was as a king"; "of dinner feasts" and tamasha dances given to all beghs; of taking poor children into food shops; of lord bountiful visits to almshouses and prisons, so that "were pleased in Keriya town all the poor, beggar, children and prisoner with us, and there were everyone happy in Keriya town"; of his sahib's exchanging those poor clothes of his for fine Chinese raiment ("but were this Chinese merchant and tailor all thief and lieful, and amban also"); of high honours paid to Rassul himself, by officials of court and city; of persistent, but vain, offers of love made him by beautiful girls ("Not I am beautiful. I am very ugly a man. They were not love on me, but they think this man is as a head-man; so that they get rich money from me; therefore they give me all the trouble.") Rassul's responsibilities were grave. His hands were full of business. But he never faltered in his study of English. "Sahib said to me: 'Rassul, you must remember, I will not let you go from my friendship until you learn English.' Yes that promise got right. At this time by his kindly, I learning this my style, which now I written as a book. No got any wrong in his matter."

Glossary

aksakal	.. A leader or supervisor, literally "white beard."
aleikum	.. Upon you [be peace].
amban	.. Chinese resident official in Tibet.
anna	.. An Indian coin; one-sixteenth of a rupee.
araba	.. A covered cart.
babu	.. A native clerk.
bagh	.. A garden.
bandobast	.. Arrangement.
bashi	.. Leader, head.
begh	.. A rich man, a noble.
bhot	.. A native of Bhotan.
bocha	.. Make oil from.
bortsa	.. A sage-brush like bush, used for fuel in Ladakh.
bottledan	.. A box for holding bottles.
calak	.. Mud. Also a kind of pulse food.
chang	.. Barley beer.
chapatti	.. A thin cake of unleavened bread.
chaprassi	.. A servant, an orderly.
charass	.. A drug having an intoxicating effect prepared from hemp.
chenar	.. A plane tree.
chit	.. A certificate of character given to an Indian servant.
chorten	.. A Buddhist stupa.
dak	.. Post, mail.
dak bungalow	.. A rest house.
dall	.. Pulse or split peas.
dan	.. "A Holder."
dastarkhan	.. A table cloth.
dawan	.. A pass.
deva	.. God (reverential title).
fakir	.. A religious beggar or mendicant.
farangi	.. Foreigner, European.

galwan	.. A robber, a trouble-maker.
galwo	.. "Little egg," an affectionate term.
hadji	.. A Mecca pilgrim.
hallal	.. The prescribed Mohammedan method of killing an animal for food.
havildar	.. Sergeant.
huzur	.. A form of address. "Your Excellency."
jamadar	.. Head of a company of men.
jhadoo	.. Enchantment, magic, charm.
joo	.. A term of greeting.
julay	.. Saddle-cloth (?).
jung	.. A high military authority.
kahtik	.. Curd (milk).
khan	.. Prince or noble.
khardar	.. Palanquin bearer.
khatangs khatik	.. A scarf given as a present.
Kirghiz	.. A Turkish tribe.
kutedar	.. Headman, merchant.
la	.. A pass.
lama lama poktak	.. A Buddhist priest.
lamma	.. lazy, protracted.
lhatoo	.. A turban (?).
lockpa	.. A goatskin to protect coat from fuel basket on the shoulder.
Masjid	.. A temple (Mohammedan).
maund	.. An Indian measure of weight, approximately eighty pounds.
mirpundtungar	.. A Tibetan official.
mulay	.. A saddle.
mullah	.. A priest.
munshi	.. A writer, teacher.
nika	.. Marriage.
numbardar	.. A Ladaki official, headman.
numdah	.. A saddle-cloth, or felt.
om mani padme hom	.. The famous Tibetan Buddhist prayer "Oh thou jewel in the Lotus, Hom."

paboo	.. A sort of soft shoe.
pakma	.. A bridegroom.
parsi	.. A Zoroastrian in Bombay.
parwana	.. A passport.
pattoo (pattu)	.. Woollen cloth. Several lengths of pattu sewed together.
pice	.. An Indian coin; a quarter of an anna.
poshteen	.. A long sheep-skin overcoat.
pugaree	.. A turban.
pundit	.. A learned man.
ramadan	.. The ninth of the Arabian months during which Mohammadans fast from sunrise to sunset.
rupee	.. An Indian coin.
sahib	.. "Lord, sir," as applied to foreign gentlemen.
sais	.. A groom or horse-boy.
salaam	.. "Peace!" a term of greeting.
scanchus	.. Pinching.
seer	.. An Indian measure of weight; a fortieth of a maund.
sepoy	.. A native soldier.
serai	.. An inn.
shikari	.. A hunter, guide, beater.
storma	
sup	.. Boiled barley.
suttoo	.. Ground, parched grain.
tagh	.. Mountain.
tamasha	.. A sight, show, spectacle, fun.
tanga	.. A copper coin used in Turkestan.
thaltuk	.. A preparation of wheat or barley.
tharspond	.. An officer in the Tibetan army.
tiffin	.. Luncheon (actually English).
tsafat	.. A small shrub used for fuel.
wazir	.. A minister, a vezeer.
yakdan	.. A leather-covered box, hung from a pack-saddle.
yumba	.. A silver ingot.
zan	.. Gruel